MENTAL CONFLICTS AND MISCONDUCT

PATTERSON SMITH REPRINT SERIES IN
CRIMINOLOGY, LAW ENFORCEMENT, AND SOCIAL PROBLEMS

A listing of publications in the SERIES *will be found at rear of volume*

PUBLICATION NO. 88: PATTERSON SMITH REPRINT SERIES IN
CRIMINOLOGY, LAW ENFORCEMENT, AND SOCIAL PROBLEMS

MENTAL CONFLICTS
AND MISCONDUCT

BY

WILLIAM HEALY

DIRECTOR PSYCHOPATHIC INSTITUTE
JUVENILE COURT, CHICAGO

Montclair, New Jersey

PATTERSON SMITH

1969

THE endowment of the Juvenile Psychopathic Institute for five years through the generosity of Mrs. W. F. Dummer first made possible the studies of which this volume represents a part.

PREFACE

THE great value of understanding the foundations of conduct is clearly shown by such living facts as are gathered together in this volume. Bearing upon one type of causation of misconduct, we have here not only a rational psychological theory, but also abundant concrete material. An important field is opened before us, especially interesting because of the revelation (*a*) of potent subconscious mental mechanisms working according to definite laws of mental life, and (*b*) of types of hidden early experiences which definitely evoke these mental processes that are forerunners of misconduct.

Troublesome behavior, originating in the experiences and mechanisms here under discussion, ranges widely from mere faults of social attitude to severe delinquency and crime dependent upon uncontrolled anti-social motivation or impulse. Cases having this causation occur so frequently that specific knowledge of their nature should be part of the equipment of all who have to pass judgment or to advise concerning misdoing and misdoers.

Much reliance has always been placed upon the idea that admonition and punishment is an effectual way of meeting undesirable conduct. However, even

the simplest observations show the very great failure
of these methods.   No thoroughly effective scheme of
punishment can be part of our civilization.   We have
set our faces against barbaric retribution and absolute
prevention of offense.   Some of us even hesitate at
corporal punishment of children.   So far as delinquency
and crime are concerned, with more or less self-con-
sciousness and with much groping towards progress,
we stand nowadays, with our reformatories and probation systems and what-not, definitely for the principle of inducing in the offender self-directed tendencies
towards more desirable behavior.   It requires little
discernment to see how deeply the success of such
undertakings must depend on wise adaptation to the
causes of misconduct.

The remarkable results following upon exploration
of mental conflicts, at least when there has been any
fair chance for building up better impulses in these
cases we have been studying, show most concretely
how earnest seeking for causes forms the effective
approach to treatment of misconduct.

Before the reader goes into the body of the work, I
would have it thoroughly understood that our studies
are tied to no one psychological school.   The efforts
at mental analysis which are here represented have
been stimulated more by uncovering facts than by
any theories, although I gratefully acknowledge the
help to appreciation of principles which has been derived
from various writers on psychoanalysis and kindred
topics.   It has been no small aid to scientific convic-
tion that many others, even though working in separate fields, clearly discern that often there are covert
mental mechanisms basically affecting attitudes and
conduct.

The reader who profits by this work is, with the author, especially indebted to Doctor Augusta F. Bronner for her studies of cases and her aid in the preparation of this volume.

WILLIAM HEALY.

WINNETKA, ILLINOIS,
November, 1916.

CONTENTS

MENTAL CONFLICTS AND MISCONDUCT

CHAPTER I

INTRODUCTION

A REMARKABLE, dynamic quality characterizing certain hidden mental reactions to experiences is responsible in some individuals for the production of misconduct, or, indeed, whole careers of delinquency. These experiences and reactions not only develop as an unrecognized background in the special case (they often are not even consciously framed as causal in the offender's own mind), but the fact of the existence of this type of mental causation is yet to be made a part of general knowledge. It is my task to set forth with abundant illustration the nature of these most important mechanisms of mental life.

In view of the newness of the idea of searching out mental factors of conduct, we have waited several years to see if the discovery of these apparently definite psychological principles held true for an ample number of cases; meanwhile watching the effects of attempts to adjust affairs in the mental life of certain offenders. Sufficient time has thus elapsed, and our studies are now ready for detailed publication. They

1

will have for many the greatest interest of any of our
findings.

Some general facts may first be stated. In the
consultation room with parents and even with delinquents themselves, or during court hearings, or in
considering the statements of probation officers who
have striven to avert further misdoing, sometimes a
curious aspect of the case becomes apparent. It
may stand out clearly that the individual experiences
a distinct inner urge towards misdoing — misdoing
that often leads to little else than anxious apprehen-
sion and other suffering on the part of the misdoer.
The painfulness of these effects, even as a repeated
experience, is not only apparent to the observer, but
may be well recognized by the delinquent. This
untoward drive of something in the concealed mental
life is seen already in young children, is much more
frequent in adolescents, and undoubtedly exists in
many adults. In the last, however, the long and
strong effects of environmental conditions and habits
cover deeply the evidences of original forces. What
do such formidable urgings represent?

It is clear to the onlooker that the inner driving
force does not proclaim itself in any way as such, that
it takes little heed of reason or prudence, that it ex-
hibits a strange energy from a source so unsuspected.
Then, if sincere and patient investigation is undertaken with the delinquent, the whole phenomenon
may be revealed as a reaction to component parts of
mental life and to certain prior experiences. Hardly
ever is the chain of causation found to have been self-
perceived or self-formulated. Relationship of the
active misconduct, regarded as effect, to the underlying cause, is anything but obvious on account of

repression of the original trouble-producing ideas and emotions. Here superficial facts are thoroughly misleading in regard to antecedents. The displayed energy is only to be traced back along devious or vicarious paths to a distant, pent-up source, where the tendency to action is generated through the high emotional import of the original experience and of the mental states superimposed. In such a case the repressions, the escape of energy along undesirable channels, the outcome in misconduct truly represent mental strife, mental conflict.

For readers unfamiliar with certain trends of thought now influencing psychology and particularly psychological medicine I may say that if the above terse statement does not seem entirely comprehensible, the subject receives further elucidation in the discussion of principles and] methods of studying cases offered in following chapters. There is no need for lack of clarity in treating this most interesting phase of mental life; I deal with it only along a road that is well lighted by ascertained data. The concreteness of the case illustrations will certainly serve to bring about good understanding of what can be discovered and what can be done in cases of misconduct of the type we have under consideration.

The study and interpretation of these specially involved *mental mechanisms,* for so they are well-termed, in their relation to misconduct, I have all along felt should proceed with full conservatism. It can readily be seen that we have not in the least overdone the central idea, have not drawn far-fetched conclusions, or been carried away by the dicta of writers who perceive the wealth of possible theory involved in discussion of hidden mental backgrounds. It is likely, rather, that some students ardently seeking mental causations in the field of medical psychology will feel that we have not done justice to the interpretation of many subtleties. More concerning the intricacies of the subject will be developed in later parts of this work, but such points always appear to us of much less importance than grappling the main issue.

The evolution of our own thought concerning the relation of mental conflicts to misconduct has been singularly simple and direct. It proceeded from no *a priori* expectation or formulation of principles. Indeed, until quite ingenuous inquiry into the springs of conduct elicited this type of fact for us, we were not aware that mental conflict played any part here. The analogy to what has been discovered in other fields by mental analysis or psychoanalysis, particularly as applied to functional nervous disorders which are, after all, largely problems of conduct, was perceived later. Starting thus firmly with actual facts, we have continuously attempted further investigation only with our feet well on the ground. I speak particularly of this because in some quarters the concept of mental conflicts seems to have offered wings for soaring high in the realms of speculative thought.

Many nonprofessional people will balk, no doubt, at the difficulties implied in our insistence on the necessity for such intensive study of not a few cases of misdoing. Certainly parents and others most intimately concerned, while often the very ones who suggest investigation, too frequently show themselves, as may be seen by our case material, quite unable to grasp the purport of the results of investigation. And seriously significant here is the well-rooted general supposition that tendencies to misdoing can be corrected by superficial attitudes towards them, such, for instance, as the administration of ordinary forms of retribution. But, indeed, in view of failures to induce moral reconstruction, ranging from attempts in family life to those undertaken by the law, failures shown by statistics and by individual cases, there should be no objections because of the comparative difficulty of getting at underlying causes.

The main situation to be comprehended is that the human mind is an immensely complex organism, and that if we are to cope with its conduct-producing powers, we must know them. Obstacles to knowledge may be encountered, but form no excuse if they are not insurmountable. After all, in at least fairly intelligent and young individuals, our experience shows that the deep-lying essentials may usually be ascertained. The task requires skill in appreciations and discernments, and acquaintance with special methods; the time demanded is only such as any serious human problem deserves.

There is no reason, with the spread of knowledge concerning this subject, why we may not rationally expect a rapid growth of demand for such thorough study of difficult cases of delinquency as may bring to light the fact of mental conflict when it exists. It would hardly do to define "difficult cases" as merely those instances of delinquency generally regarded as hard to explain, because superficial accounting for wrongdoing is altogether too common. We continually meet all sorts of rough-and-ready explanations of delinquency offered by everybody, from parents to experienced judges — explanations which seem entirely satisfactory as a theory to the person offering them, even when the field of inquiry in the given case

has not in the least been covered. In our case-histories, if it were worth while, considerable space might
be given to citing the various false causal interpretations which had been passed along as if they represented
known facts.

As a contrast to this, I may insist that other workers
will have just our experiences in discovery if they
assume the highly practical task of intimately studying the causative factors of delinquency. It was not
long before we were forced to the conclusion that such
information as might be obtained by mental testing,
physical examination, by learning the main points of
developmental and family history, and by inquiring
into companionship and other environmental conditions, was absolutely insufficient to explain the essentials of the development of a marked tendency to
delinquency in certain cases. Certain elements of
inner mental life had to be sought out and invoked
for explanation, even if practical issues alone were in
view.

If there is practical value in this deeper investigation
it must be evidenced by positive, determinable, therapeutic results. Not only do I grant this point, but
I have always insisted on it since I first realized how
mental analysis, as a general method, tends to work
over into the field of psychology of conduct. It may
be said at once that some early cases gave such unmistakable proof of the possibility of great service
being rendered through ascertaining the mental conflict back of the misconduct, that since then there has
never been with us serious doubt of the worth of this
method. Our case-studies, as given later, will sustain
the point. In fact, even the failures — from which I
contend we may learn nearly as much as from suc-

cesses — often show the continued existence of just those elements which we clearly recognized it was necessary to eliminate from the environment or from the mind in order that the correlated conduct-tendencies might be altered.

In the literature dealing with delinquency and crime we must plead that practically no help or hint was to be found concerning the import of mental conflicts for the production of misconduct; as a matter of fact the present volume offers the first approximation to a careful study on the subject. However, in the publications of a number of students of mental analysis or psychoanalysis, we have found much that has aided our understanding of the mental life uncovered to us by our own cases. Something of our debt to other investigators will appear in later chapters; here I will merely state, in general, that the deeper strata of the mind that experts have tapped in their endeavor to study the foundations of the neuroses have revealed data that serve to strengthen greatly some of our findings.

How important this subject of mental conflicts really is in relation to delinquency, as witnessed to by the proportionate number of cases, is a question already, no doubt, in the minds of some readers. It would be difficult to give an estimate that might serve as an indicator for any given situation. We are uncertain even about the totals in our own series. (We find no practical difference between the proportions for each sex.) In our first thousand cases of youthful recidivists we found seventy-three instances where mental conflict was a main cause of the delinquency, but during the first year or more of our work we were not aware of the possible frequency of this factor and

very likely did not always discover it. Even later
we have undoubtedly failed sometimes to ascertain
this essential fact; it is by no means always easy to
uncover the conflict. In the second series of a thousand recidivists, studied by Doctor Augusta F. Bronner
and myself during two years, although we found
seventy-four examples of mental conflict, we, again,
would be far from contending that this number represents the true total. Many times, in the exigencies
of court work, only the comparatively superficial
facts of mental and physical conditions, with some
points about family and habits and environment, have
been elicited. But even our incomplete showing of
over seven per cent. for each series looms large enough
to demonstrate the considerable importance of this
cause, and to show that any student of unselected
delinquents is very likely to see many of these particularly intricate cases.

Much more important than the matter of numbers
is the fact that, on account of the recurrence of the
impulse to misbehavior, amounting at times almost to
a criminalistic compulsion, some of the most important cases of delinquency are those involving the problem of mental conflict. The cases cited will amply
demonstrate this. Over many years conduct may be
tinged with a malign show of anti-social tendencies,
and in some cases a very definite, unfortunate social
attitude is assumed. Indeed, a long career of misdeeds may be evolved from the primary cause and its
renewals.

Even in this introductory chapter I would emphasize
other incident factors, over and beyond the original
mental experience and its repression, which enter
into the making of delinquent careers upon a basis of

mental conflict. In the first place it may be, as often suggested, that a special type of temperament is in part responsible for this given reaction. Possibly this is so, but, of course, the fact implies no mental abnormality; indeed, it may well be that individuals particularly well endowed in emotional qualities and finer feelings are the more prone to suffer from mental repressions and conflicts.

Then, next, may be mentioned certain superimposed elements entering into the making of delinquent tendencies in these cases of mental conflict, not that they are always present as major factors, but the chance of their playing an important part is so great that consideration of them is ever necessary. To enumerate: the thought or impulse as once held may very likely crop up again in the mind through the active forces of memory and of association and habit formation. Then there may be persisting environmental influences which further the development of the delinquent tendency, even though the genesis of the latter has been for the most part a matter of the inner mental life. There are the suggestions coming from various features of living conditions in an old neighborhood, from an already achieved reputation, from old associates in delinquency, or from companions known while under detention. There is the sorry effect of a bad reputation upon chances for employment, and the effect of police surveillance, — warranted, of course, but which leads to the former delinquent continually looking upon himself as a possible offender. Even a family attitude towards an offender may have the same result. We have watched all of these adventitious forces at work in some cases and have observed that where no change of conditions has been carried out,

the continuance of the tendency to offense has seemed
inevitable. Complicated and difficult for treatment
as the situation may sometimes appear, the various
elements are not indistinguishable. The problem in
any one of these cases where other elements are added
to the original mental conflict is typically the problem of reformation of criminals in general; there are
many social maladjustments which stand in the way
of betterment.

The interest and import that this whole subject of
the relationship of mental conflicts to misconduct
should have for a wide range of readers is just the
interest and import that the study of causations should
have for all those concerned in any way with the
problems of conduct. First there are the parents; they
could be saved a vast deal of trouble and disgrace if
they understood and could head off delinquent tendencies at the time of beginnings. Perhaps nothing
stands out any clearer in our cases than the fact that
those nearest have been totally ignorant of what has
been going on in the mental life of the young persons
in question, and often have not known of exceedingly
important experiences. Then, teachers, if acquainted
at all with this subject, might often surmise enough to
at least advise professional investigation. Judges and
probation officers, who see the well-defined cases of
delinquency, often gather facts concerning the delinquent which should suggest every reason for deep
inquiry into causes and beginnings. The observed
ineffectiveness of attempted superficial remedies under
the law, in many cases, should be sufficient to demonstrate the necessity for thoughtful, patient, professional consideration of *all* that could possibly cause
the misconduct. Perhaps we might also say that

institutional people, by vocation engaged in handling delinquents, are falling short of their highest duties and greatest possibilities if they, in their turn, are not searching for all things curative. And as for pastors and all who attempt moral guidance, it is perfectly patent that they can hardly be thoroughly qualified for their attempts in many directions if they do not have as part of their armamentarium knowledge of the essential facts pertaining to the genesis of misdoing.

Who professionally shall be the analyst to delve into genetics in the actual case depends in any given situation upon who is personally suited and educated for the task. It is a work for medicopsychologists and perhaps for psychologists untrained in medicine, but it also strikes one that it is a rich field for properly equipped pastors, — men who, on account of their very calling, should be trained to fathom the foundations of conduct.

The bearing of such findings as ours on the whole scheme of handling offenders under the law is as striking as it is obvious. It might well serve as a theme for many a discussion. Few words are here necessary; we and many others have long since dwelled on the to-be-expected inefficiency of any system constructed by the law for handling human beings which is not founded on first principles of understandings. What can be expected if no early effort is made to discover the dynamic sources from which delinquency emanates?

A great variety of misconduct arises upon the basis of mental conflict. In our observed cases, the range is from the less serious, but sustained bad behavior of childhood, to deeds of actual crime. As will be seen in the following list, there is little in the way of misbehavior to which mental conflict may not lead. We have seen examples of :

General troublesomeness and mischief making, including destructiveness.

Stubbornness, obstinacy, chronic willfulness.

Truancy.

Remaining out over night and running away from home.

Vagrancy.

Stealing, including pathological stealing. (We desire to avoid the use of the ill-defined term "kleptomania.")

Obtaining money by false representations. Forgery.

Exhibition of bad temper. General violent behavior.

Deliberate malicious mischief and violence.

Sexual offenses.[1]

Cruelty — sadistic offenses.

Self-injury of the nature of masochistic offenses.

Injury to others, or attempt to injure.

(It should be readily conceded that the social sins defined by the law do not represent any deeper perversities and often are not as significant for the production of unhappiness as are many of the chronic exhibitions of ugly family attitude, of selfishness, miserliness, bad temper, of overbearing or unfair business methods. And we doubt not that many of these other forms of ill conduct also may arise from subconscious mental conflicts. Indeed, analysts of mental processes have recently been showing this to be true.) [2]

[1] In our chapter on Applications we have given the reasons for limiting our discussion of sexualistic offenses.

[2] O. Pfister's analytic researches into the causes of family hatred offer an instance. *Jahrbuch für Psychoanalytische Forschungen*, Bd. II, Heft 1, 1910.

In the detailed histories of specific cases which follow my general discussion, nearly all the above offenses are represented. Cases have been selected as they portray types of causal experiences, of mental content induced by these experiences, of varieties of resultant misconduct, and sometimes to illustrate other features of special importance. The cases are placed in chapters, according to their emphasis of some particular point. Since the general elements are active in each instance, much overlapping is unavoidable; cases of stealing, for example, are depicted in other chapters than the one especially devoted to stealing. It will be readily understood that space for our very long records cannot be afforded, since it seems desirable to give a considerable variety of cases, that the abridgments indulged in omit the details of the actual difficulties encountered in getting at the conflicts, that investigations resulting negatively and many other minor points are neglected, that personalities and places are always disguised beyond recognition. Those who wish to understand the subject and its bearings are invited to read closely this most informing concrete material.

As a final introductory word, I would suggest that if motives and impulses, acting recurrently until they signify tendencies and careers, arise out of the subconscious mental life of the individual, the fact must imply vastly more than is involved in the discussion of delinquency. We may reasonably at once think of such possible origin for other kinds of behavior, for social self-assertions, for the pettier unpleasant attitudes and frames of mind, for undefined dissatisfactions and social dislikes. Even many impulses to good behavior and to select desirable paths of actions probably arise from mechanisms active in subconscious mental life. At present one may look forward to extremely interesting investigations along this line, with considerable hint of possible accretions to our knowledge already appearing in recent literature on human motives and conduct. At least, the significance of genetics in the field of conduct problems is not limited to behavior of a special group, or to society's interest in delinquency and crime. Broader horizons dawn for the student of origins of conduct-tendencies.

CHAPTER II

GENERAL PRINCIPLES

CONCRETE findings, rather than theories, have gradually formed the framework of our ideas concerning the relationship of mental conflicts to misconduct. The whole conception is valuably strengthened, however, by formulation of such generalizations as may be rationally evolved from our collected data. Then, there is much of interest in reviewing these larger considerations by the side of certain psychological deductions developed through analogous work in other fields. It has been most fortunate for our investigation that in the last decade or so working methods and principles of dynamic psychology have been established which are especially helpful for the understanding of certain causes of conduct disorders.

At the very outset of any setting forth of principles, I would emphasize the most fundamental of all facts concerning this subject, namely, that the use of the genetic method opens the way, as nothing else does, to the most formidable attacks upon misconduct. One might expect any thoroughly common-sense method to include an effort to go back to beginnings in order to arrive at understandings, yes, and in order to accomplish reformations, although this only too seldom accords with actual practice. But through results

15

actually achieved — in the form of wider explanatory
vistas gained and conduct-tendencies altered in individual cases — there need be no mere conjecture
about the matter; we discover many definite evidences
of the practical utility of studying causations.

Another main consideration is that we find ourselves here working in the field of dynamics. It is
not so much what the individual is structurally, so far
as the mental powers are measurable, but what the
mental forces may be that are at work creating the
undesirable behavior. As I have often maintained,
there is much to be gained by the logical procedure of
primarily considering conduct as the direct offspring
of mental activity. And where mental conflicts are
involved, the study of dynamics must go deeper than
usual; investigation must be carried out that shall
reveal much more than superficial facts and the
obvious workings of the mind. We may, perhaps,
without much harm to the situation, neglect the mental forces at work in some instances of misconduct, but
in cases of the type now under consideration, the study
of mental processes affords a master-key for opening
to the light the essentials in the background.

Then, it is not merely the fact that there are driving
forces of the inner life making for misconduct, but it
is a matter of much import that these forces prove to
be so powerful and are so persistently recurrent. Many
of our cases exhibit the most remarkable energy of
impulse in untoward directions. The determining factor of action arises and recurs with a show of strength
all out of proportion to any readily perceivable source
of motive power. It would seem as if this feature
alone of the offender's conduct would be sufficient to
call for deep reflection and analysis.

Another point concerning these remarkable cases has heretofore been made very little of, so little that it affords complete evidence of the superficiality of ordinary appreciation of motives. We find that some misdoers do not, in their misconduct, appear to be in the least carrying out their keenest desires. Their actions are forced, as it were, by something in themselves, not of themselves. If we judge by the repetition of misdeeds in the face of possible punishment and other suffering, we might suppose that these misdoers were impelled by their very strongest conscious wishes. But we know that this is often not the case, because the effect of the conduct in question is not in any ordinary sense pleasurable to the misdoers, nor do they regard it as such. The wrongdoing is not even primarily contemplated as likely to give them high satisfaction. So far as we can learn, the impulse arising from mental conflict has no penumbra whatever of delightfulness; on the contrary, it seems as if one of its most noteworthy characteristics is the curious absence of any idea of pleasure to be derived from following it. We have heard the expression from not a few misdoers, "I don't know what makes me do it. I don't want to do it, and I feel sorry afterwards." It would seem that students of human motives should long since have been attracted to this curious phenomenon of conduct, because, results not being even contemplated as pleasurable, ordinary motives are not plainly involved.

In investigation of mental conflicts as causes of misconduct, we are bound to contemplate the mental life of early years, not because of *a priori* considerations, but through being led back, step by step, to influences active then. We sometimes find a very direct route

leading from emotion-provoking experiences and reactions of childhood to even major offenses of adult
life. How many cases there may be where the causes
date back to childhood with intervening years free
from misdeeds, it will need further development of
studies of this subject to show. From our observations we should say that this intermitting type of evolution of misconduct will seldom be encountered.
As far as examples of long-standing, overt tendency
to offense are concerned, of course such cases must
have had long-standing causes.

In passing from these prefatory generalizations to
discussion of the mechanisms involved when mental
conflicts result in misconduct, I must first attempt
some clear statement of certain concepts, deductions,
and terms developed in closely allied fields. While
this exposition is mainly in the interest of the general
reader, it may serve to show professional students also
how far our practical experience tallies with the deductions of others, and in what measure certain
psychological conceptions may be utilized in studying
misconduct.

The general method of psychological investigation
with which we are now concerned has been much
under discussion recently, and has been usually spoken
of as *psychoanalysis* or the *psychoanalytic movement*.
These terms have become familiar to medical men and
psychologists, and the laity has now heard much of
their purport, but still we are doubtful about adopting
them for our uses. The terms are not thoroughly
serviceable for all students of mental mechanisms
because of specific connotations which have been given
them. We find that followers of Sigmund Freud, the
great sponsor of the psychoanalytic movement, rather

object to application of the word psychoanalysis to the work of those who do not in fairly full measure follow the theories and practices of the master. On the other hand, some of us who are not complete psychoanalysts in that sense, do not wish to mislead and make it appear as if our studies implied the use of the fine technic of interpretation and the extremely prolonged mental analyses which the principal exponents of the Freudian school deem desirable in their exploration of the neuroses. Whether or not practical results are obtainable through studies of misconduct by less thorough-going analysis, I leave the reader to judge later for himself; just here the point is that our work is not based on psychoanalysis to the complete Freudian extent. It seems much better for our purposes, then, to follow the suggestion of Meyer Solomon,[1] and speak of *mental analysis* — a phrase that can be "adopted without offense to anybody."

For a clear general statement of the method of mental analysis I can do no better than cite from an expert analyst, Doctor Putnam:[2] "The psychoanalytic method is the name given to the special means by which the memory is aided to penetrate into the forgotten portions of one's life, with the view of bringing to the light of clear consciousness the details of emotional conflicts which, in spite of being out of sight, exert an influence, often of an unfavorable sort, on the development of character and temperament, as well as on the motives, the habits, and the thoughts." Though this definition is admirably stated, for our ends we might paraphrase the first part of it and state that:

[1] Meyer Solomon, "On the Use of the Term Psychoanalysis and Its Substitute." *Medical Record*, New York, September 18, 1915.
[2] James Jackson Putnam, M.D., "Human Motives", p. 68.

Mental analysis is a name given to the method of using the memory to penetrate into the former experiences of mental life.

It is of great significance for understanding or undertaking our type of work with offenders that the use of artificial devices to aid the memory, at least in most instances, appears quite unnecessary. To be sure, nearly all the cases of mental conflict we have studied are purposely those of decidedly young people in whom the memories of the early unfortunate experiences are much fresher; there has been with them less to obliterate the outlines of the original stirring event or emotion. Then, no doubt, the retracing process in misconduct cases is much simpler and more direct than in cases of functional nervous disease, with which the psychoanalysts have busied themselves. It is rarely necessary to dig up "a long series of events related to each other by ties of the most varied sorts", or to encourage the memory, as Putnam adds, "to go on a voyage of discovery without reference to what may be discovered."

If one were working with older misdoers, probably the genetic search would have to be much more prolonged and intricate, and much more that was irrelevant would have to be dug up for examination. I say probably, because we cannot safely state this from our own experience nor from data acquired by others. Practically nothing has been written on this point, and it must be acknowledged that efforts with old offenders are not particularly promising on account of the many deteriorations, mental, physical, and social, which usually accompany a prolonged career of delinquency. Here, as in other aspects of clinical criminology, much the best returns, scientific as well as redemptory, are to be obtained through working with misdoers at a time not far from the beginnings of their misbehavior.

As suggested above, it appears more than likely that the pathway from mental conflict to misconduct is straighter than are the steps between mental conflict and nervous disorders. It is emphasized by many analysts working in the latter field that they discover mental processes pursuing their activities through the most remarkable transformations and by way of shuntings off and circuitous paths. In their cases, the seizing hold by the subconscious mind of some particular association of environmental or mental experience and attaching it strongly to the original emotion-producing event in a way that makes for abnormal manifestations in body or mind, is not nearly so direct or understandable a phenomenon as what occurs in the cases of misconduct that I cite. It appears to be a much farther cry from a neurosis than from delinquency to genesis in mental conflict. The technical studies of the various mental reactions, the knowledge of which the analysts, particularly the Freudians, have given to the world, appear not nearly so essential to the student of misbehavior. I have little doubt that there is more to this whole subject of the relationship of mental conflict to misconduct than we have developed while attempting during these years to base our investigations on thoroughly firm ground. I see the human mind as too complex an organ for me to suppose that in these comparatively simple phrasings of mental analysis all is explained. Following this effort to clear a way, there should be deeper explorations in various important regions where mental life and social conduct are interrelated.

The great desideratum in all work of this sort is to bring "to the light of clear consciousness the details of emotional conflicts which, in spite of being out of sight, exert an influence." Whatever the victim's troubles, whatever the special technic employed, exploration is the aim of mental analysis. What there is further to be said in exposition of the mental mechanisms pertaining to our subject is all by way of filling in the outlines of the main conception or fact.

We may now go on to consider some of these mechanisms. The term *mental conflict* represents an idea that is not at all difficult to understand. Few would question the existence of such a phenomenon. Technical discussion hardly makes the concept any stronger, and, yet, perhaps some attempt at definition is desirable in order that there may be no misunderstanding whatever about what is meant. A mental conflict, then, is a conflict between elements of mental life, and occurs when two elements, or systems of elements, are out of harmony with each other. This is the barest possible statement. Why do mental elements in the same individual become conflicting? This question leads us, in turn, to consider other mental mechanisms.

Memories or ideational elements forming the content of our mental storehouses are largely constellated; on account of the activity of various laws of association mental elements are so related to each other that there is a bond between them. The particular form of a constellation is the result of the special grouping or linking together of perceptive experiences or of their reproductions as they arise in the mind. A *constellation* of ideas is thus a system of mental elements having some special relationship of the elements to each other.

We must next consider the *complex*, the theory of
which is at the heart of the psychoanalytic method;
this according to our own findings in mental analysis represents a vitally important subject. Various
authors have sketched their conceptions of a mental
complex, particularly as they have taken or modified
the idea from Freud, who develops such an extensive
psychological superstructure upon this foundation.
(There is no doubt that the concept of a mental complex existed long before Freud's day, albeit with little
consideration of the phenomenon and no attention to
practical applications.) We may gather from all
these writers that a complex is a constellation of mental elements permeated with a vigorous emotional
tone, a system or association of ideas grouped about
an emotional core or center. The existence of such
peculiarly disposed constellated systems no one can
doubt; how important they are for us as students of
misconduct will appear many times to our readers.

The complex has other essential characteristics.
Being possessed of an emotional tone it has energy-
producing powers; by reason of this it may be, and
often is, a great determiner of thoughts and actions.
This is merely following the general law that emotion-
tinged portions of the mental content are the dynamic
elements of mental life. And it also appears that only
parts of complexes active as producers of behavior
appear in consciousness. This is proved by the fact
that a very distinct effort or exploration is necessary
to bring any such entire system of ideas into view.

Discovery that portions of an active complex are
left in the mental background as subconscious led
to study of the phenomenon known as *repression*.
When a mental experience, or group of thoughts with

an emotional tone, or part of such a constellated system of ideas, is pushed back, "put out of mind", "forgotten", it is said to be repressed. This seeking oblivion for an experience may be more or less of an automatic, hardly conscious reaction, perhaps directly dictated by naturally falling in line with social conformities, either family or general, or it may be a thoroughly deliberate attempt to get rid of something conceived as undesirable.

Here we are brought sharply up against the question of whether there can be any real "forgetting" and "putting out of mind." Above all, we know that anything once experienced as mental content is subject to being stored. And it is a matter of everyday knowledge that the storage places of the mind contain many things that the conscious self is not aware of, either in detail or as being stored. No one has had a keener insight into the nature and importance of memory processes than the philosopher Bergson, and our own appreciation of this side of mental life may well be served by quoting from him a paragraph [1] that must have caught the eye of many students of mental analysis. Speaking of memory he says, "And as the past grows without ceasing, so also there is no limit to its preservation. . . . In reality, the past is preserved by itself automatically. In its entirety, probably, it follows us every instant; all that we have felt, thought, and willed from our earliest infancy is there, leaning over the present which is about to join it, pressing against the portals of consciousness that would fain leave it outside. The cerebral mechanism is arranged just so as to drive back into the unconscious

[1] Henri Bergson, "Creative Evolution", p. 4; translated by Arthur Mitchell, 1911.

almost the whole of this past, and to admit beyond the
threshold only that which can cast light on the present
situation or further the action now being prepared.
. . . Doubtless we think with only a small part of
our past, but it is with our entire past, including the
original bent of our soul, that we desire, will, and act.
Our past, then, as a whole is made manifest to us in
its impulse; it is felt in the form of tendency, although a small part of it only is known in the form of
idea." From these words we get a picture of mental
life that is peculiarly valuable as a background upon
which some fundamental conceptions of mental analysis in relation to misconduct may be developed.

The analysts all insist from their explorations of
mental content that repression does not signify kill-
ing off the undesirable portion of mental content.
Indeed, the word repression, so far as the complex
is concerned, has come to mean merely the splitting
off from consciousness of part of what would naturally,
through the original bond of association or constellation, be represented in its entirety in consciousness.
Repression is a form of *mental dissociation*, — a term
used long before the present development of the science of mental analysis. The conscious mind chooses
for its own reasons to consider some undesired portion
of a complex as forgotten, but, unfortunately, the
process of forcing it "out of mind" does not lead to
quiescent assimilation of it with more normal material
of prior experiences, assimilation into the great organ-
ization which we call the subconscious mind. The
dissociated portion is left with its original emotional
tone still attached, and through this fact anything
but quiescence may ensue. As the psychoanalysts
have put it, a complex dissociated by repression con-

tinues to have its own existence as a separate unas-
similated entity and to be possessed of special energy.
Repression, then, does not imply suspension of activity.   Clear exemplifications of the truth of this are to
be perceived in many of our case-histories.

The term *mental infantilism*, often applied by
psychoanalysts to the type of reactions which produce
neurotic symptoms, appears to have special significance for us. If it is an infantile reaction to attempt
to dispose of an idea by repressing it and at the same
time to keep it alive by getting some satisfaction for
the instinctive demand which it connotes, then surely
our cases demonstrate mechanisms of this earliest
psychological type.   Instead of a mature facing of
reality we discover these curious compromises where
some delinquency is indulged in as an expression of the
existence of a complex; the main elements of the complex are not expressed because they do not harmonize
with the individual's conceptions of personal or social
morality.

Subconscious mental life, which is one of the main
concerns of dynamic psychology, although hardly
mentioned by name in many textbooks of psychology,
requires from us some discussion concerning certain
points of special import.   (I hold no brief for the term
subconscious as opposed to or distinct from the meaning
of the word *unconscious*, which is sometimes used in
this connection, but it does seem more serviceable,
since the latter, as applied to mental processes, seems
to offer a contradiction in terms. As might be expected in a newly developing science, words have
been utilized that have meanings attached not altogether suitable for subsequent finer discriminations.)
The subconscious part of the mind may be defined

in its widest significance as that portion of mental life which, at least for the time being, is outside the general field of attention. Of course, the only proof of the existence of this background of mind material is the fact that on occasion portions of it are presented above the threshold of consciousness, namely, in the field of attention. Now, part of what is subconscious may be voluntarily recalled, with small or with greater difficulty. Some of it only makes itself known by involuntarily flashing or jumping into consciousness. Still other portions, in order to get above the threshold of conscious thought, need the use of artifices, such as hypnotism, hypnoidal states, or the free association methods, or require directive insistence on closely tracing associations for special memories. That an enormous number of past experiences cannot be voluntarily remembered is undoubtedly true. In the storehouse of the subconscious mind some of the material is near the portals of easy exit, some material is far off in dark nooks and crannies, far from the doorway and the light of conscious thought.

Particularly well conserved in subconsciousness, as I have already stated, are mental experiences or groups of mental elements which were stored away accompanied by a strong emotional tone. This is a matter of common-sense observation with all of us. These special constellations are peculiarly the ones of which parts flash up into the field of attention, and which cause substitutive reactions of various sorts. The most virile of these complexes are those in which the original emotion or "affect" was powerfully repressed, totally unreacted to, strangulated. The strength of a complex as a producer of unusual and abnormal mental, physical, or social behavior is not

measured by the length of time since it was repressed.
Neither is its force to be judged by the fact of easy
recognition or of complete disguise of any part which
appears at the surface of consciousness, nor by the
comparative difficulties experienced in pulling the
complex up to the surface to be seen and known for
what it is.

Variations in the difficulty of this task of getting at
and exploring the real nature of a complex are undoubtedly due to a number of differing conditions.
Among other things there are the innate traits of the
individual, the reaction tendencies acquired through
environmental and educational circumstances, the
force of the original emotion belonging to the complex
(sometimes amounting to an emotional shock or a
psychic trauma), the possibly continued repressive
activities exerted against any attempt at exploration.
This last is termed *resistance*.

The peculiar energy belonging to some complexes
calls forth frequently renewed efforts at repression.
In such instances the repressed ideas are of a nature
incompatible with the trend of personal consciousness,
and conscious reaction is therefore not permitted.
In describing this mechanism, Freud speaks of the
activities of a mental *censor* watching over certain
elements of complexes and preventing them from becoming associated with those in consciousness. But
more than this, there is the important phenomenon
which shows itself during professional mental analysis,
namely, resistance. To comport with special desires
and ends of the personality, there may be resistance
against any attempt to bring certain complexes to the
light. Many of the reasons for this resistance are
peculiar to the individual and to the situation. Just

as analysts in exploring the psychopathology of functional nervous and mental disorders, so we in our work with cases of misconduct sometimes observe this phenomenon of resistance most distinctly.

Any thinking person can readily conceive the leading cause of mental complexes and of repressions and resistances. All of these mechanisms depend for their existence upon feelings or emotions, and what is there to compare to various phases of sex life and to sex ideas as producers of emotion? And then, in strange contradiction to this is the opposition which the person finds, through social customs and taboos, to any expression of what may have been experienced and inwardly felt with such intensity. Thus, from an *à priori* standpoint, we shall see no cause for wonder if a great deal of emotion is found attached to repressed constellations of mental elements which center about sex experience. and ideas. Many objections have been raised to the work of the psychoanalysts because it deals so intensively with sex material. I am not at all inclined to defend these students on all issues which can be raised, but no doubt our own findings could be used by them in support of many of the positions which they take concerning this matter. We ourselves have been utterly surprised at the development of so much delinquency of various sorts from beginnings in unfortunate sex knowledge which has come into the mental field as a psychic shock, producing emotional disturbance. To be sure, we have heard some widely experienced, intelligent observers of delinquents, knowing nothing of mental analysis, state that they consider sex affairs to be at the root of a tremendous number of criminalistic impulses, but yet the direct connection and the clearness with which the

mental mechanisms may be observed in these cases
has been a constant source of wonderment to us.

One of the great contributions of the psychoanalysts
has been that they have discovered the very early
roots of sexual life in the individual. They have
proved that in childhood, even in early childhood,
there is mental life, exhibited perhaps as instinct or
imagery or idea, centering about sexual components.
Not that this school of psychology is alone in this discovery; a number of other thorough investigators,
for example, Moll,[1] have made similar observations.
If, then, we find the development of sexual complexes
and repressions years before the advent of puberty,
we need not be astonished. That there are many
social as well as psychological implications in this
fact goes without saying.

Analysts, in studying the causes of functional bodily
disorders, have discovered the process which has been
termed *conversion*. This is the mechanism of convert-
ing a mental phenomenon into a physical manifesta-
tion. As some analysts put it, certain physical
symptoms are produced by liberating from a mental
complex emotional energy which then innervates
abnormal neural pathways. This changing over of
energy from restrained and hidden to active and overt
manifestations is analogous to what we observe when
mental conflict finds expression in misconduct.

Other mechanisms, less traceable in physical aspects, have been discovered which offer even closer
resemblance to the nature of our own findings and
interpretations. There is *substitution;* this may be defined as what occurs when emotional energy, escaped

[1] Albert Moll, "Das Sexualleben des Kindes", Berlin, 1908. Also
translation by Eden Paul, "The Sexual Life of the Child", New York, 1913.

from the repressed parts of a constellation, becomes attached to associated, but not unbearable and, consequently, not necessarily repressed elements. The usefulness of this conception will appeal strongly to all readers of our own case-histories. Another term much used is *abreaction* — signifying the general phenomenon of liberation of energy belonging to a complex, a working-off of the latent, stored-up emotional force. When this occurs, activity takes place along paths of less resistance than those through which the complex has been repressed. (Of course, abreaction would also include fulfillment of the whole trend of desire of the complex.) It will gradually appear that several features of the theory of abreaction have their significance for our studies of misconduct.

Some of the larger conceptions of mental life as developed by analysts are of considerable interest to us here. It is one of the theories concerning the subconscious mind that no psychical energy which enters this realm is ever lost. Conservation of energy takes place here as in the world of matter. If, then, an experience is thrust back into this storage place with a strong emotional tone attached to it, this means that the experience or complex may remain below the threshold of conscious attention, but exists there with a capacity for releasing energy and creating much disturbance. Another conception, in like manner, specifies the fact of transformation of energy in the world of mental processes. Stoddart compares psychical to physical energy and speaks much of the driving force of mental life. Jung has offered the name *horme* to apply to the energizing principle in mental life. Stoddart suggests that if a certain amount of horme or psychical energy, once known to exist, appears to

be lost, it may be just the business of the analyst to
find out what has become of it.   In our own field we
readily see the value of following the long effects, even
over periods of apparent discontinuance, of some
previously evoked emotional experience.   The histories which are here related show certain types of
experience as highly provocative of emotion and
inner urge, with fixation of the energy on some portion of mental life which, in our cases, is directly
responsible for the production of misconduct.

Another main theory is concerned with *determinism*
in mental life.   Influencing the nature of every thought
there is some past idea linked to it by the laws of
association; for every impulse there is an immediate
cause in some phase of present mental activity, as
well as a preceding cause in mental experiences farther back.   No impulse to action is to be regarded
as a meaningless phenomenon, it is always determined
by foregoing elements of mental life; even no idea or
image can spring up without relation to the past.
Without stating this theory at any greater length, I
may say at once that determinism in mental processes
is the backbone of the psychoanalytic method.   Now,
whatever may be urged against the extremes of this
conception of psychical laws, exhibited, for instance,
in sanguine attempts to find reason in the gibberings
of dementia or the railings of mania, the fact is that
mental analysis has proved most clearly the existence
of a vast amount of determinism that was not known
heretofore.   For our studies of misconduct, these
determining factors in mental life, so frequently not
realized in the least, even by the agent actively producing their effects, prove to be of vast importance.

A number of mental mechanisms other than those

considered above have been enumerated by the exponents of psychoanalysis; most of these are of comparatively slight interest to us here and will not be discussed, but certain of them represent mental processes which are of great importance for the possibilities of treatment of tendencies to misconduct. These, together with several points concerning practical applications and methods of mental analysis in our field, will be taken up in the next chapters.

CHAPTER III

APPLICATIONS

THE practical application of mental analysis to
problems of moral reconstruction properly forms the
center of our discussion. It was in order to reach this
central point by rational, explanatory steps that we
found it necessary to take some account of certain
theoretical conceptions developed as fundamentals of
psychoanalysis. A direct answer to the reasonable
interrogation, *Cui bono?* concerning mental analysis
as applied to conduct problems is given through our
case-histories, which clearly demonstrate valuable
understandings gained and delinquent tendencies
altered by use of this method. Still further inquiries
are naturally concerned with peculiarities of the mental
processes implicated in the conflicts that cause misconduct and with details of the procedure that offers
most chance of achieving the desired reformation.

The first suggestion of the value of mental analysis
in the problems of misconduct should come through
considering one of the main laws of mind, namely,
that the direction and content of every mental activity
stands in definite relationship to previously active
elements of mental life. Of course, no intelligent
person could believe for a moment that ideas of misconduct, or even impulses thereto, arise by chance.

The constitution of every idea and impulse is largely predetermined by antecedent ideas and images. Every thought arises as a link in a chain of mental associations joined together by various psychological conditionings. Misconduct as a reaction to stimuli received from the outer world — stealing, for instance, of objects temptingly displayed — may seem so obviously explicable that the observer neglects to look for other causal considerations. But when the impulse to misconduct arises from an internal stimulus and, particularly, when individuals subject to such impulses may be found vividly conscious of struggle against them, the phenomenon is most striking, and the behavior appears inexplicable by any of the ordinary conceptions of objective causation. And as for inner stimuli and their origin, it seems nothing short of amazing that scientific studies have not long since been directed towards ascertainment of what these may be.

While there has been no general application of mental analysis to the study of delinquency, there has been gradual appreciation of the wide bearings of the method, both by the specialists who use it in treatment of the psychoneuroses and by a few others who have recognized it as a method which reveals important facts of mental life.[1] Mental conflicts certainly must react in many other ways than by setting up the abnormal

[1] For readers of English we may cite here, as showing something of the broader aspects of mental analysis, "Mental Mechanisms", by W. A. White, 1911; "Human Motives", by J. J. Putnam, 1915; "The Freudian Methods Applied to Anger", an article by Stanley Hall, *American Journal of Psychology*, July, 1915; "The Freudian Wish", by E. B. Holt, 1915; "Psychoanalysis and the Study of Children", an article by O. Pfister, *American Journal of Psychology*, 1915, p. 130; "Psychopathology of Every Day Life", by Freud, and "Psychology of the Unconscious", by Jung — both of the latter recently translated. Then, lately has appeared "Mechanisms of Character Formation", by W. A. White.

manifestations which the neurologist is called upon to treat. There have been a number of definite suggestions by analysts that mental analysis might prove particularly valuable for students of criminalistic behavior, but no account of systematic work in this direction has appeared [1] and there has been no publication heretofore of any considerable number of misconduct cases originating from mental conflict.

Interpretations and technical considerations in the field of psychoanalysis have already gone far, and to what extent these — many of which we have not in the least touched on — may be at all useful in treatment of misconduct remains for the future to determine. (I desire here to state that I am far from believing that our studies have explored the deepest mechanisms conceivably at the roots of misconduct, even though what we have discovered has proved to be so practically important for understanding and treatment.) At present, however, it is clear that mental conflict does often stand in causal relationship to misconduct and that this vital fact may be brought out by even a moderate amount of analysis and, in general, is understandable when discussed in nontechnical terms. Beginning with these main points we may pass on to the special features of applying this method.

The symptoms of certain functional maladies of the nervous system are strikingly allied to definitive misconduct. In a case of hysterical paralysis, for instance, the picture closely resembles an exhibition of obstinate self-will; it is the assumption of an attitude directed against and actually conflicting with normal environ-

---

[1] Oskar Pfister, in his book "Die psychanalytische Methode", Leipzig, 1913, insists on the importance of mental analysis for treatment of misbehavior, but gives only a few minor cases at no great length.

mental demands. The extreme troublesomeness of psychoneurotic cases in family life, or even in courts of civil law, indicates that they may be partly considered problems of conduct. Certainly the background of the mental and social attitude of the individual is properly a matter of study in both types of cases — those where the abnormality is termed misconduct and those where peculiar behavior is regarded merely as evidence of a psychoneurosis. Indeed, the development of some peculiar and abnormal attitude towards family relationships or the world in general sometimes is directly responsible for misconduct exhibited in many forms. We have seen numerous examples of offenders holding such a definite attitude or grudge, which has often been formed at a surprisingly early age. I may refer to our case-histories for details. It seems reasonable to conclude from this general fact that analytic studies of mental attitude and of grudge formation might be widely undertaken with much promise of helpfulness to both those who are actively and those who are passively concerned. Even where no actual criminalistic conduct is engaged in, the faulty attitude may give rise to great irritability and may produce much unhappiness for others. Do we not know men and women whose main trends of behavior show almost vindictiveness towards their fellow-beings, and this without any cause whatever except their own inner set of mind? Entirely applicable to our study of general tendencies of conduct is investigation of what in the inner mental life gives rise to attitudes which are factors at the base of such tendencies.

Preceding any attempt at explanation of the general fact of disordered behavior, even in a particular instance, Freud maintains that there must be inquiry into the origin of the specific form of disorder displayed. It is best not to take up first the question, for example, of why this given individual suffers from a neurosis, but why does this special type of neurosis appear. For answering all aspects of the problem in any case, Freud maintains that it must be known both what the patient brings to the situation by way of innate traits, and how special mental experiences have been effective. The value of these points for our method is very clear. We, too, must go further than the mere fact of impulse to misconduct; we must know the actual content of the impulse, be it towards stealing, or running away, or anything else. Then in studying sources we, too, may not neglect either the reaction-type of the individual or the mental experiences which have been determining factors in the behavior. Moreover, as Freud says, by working in this well-balanced way we are likely to make important scientific discoveries about the causation of behavior trends in general.

For understanding our cases we are under the manifest necessity of digging up earlier mental associations. Proceeding to the task, we find that we encounter many rich deposits of explanatory facts. The discovery of important associations, as I have stated previously, is made with greater or less difficulty, and when brought to the light, they may show the most unsuspected chaining together of mental elements. The connecting links may be just such as Prince [1] found in a case he has published, where the patient suffered greatly from phobia (obsessive fear) related to the ringing of bells. It was finally dug out of the patient's subconscious

[1] Morton Prince, "The Psychopathology of a Case of Phobia", *Journal of Abnormal Psychology*, October, 1913.

mind that many years previously she had passed
through a time of mental anguish while her mother,
who died soon afterwards, suffered from a severe illness
and operation — and frequently during this period of
anxiety bells had chimed. She later knew nothing
of any relation of her phobia to this particular event;
she could not by conscious effort recall any emotional
shock connected with bells; by no ordinary means
was the subconscious memory of the effective association finally uncovered. There had been this conjunc-
tion, direful for her, of a terrific emotional strain with
a strong sensory impression. Investigation of such
associations of unusual perceptive experiences of many
sorts — especially hearing something said or seeing
something out of the ordinary — with high emotional
states, offers much of value for the student of misconduct.

How much of the specifically genetic mental background of misconduct is unrealized or forgotten, is a
matter that varies greatly and depends upon the age
at which investigation is begun, upon experiences
that have been added, upon the mental make-up of the
individual, and so on. As I have intimated previously,
the procedure necessary to bring up the memories into
active conscious life may be quite different in different
fields of work, in studying misconduct, for instance, as
compared to investigating the psychoneuroses. The
very same kind of fact may be much harder to dig out
of one type of subconscious mind than out of another.
We note also the great variations which may obtain
in studying the same individual at different times.
We saw a boy of twelve, a naïve, straightforward
type of lad, who had recently begun his delinquencies.
He told us of the hold which certain other delinquent

boys had gained upon him, how they had informed him concerning sex matters. He had worried much about these things, he had repressed impulses and feelings of which he did not approve, but he did not hesitate to follow his companions' example in venturesome stealing. This lad later became notorious on account of daring burglaries. We saw him repeatedly when he was sixteen years old, and then he seemed to be totally unable to remember anything of the earlier conflict which he had so vividly described to us. He had remained free from the vices of sex life. Concerning his failure to remember, the fact that this boy, though not feeble-minded, was mentally somewhat subnormal, might be thought to complicate matters, but his memory processes in many ways were found to be excellent. Although we repeatedly tried without success to get him to recall what we knew had been in his memory, we should hardly care to allege that this was entirely impossible; perhaps more vigorous measures might have brought the facts to consciousness. Early associations, as in the case of the ringing bells that Prince cites, may sometimes be evoked under hypnosis. With this young burglar, seen only at the later date, it would have been quite impossible for the observer to have known that the beginning of his career was influenced by mental conflict.

Mental repression is active in most remarkable fashion in the cases of misconduct to which we call attention. The facts as they appear in the concrete examples seem thoroughly understandable. The alternatives in their simplest terms, repression as against expression, are not evaluated usually as they were by the boy in John Muir's anecdote: The lad used a forbidden word, and to his upbraiding sister he retorted, "I couldna help the word comin' into me, and it's na waur to speak oot than to let it rin through ye." That repression takes place in our cases is clearly shown by the ingenuous accounts of efforts to jam certain experiences, images, or memories into the forgotten, into a region below the threshold of conscious thought.

The reader will also note, however, in our case-studies the expressions, in varied phraseology, indicating how portions of some particular constellation of ideas unwilled flash up into conscious mind. But frequently the very same misdoers who tell of this unbidden entrance of certain ideas into the mind maintain, "I never think of these things." Then it is to the observer as if glimpses were to be had of an automatic psychological mechanism at work behind doors usually closed. The explicit distinction so often made by our young individuals between an idea or memory flashing up in the mind and their *thinking* about such an idea or memory, shows how early and in what naïve minds the phenomenon of repression can be forcefully at work.

Leaving the fact of repression as clearly established for us, we next may take up some particular applications of the mechanisms of mental conflict. At the outset I must insist again upon the impulsive and obsessive nature of the mental activities which follow in the train of conflict. It is anomalous and amazing that any delinquents should experience little or no pleasure in the doing of misdeeds, or that misconduct is undertaken by them without any particular expectation of pleasurable returns. Yet such appears to be the fact in many cases where the misdoing results from mental conflict. It is not, in these cases, for an end as judged in terms of gains in the outer world, but only

as a response to the dictates or urgings of an inner
wish, unframed in terms of objective profit, that the
misconduct is engaged in. Perhaps no one better
than Holt [1] has brought out the distinction which
obtains between an objective end mentally represented
and a bare wish or urge, either of them as a motive
force. It is the wish, often subconscious, which is the
dynamic component of mental mechanisms set in
activity by mental conflicts. We may frequently
perceive the development of conduct impulsions, and
even of obsessive imagery, quite apart from any
rationalized will to action. To the delinquent himself
his misconduct often does not appear at all as a particularly reasonable or explicable act; in later contem-
plating it he may state that he perceives it to have been
merely a following out of an impulse. He gained
nothing, and really had no anticipation of gaining
anything.

All who professionally employ mental analysis are
impressed with the phenomenon of *resistance*. Often
when some point, frequently an important one, is
reached in the course of the analysis, a barrier to
further progress is suddenly raised. There is evasion
of the question immediately at issue, perhaps a defen-
sive forgetting, or even deliberate refusal to go further
in the given line of inquiry. With the neurotic patient
it seems sometimes as if there was no genuine desire
to get well; the ailment itself is cherished. Or, it is
the inquiry that is disliked; it bids fair to open up the
mental life in a way to be shunned. In some of our
cases resistance is plainly observed, and at times it
causes an attitude that is quite impenetrable. I have
outlined an instance (Case 12) of failure of analysis

1 "The Freudian Wish", 1915, p. 100 ff.

through this cause. Repeatedly we have seen offenders who have committed crimes over and over again without any returns except suffering, seeming thus very possibly victims of mental conflict, who showed an obstinate attitude of unwillingness to go any distance in the exploration of their own inner mental life that was itself convincing evidence of existence of mental conflict. In such fashion a wall of complete inaccessibility is in rarer instances built up about the deeper mental life. Experienced reformatory workers have recounted to me instances where the offender, for instance an intelligent young woman convicted repeatedly of crimes indicating a special trend, the genesis of which must inevitably have been in some restless fermenting of the inner mental life, persistently refused to yield to the most kindly advances toward penetration of essential mental mechanisms. This hidden life was cherished as if the telling of it would shatter the most valuable of all personal possessions. We shall welcome the day when competent studies are recorded of such cases of extravagant resistance.

Of main importance, naturally, in the application of mental analysis to our field, is the resolving or in any way getting rid of a mental conflict. It is undoubtedly true, as some one has suggested, that a mental conflict cannot last indefinitely. In the course of time, with the press of accumulated new experiences and interests, the complex is bound to become attenuated and lose power, or there may be other ways in which it is disposed of. The activities, pernicious and other, which are suggested by the original complex may be given way to, and thus the latent energy be used up. Some writers have depicted a process called *rationalization*, through which there is the building up of a reasonable attitude towards the complex, which is then met face to face as a bare fact, unexplained and unexplored, and, even if not resolved, is retained in one special mental compartment; the rest of mental life is kept entirely aloof from it and is not swayed by energy liberated from the complex. This, of course, is deliberate dissociation; it is difficult to believe that a mental conflict is thereby in any fundamental way overcome; the complex is merely isolated.

It is self-evident that if a complex has latent energy-producing powers, and conflict results in the accumulation of pent-up energy, this, in turn, has to be released, worked off (the abreaction spoken of in the last chapter). For the different directions which the energy may take, separate terms have been offered. There is the phenomenon or mechanism of *conversion;* in this there is transmutation of mental into physical manifestations, as in hysteria, but with this we have nothing to do here. There is *sublimation* and *displacement* and *substitution* — these terms indicating mechanisms by which there is diversion of the energy of a complex into channels apparently not the main ones suggested by the complex. These diversions of energy (as well as repressions of complexes, for that matter) are not always abnormal and provocative of nervous manifestations or misconduct. In any case, the transference of energy is into secondary, and what seems to the subconsciously directed individual as more permissible forms of activity than are represented by the ideas most closely associated with the emotional elements of the original complex.

The operation of the substitutive type of mental mechanisms in diverting energy is to be seen in many of the cases of mental conflict we have investigated.

Without understanding the phenomenon, one understands little, indeed, of the case. Substitution, or displacement, is very frequently the method by which energy is conducted into the channel of misconduct that is explicable in no other way. It is only as we learn the facts by studying the deeper associations that relationship between some important earlier mental experience and the misconduct in question is discernible. Our case-histories show us most clearly how the conative element of the mind (Kant's "Streben"), the energy or striving in mental life, is released through the activities of what the outsider calls misconduct, but what to the doer seems a lesser delinquency.

Sublimation is a word more properly applied to diversion of energy derived from a mental conflict into useful lines of conduct. This may sometimes take place without help from the outside, but unfortunately, only too seldom. With other forms of transmutation of energy in the mental life we need not concern ourselves here, since they hardly belong to the discussion of misconduct in the ordinary sense. But there are many interesting pages of discussion to be found in the literature concerning this basis for the development of prudery, excessive religious tendencies, and other reactions.

The therapeutic aspects of dealing with mental conflicts which, being repressed, react in the form of misconduct, require detailed discussion. In considering, first, the general theory of treatment by the method of mental analysis, I may cite Stekel, who asserts the task of psychoanalysis (for us, mental analysis) to be reconciliation of the patient with reality. Expressing this differently, Putnam states, "Every psychoanalytic treatment is a phase of an educational process which

necessarily has, as its ideal goal, some sort of sublimation."

The ultimate aim of mental analysis is synthesis, its
immediate method is the digging up links of mental
association out of the past for the purposeful building
of conscious knowledge of causal relationship.   The
neurologists, analyzing functional disturbances of the
nervous system, are impressed by the fact that parts
of the complex that escape from repression are discovered distorted and disguised by way of attempt to
render themselves acceptable to consciousness.   Something of this distortion and disguise is seen in our cases
of misconduct; conscious sanctions of the misdoer will
not tolerate for a moment expression of certain elements
of the complex, while other elements surreptitiously
flare up in ways so altered that their relationship to the
repressed material is often not guessed.   The solution
of the problem and the cure of the trouble mainly
lies in developing the individual's own cognizance of
the essential association of facts.   The task, thus, is the
synthetic, conscious establishment of reality within the
mental life.

At this point a word on variations in methods and
results is in order. Many writers have commented
on the immediate therapeutic value of exploration by
mental analysis. We have seen it ourselves. It is
in some cases as if the cause of trouble had only to be
seen face to face when it was at once vanquished. The
complex brought up into consciousness and observed
there as a causal agent is shorn of its power; out in
the light its conative elements vaporize. The educational process which Putnam speaks of is not always
necessary beyond the analysis itself — the proof being
that if with the analysis unfortunate manifestations of

the energy of the complex disappear, socially satisfactory abreaction must have taken place. Of course, in many cases the conflict cannot be devitalized in this way; the complex may consist of material too solid to resolve so easily. Here is a boy, for example, frequently a runaway from a good foster home because of conflict concerning his parentage. He has secretly heard that he is an illegitimate child, it has been whispered to him as a taunt by a neighbor's boy who overheard the scandalmonger's tale. For long, without a word spoken, our boy has tried to down the shock; his delinquencies are the reaction. When we explore the causes of his misconduct, the material of the complex cannot be rejected; we find by inquiring that he really was born out of wedlock. A definite educational process in such a case is absolutely essential, with every sort of attempt at sublimation. Exploration was necessary, but in this instance was only a first step. Much mental and, perhaps, social readjustment must follow.

Some applications of mental analysis to certain types of offense and to certain classes of offenders we may outline. Problems involving specific sexual offenses as possibly related to mental conflicts I shall give little attention to, because many writers have previously treated this topic. The cases themselves should be handled only by specialists who are well acquainted not only with theories, but also with such therapeutic possibilities as have been already worked out.

About the following types of delinquency, indirectly sexual, a few words are here in place : *Fetishistic stealing* as a crassly symbolic performance is well known; it requires no acute discernment to see that there must be underlying connections of imagery and association between the thieving impulse and some sexual idea. What there is by way of mental processes back of the stealing of fetish objects, Freud,[1] more than any one, has shown us, although Binet [2] earlier elaborated many of the salient facts.

Exhibitionism, except the innocent variety in the curiosity stage of childhood, is another delinquency which is absolutely impossible to understand without mental analysis. Most complicated are the subconscious motives of those unfortunate and occasionally intelligent persons who are obsessed by the exhibition impulse. Even in those partially demented alcoholics and senile individuals who indulge in this misdemeanor, the act is to be regarded as representative, the object of it not being consciously framed by the misdoers themselves, and the mental mechanisms back of the impulse not being readily discoverable. Some of the same indirectness of motivation exists in cases of *voyeurs*, those beset by the impulse to peep. All of this, too, has been dealt with at length by writers on psychoanalysis. Homosexual and other sex perversions have likewise formed an extensive theme for the analysts, who have discovered mechanisms and types of mental conflict responsible for these abnormal tendencies. An immense literature has grown up on this topic since the days of earlier writers who merely dealt with these peculiar conduct-tendencies descriptively.

The infliction of cruelty, *sadism*, is an offense based

---

[1] Several sexualistic types of misconduct are dealt with succinctly in "Three Contributions to the Sexual Theory", translation by Brill, New York, 1910.

[2] A. Binet, "Le Fétichisme dans l'Amour", O. Doin, Paris, 1891.

on mental mechanisms directly related to the sex
impulse. Even casual accounts of some cases show the
connection; very deep studies are necessary to get
at the basic facts in others. Mental complexes and
conflicts and repressions undoubtedly play a great
rôle here. While the relationship of mental repression
to sadism is clearly enough to be perceived in many
instances, it has been stated by experts that no instance
has been completely analyzed.[1] The cases we have
seen have proved extremely refractory to study, on
account, so it has seemed, of resistance from feelings of
shame entering in so largely when the matter was up
for discussion. *Masochism*, a pathological enjoyment
of the infliction of pain, is also well known to be based
upon repressive mental mechanisms. Masochists show
characteristic outbreaks of misconduct apparently not
connected with the fulfillment of any normal desire.
There is no need for us to elaborate this subject; curious self-infliction of wounds has been described at
great length by various authors, and the genesis of this
impulse in conflicts centering about sexual matters is
well known. None of the foregoing types of misconduct, so intimately related to the mental side of sex
life, can be understood without knowing the detailed
studies of authorities on these matters.

About types of individuals especially benefited by
mental analysis, professional men who have used the
method have had much to say. One of the main questions that has arisen with us concerns the possibility
of working with adults involved in misconduct. There
can be little doubt that the difficulties are much greater
than when working with younger people. I have

---

[1] *Vide* Hitschmann's "Freud's Theories of the Neuroses", translation
by C. R. Payne, New York, 1913, p. 37.

allowed myself little time for adult delinquents because
of the vastly greater promise of practical returns
through dealing with young misdoers, but even a slight
experience with older offenders makes the complexities
for analysis of their problems loom large. Several of
the many contingencies are suggested in the following
paragraph :

Through longer repression into the subconscious
mental life there is vastly greater hesitation, namely,
resistance, at opening up the mental past. Outbreaks
of misconduct, even crime, have been the events be-
tokening the activity of the complex, and there is
natural unwillingness to bring these to light. Also,
it is plain that memories of trains of thought succeeding to the old psychic trauma, to say nothing of remem-
brances of that experience itself, have been very deeply
banished. Then there is the peculiar attitude of the
offender towards society and towards himself, a curious
mood for misconduct — a product of attempt to conceal guilt, of reaction to incrimination, of incarceration,
of acquirement of bad habits, of lack of opportunity
after incarceration to compete on equal terms with
his fellow men. The existence of these various phases
of the situation and of the attitudes which they tend
to create, plus established mental habit, stands heavily
against the success of mental analysis with any ordinary type of adult offender who might be supposed a
favorable case for use of this method.

It has been stated by experienced analysts that little
is to be expected from work under dispensary conditions, with any case coming to a public clinic. They
remark upon the entirely different results obtained
through work with private patients. We should deem
this likely to be true of the analogous application of

mental analysis to problems of adult misconduct, for it may be that with the more elaborate methods which it is possible to use in the case of a private patient, analysis with older offenders might succeed beyond our expectation. We hope some day to see studies contributed on this point. With the development of broader social interests by competent medicopsychologists, perhaps the conditions which now bar success can be somewhat altered, but for the present, when there is so much to be done with young people by way of preventing adult careers of misconduct, we urge greater attention to the more promising field.

The point made that successful coöperation with the patient obtains only when there are willing visits to the office and when payments indicate appreciation of the gravity of the trouble and of the sincerity of therapeutic efforts is not borne out in our work with young people. Perhaps the point would hardly be made with adolescents and children, who ordinarily rely on others to make their engagements and pay all their obligations. Certainly on the basis of our long experience I would confidently assert that mental analysis, if undertaken during the more plastic years of life, is a potent agent for altering conduct tendencies, even among those unable to offer adequate recompense or those held in institutions for delinquents.

The several types of individuals particularly to be warned against as unsuited to mental analysis for treatment of misconduct are those showing essential mental disabilities or instabilities, whether the abnormality rests on a deeply constitutional, temporary developmental, toxic, or traumatic basis, or is the immediate result of some disease process. The actually feeble-minded and insane are in a class by themselves for consideration, but giving rise to misconduct there are also other well-defined abnormal mental conditions, the treatment of which calls for much more than mental analysis can offer, even when the mechanisms of mental conflict are apparently active in producing undesirable reactions. I may merely mention constitutional inferiority, with its chronic states of mental instability and inadequacy; cases of traumatic disposition or constitution, characterized by erratic conduct reactions to the minor stresses of life; and instances where slight aberrational tendencies are shown as the result of bodily disease. These three classes cannot be regarded as having normal self-control, at least in the face of specially trying conditions. While, perhaps, they may be somewhat helped by mental analysis if there is mental conflict in the background of their misconduct, yet it is too much to expect that they steadfastly maintain tendencies towards good conduct in the face of temptations and other adverse conditions. Much more must be done for them.

Rarely to be benefited by mental analysis are adolescent girls showing hypersexual tendencies, even though mental conflict plays a part in the case. They are properly subjects for educational discipline and environmental control. We have watched with peculiar interest a case of pathological stealing and other misconduct proving to have typical mechanisms of conflict, in a sexually inclined bright girl of nineteen, which a competent psychoanalyst with fine spirit faithfully endeavored to treat in private practice. The outcome was practically fruitless, the girl proving too unreliable in word and intention; her instabilities were excessive, perhaps as the result of exaggerated phases of adolescent mental turmoil, or defective mental make-up, or unusual physical demands. Pathological lying, which sometimes arises, as I have elsewhere [1] pointed out, upon a foundation of mental conflict, presents also grave difficulties for treatment. The falsification as an active tendency may be carried into the consultation room. Yet we can bear witness to the fact that in some, even unexpected, instances mental analysis has gone far towards clearing up a situation that ultimately was righted.

The possibility of mental complexes and repressed conflicts being sources of misconduct in well recognized cases of mental abnormality, either in defective or aberrational individuals, I have hardly any reason to consider in this volume, although I conceive it quite likely that from studies of cases of recurrent impulse to misconduct in such mental types we might elicit information of great theoretical and practical import. Certainly, in some of these abnormal cases, it is quite evident that the tendency to offense arises from active mental mechanisms identical with those displayed by normal individuals. Thorough studies, such as hardly any one but Glueck [2] has begun, of the dynamics of misbehavior in these types promise much. I have never felt, for example, that it is psychologically quite sufficient to say that many a feeble-minded delinquent is delinquent because he is feeble-minded. The questions may also fairly be put in such a case, Why is this particular form of misconduct displayed? Why this impulse at all to misconduct? Why not an easier-going tendency to good conduct? Evidently even in

---

[1] "Pathological Lying, Accusation, and Swindling — A Study in Forensic Psychology." Little, Brown, and Company, 1915.
[2] Bernard Glueck, "The Malingerer: A Clinical Study." *International Clinics*, Vol. III, Series 25, 1915.

these cases, there are effective mental mechanisms with which we are not as yet familiar.

Mental analysis may be presumed, according to many analysts, to be an effective agent for treatment only when used with intelligent individuals. It should be noted that so far as our own material is concerned, we find, perhaps for obvious reasons, almost all the cases of mental conflict in offenders of more than average ability. We have occasionally gained some insight into the psychic mechanisms (*vide* Case 28) of even mental defectives, but interesting and valuable for human understandings though such explorations may prove, the outlook for treatment by analysis in these cases is, of course, very limited. Memory powers in the less intelligent may be sufficient to bring to light the genetic facts, but more than this is required for effecting the important desired changes in behavior. There must be clear apperception of the relationship of cause to effect; there must be self-perceived desire for relief from the burden of anti-social impulse; judgment must be sound to avoid the snares of old habits, and good intention must be backed by normal will power. Leaving the question open concerning whether or not our findings were due somewhat to the greater attractiveness of the brighter misdoers for psychological inquiry, we can at least be sure that the promise of practical returns from the use of mental analysis in cases of misconduct caused by mental conflict is much greater with the more intelligent.

CHAPTER IV

METHODS

DISCUSSING methods of mental analysis suitable for attacking conflicts as causes of misconduct, we can at once state that these may well show variations from methods primarily adapted to treatment of the psychoneuroses. It has been suggested by competent students of mental analysis, looking over our case-studies, that our field offers material susceptible to a simpler and less roundabout approach. If we are asked to frame reasons why a less elaborate method may prove sufficient, we can suggest the following points: In working with young people, both children and adolescents, we are nearer the original experience from which the conflict arose; it is fresher in the mind because it is less covered with added experiences and their accumulated memories, and because it is less confused with the sources of a myriad of later impulses. Other things being equal, the less remote the experience, the better the memory of it, the less effort is required to bring it back into conscious mental life.

Then, at earlier ages, repression of a mental complex, though to be found as a very real phenomenon, is less strenuously maintained than during later years. Even when the conflict has been tremendously active and direful in its consequences, a first simple inquiry into its existence and nature may be fruitful. Very likely the slighter consciousness of conventional standards that characterizes youth is a reason for less resistance. Then, it is more natural at this age to be confiding, all expect confidences from the young, and the great difference between the ages of subject and analyst tends also to increase willingness to confide. Altogether, it is our experience very rarely to find, as in Case 12, complete inaccessibility to the simpler methods usually employed.

Another feature of youthful cases makes for ease of ascertaining the genetic facts. Disguise of the form and distortion of the path of the energy escaping from the complex is likely to be slighter than in later years, and is much less than when the objective reaction is a mental or physical ailment. There are many important instances where the analyst can very quickly with the misdoer find clear memories of a highly emotional experience, from the time of which the birth of misbehavior tendencies dates. In many cases the same person who caused the emotional disturbance gave the first acquaintance with the special form of delinquency toward which impulse is shown. The emotion is evoked by introduction to facts of great personal and social importance. To have learned about sex affairs, for instance, and stealing from one and the same person has been the lot of many delinquents who proved to be the victims of mental conflict. In the original constellation of ideas, which soon became a complex, stealing was a specific component part. Indirect and vicarious and not understandable by ordinary observation though the escape of energy in the form of stealing may be, its dynamic origins are simple indeed as compared to the mechanisms of later life and especially those of nervous or mental invalidism.

The repression itself, we find, is frequently spoken of by young people in the most ingenuous fashion when once there is sincere and skillful attempt to tap the real source of trouble — the mechanism does not have to be merely inferred, or, as in the classical cases, learned by elaborate analysis. In these more naïve individuals who know nothing of mental conflicts as such, the straightforward recital of repression is most striking. In not a few instances the fact of repression is sooner or later specifically offered to us as evidence of the possession of moral attributes; the form of delinquency actually engaged in is not nearly so bad (says the delinquent's censor) as certain other activities, the ideas of which are repressed. The represssion seems many times to have been undertaken in direct fashion, in a sort of get-thee-behind-me-Satan spirit, and, indeed, may be later regarded as having been entirely the result of a conscious process.

Then, too, the analysis is frequently easier because of the misdoer's awareness that the unfortunate impulses are subconsciously stimulated. The sequence of mental events may be narrated with considerable clearness and there may be apperception of the initiation of misbehavior tendencies by some inner mental activity not the result of conscious will to action. The production in subconsciousness of energy, of *horme*, of *libido*, or whatever it may be called, is thus directly felt as an actual and strange determiner of action.

One of the leading points in method is concerned with the attitude of the one who would, for the purpose of therapy, assail these problems with the individual offender. It goes without saying that only those who are students of the science and art of mental analysis should undertake the task, and these should cultivate the most sympathetic and patient approach. The experience of very many delinquents is that they have been met either with punishment for their misconduct, or with mere injunctions to do better. The attitude of the analyst should be the antithesis of one who settles a case without full inquiry, or who in an offhand way gives an opinion of why certain misconduct has occurred. The approach should be such that the delinquent himself feels that the inquiry into foundations is born of the desire to help.

The response shows that frequently the offender is fairly hungry for the chance to delve with some understanding person into the real inwardness of his tendencies to misconduct. Even when there has been not the least understanding of the particular nature of the mental forces felt to be at work, often there has been expressed a great desire to search out the facts. We have seen striking examples of this. No wonder that in such cases the arguments and moral enjoinders of ignorance fail.

The analyst, taking the true professional attitude, will make it plain that he is not shocked by disclosures, that the facts confided are such as frequently form the burden of communications in the consulting room and are no reflection upon the innate moral qualities of the confider; rather they are evidences of a genuine desire to be clean-minded. This method of attack is particularly effective when resistances appear; then every effort should be put forth to persuade that there is nothing to be ashamed of in what arises involuntarily within the mind.

At this point several suggestions of methods to aid in overcoming resistances may be offered from our experience. We can confirm what many analysts have said about the necessity for cutting short the interview when strong barriers to further progress are raised. On another day a different approach may carry us easily beyond the place that previously seemed impassable; other words may not provoke the former inhibitions. A variety of devices, all fair enough, may be considered when working with children. Occasionally a real reward for truth-telling is justifiable, and not rarely a promise of immunity from punishment by parents is securable, to be offered, in turn, to the child. I have mentioned that an immediate appeal for truth is sometimes readily successful, but in other cases only resistances are encountered by the procedure; then any one of the indirect routes of inquiry is to be used. These pages contain numerous hints of these more roundabout paths. One final thought on this topic is important: We often find we cannot go far in the analysis until the misdoer knows that we have special and specific information concerning at least some items of his misconduct. It thus saves time to be forearmed with detailed knowledge of some definite delinquencies.

A danger in starting mental analysis with offenders is in laying stress upon recent delinquencies, those, for instance, with which they are at present charged. It requires little insight to understand that for many reasons there may be desire to keep these affairs quiet; even after a case has been satisfactorily settled, the feelings of shame, chagrin, etc. may cast an emotional pall about the events, making an entirely different setting from that surrounding older delinquencies. Time weakens emotional elements; any one can look calmly back upon experiences which formerly covered with confusion; and so it is with misdoers. After

slight inquiry about the present circumstances (often
the details can be learned well enough from others),
attention should be directed to preceding periods of
mental life.

We have found that a short cut to unearthing the
conflict is through persuading the delinquent to hark
back to his earliest knowledge of social offense.   Sometimes we are met by the first assertion there has been
no long familiarity with stealing, for instance, or that
acquaintance with other delinquents has only been
recent, perhaps merely since the offender has been
within the clutches of the law.   These statements are
unsatisfactory and simply mean that the individual is
not bringing up enough from the realm of memory, at
least in these cases which involve mental conflict.
Gradually, by skillfully inquiring about the beginnings
of ideas of delinquency, one does hear about very early
experiences, such as are given in detail in our case-
histories. The memory of these may finally stand
out very clearly.   Of course, indirect inquiry, such as
concerning the doings of early playmates, the first
knowledge of the particular form of delinquency to
which the offender is prone, the worst person among
former or present acquaintances, the source of earliest
knowledge of sex affairs, the person who may have
shown bad pictures or taught bad words, any of these
may revive a memory that brings to light the components of a complex. It may take long to go over
the memories of early playmates and of experiences
obtained from them or through other sources, but the
essential information is usually sooner or later to be
obtained.

Let no one suppose that these memories are to be left
without corroboration. I still am unable to restrain

my native skepticism concerning some of these remarkable revelations of seed sown years ago which produces fruit at the surface after long periods of growth underground. Generally it is possible to get considerable corroborative information from relatives, and indeed, sometimes the first hint of possible sources of trouble has come from relatives themselves in response to inquiry about companions who might have exerted a bad influence, even though not known to have done so. We have had instances where it was at first impossible to awaken subconscious memory of bygone influences until the clue obtained from parents was followed and served to stimulate the dormant power of recall. Our confidence in the fact of the early establishment of complexes and succeeding conflicts and repressions has been strengthened perhaps more by corroborative histories obtained from relatives than by anything else. They may have known nothing of the actual experiences or significance of influences, but often were aware of the character of a certain individual who was a part of the former environment. I advise all analysts to seek such corroboration. Not that we are met, after all, by many falsifications in these inquiries, but one is always scientifically justified in assuming that any statement may possibly be untrue, and lying is commonly supposed to be prevalent in the world of offenders.

It is almost needless to state that for the sake of avoiding any misrepresentation on the part of the young person, suggestive questions and premature explanations of causation must be strictly avoided. As a matter of fact there is little need for any suggestion of the details of causations. Once the offender perceives the open-minded inquiry into foundations, he usually of his own accord goes on and on with the analysis, following the lead of skillful non-suggestive questions, thereby showing his real desire to be relieved of his impulses.   It is not a matter of starting out by saying to the individual, "Now, I want you to tell me what is the matter, why you act in this way."   Nor does one ask whether the misdoing was started by such and such types of specific experiences.   Rather, one leads on the inquiry in simple, patient fashion, till the facts of causation develop in consciousness, and the subject of the impulses realizes the genetic facts or even explicitly states, "Now I see what is the matter, why I am doing these things, how I got started."

The force of such a statement is all the more impressive because in our cases it is frequently made by a thoroughly naïve individual, one who knows nothing of theories and laws of mental life.   And the directness of the phraseology shows that the misdoer himself has made an unexpected discovery.   From another viewpoint the obtaining of such a forceful expression, showing a new-found realization of causations, establishes firm confidence in the validity of the method and its possible therapeutic results.

So far we have found in our efforts no value in working with the artificially controlled association reactions that some analysts have used.   We have elaborately tried this in a few cases, with no success whatever, and in hardly any instance has there been need for it.   I freely confess, however, that in the cases where we have failed, perhaps had we had the opportunity for still more intensive studies such devices might conceivably have proved useful.   Nor have we discovered anything significant by using the "Tatbestanddiagnostik" test — where it is sought to learn important facts through the revelations of lengthened verbal association reaction times. We have concluded through our long laboratory experience that there is a great deal to be said in this connection, as in general, about possible differences between the reactions of young people and adults. Of course, associations are just what the analyst is unearthing by his method, but the desired significant associations are brought out best by tracing them freely, by unwinding the chain of thought link by link.

Nor have we for elucidation of the etiology of misconduct found it necessary to invoke the symbolism so much in vogue with psychoanalysts. Again here it may be that we thus overlook some deeper mental mechanisms, but our task is so directly practical that one does not wish to inject into it any such considerations of theoretical value. Regarding this apparent lack of necessity for utilizing the psychoanalytic system of representative meanings of things, Doctor Putnam suggests that in our field it may be that types of activity (rather than any detail of an end attained, such as the peculiar nature of some object stolen) are the symbolic manifestations. We should be inclined to acknowledge the possibility of this or of the alternative, namely, that misconduct tendencies may be merely vicarious, leading off energy along paths divergent from the original direction which the complex indicated.

For the analysis of dreams, so widely used in the investigation of the psychoneuroses, we have also found little demand. In the first place, they offer for us a much less direct method of getting at the etiological facts. Then, although we have made many inquiries about significant dreams, it is rare indeed that we found the slightest suggestion of anything that would warrant analysis of them. It has seemed to us very likely that dreams may be much more vital for understanding nervous troubles than misconduct; certainly in some of the misdoers who had symbolic dreams there were also clear signs of nervous disturbance, particularly hysteria. In rare cases, to be sure, the content of dreams of offenders does certainly suggest the content of subconscious mental life and the symbolisms of which the Freudian school in particular has made so much, and so occasionally may offer help for understanding the basic nature of conduct tendencies.

Many of our cases of mental conflict have been elaborately studied by tests for determination of mental ability. As a result of our findings, I can make the general statement that in no one mental test or group of tests are reactions found that safely indicate the presence or absence of mental conflict. Nor do we find any characteristic attitude that is assumed towards tests or towards the examiner. But this is not saying that the giving of mental tests is useless, even for other purposes than the determination of the general mental status of the offender. One of the points that we see the need of continually emphasizing is the carrying out of really constructive efforts for the reformation of misdoers. To this end studies serve greatly which may establish the fact of special disabilities which interfere with school or vocational success and, even more particularly, special abilities which may be utilized for the direct development of satisfying interests. These are of the utmost importance for the reconstructive measures we have attempted so often to point out as vitally necessary for the supplanting of pernicious mental activities resulting from conflicts.

It is impossible in any chapter on method to enumerate all the possibilities of inquiry suitable to ascertaining the varieties of experience that may be in the background of mental conflicts. But certain types of experience we find so common that some specific directions may be offered. I have already mentioned inquiry into early companionship. Then, perhaps nothing so frequently taps the source of trouble as sympathetic questioning about worries and persistently recurring images or ideas. The simple asking, "What is it that bothers you?" or, "Do you worry about anything?" is often sufficient to bring out facts that brightly illuminate further progress in the analysis. The recurrence of particular words which connote disturbing ideas, or of pictures that stir up the mind, or of obsessional ideas must be made the subject of careful, detailed inquiry. Still another specific question that sometimes proves of importance, concerns whether or not the offender is the victim of emotionally disturbing wonderings centered about acquired items of half-knowledge.

Familiarity with types of troublesome mental content, whether auditory or visual, whether words or pictures or ideas, is to be best gained from perusal of our case-histories. Indeed, the careful reader of the histories will learn these facts and many other points that bear upon the practical elaboration of good methods of mental analysis in cases of misconduct. If the main principles given in these earlier chapters are grasped and acquaintance is gained with a good range of concrete illustrations, common-sense variations adapted to the study of individual cases should readily suggest themselves.

The exploration having been carried on far enough to find the probable genesis of the given impulse to misconduct, what next? As may be seen in a few of our

cases, the genetic factors once brought into consciousness, the individual is sometimes able to take care of
the situation.   But this bringing into consciousness
must mean the full realization by the subject of the
causal connections that the analysis has revealed.   The
enemy in the open often can be successfully combated
if other conditions are favorable.   One of the most
essential of favorable conditions is a good home environment, good in the sense that the causes which
led to the conflict did not arise in home circumstances,
or, if they did, that they are entirely altered after they
have become known.   Further, in the home there must
be sympathy and understanding and the best opportunity for the establishment of confidences.   It is
notable that a goodly number of our cases of conflict
come from homes where the offender, as offenders go,
had unusually good opportunities and interests, but,
of course, the element of confidential relationship was
lacking.   (Indeed, this incongruity of misconduct
arising in a good environment often leads one to suspect
mental conflict.)   In our cases that were successful
immediately with the analytic exploration, competent
relatives have nearly always had a hand in the result
through following our advice in getting even more completely at the needs of the individual and building up
new interests.

   We have questioned the rationale of our own therapy,
whether it did not largely consist of what is technically
called "side-tracking", that is, attempting *merely* to
replace the misconduct impulse by better interests,
without resolving the real conflict.   We have decided
that inasmuch as we attempt to deal with the specific
nature of the actual factors producing misconduct,
digging up the subconscious memories to get at causes,

it is much more than that. But even with this deeper study, the diverting of energies to better channels must follow; there must be sublimation. Young people must have somebody in whom they can confide, or some activity in which they can indulge whenever there is renewal of old impulses. With such "after-care" the impulses themselves gradually cease; it is only where these matters are neglected that they persist. Sometimes, then, final success does not signify a continuance of sublimation as need for it arises, but means complete dissolution of the original conflict.

At this point should be stressed the contrast between mental analysis and the method of suggestion so often exploited as a possible treatment for misdoing, suggestion either in waking or hypnotic states. As Jones [1] so clearly points out: "The great disadvantage of any treatment by means of suggestion is the blind nature of it. It achieves its results by substituting the idea of the physician for the previous expressions of the pathogenic effects." Through the use of mental analysis, the source of trouble is directly faced and the individual develops himself in perceiving it and attacking it. The victory is his with as little dependence as possible on others. No one doubts the greater strength that character possesses when built with forces and materials produced from within.

Exploration without *re-education* is a failure — analysts have long stated this as a truism; there are rare exceptions. What is the meaning and program of re-education in this connection? It is the making over of certain ideas, the re-interpretation of experiences and portions of the mental content, the changing of

[1] Ernest Jones, "The Treatment of the Psychoneuroses", in "Modern Treatment of Nervous and Mental Diseases", Vol. I, p. 376.

connotations of words and pictures. It is the cultivation of openness, leading to the cessation of mental repressions of experiences and thoughts. It may be the supplying of knowledge and the satisfying of questions and doubts. It is the supplanting of undesirable elements of mental life by the centering of attention on new interests; the furnishing of new outlets for activities. It may be the establishment of a new attitude and outlook on life. Of course not all these measures are necessary in any given instance, but the importance of the process of re-education becomes clear from their bare enumeration. Just what concrete means should be used depends upon the specific, detailed needs of any given individual as revealed by the analysis of inner causation and the study of external factors in the situation.

Not the least of difficulties in readjustment arises through necessity for alteration of previous environmental conditions. We have been plainly told by offenders, after they had ferreted out with us their own conflicts and complexes, that it was useless to go back to old living conditions where the conflict was bound to continue; only in a new environment would there be any chance at all for success. One boy tells us, for instance, that when working on a farm or busy with the varied opportunities of a fine institution, as compared to the meager interests of his own home, he is free from conflicts about sex matters. When conflicts are built up on sex instincts, it is useless merely to say to the offender that they must be downed. The development of new activities is a common-sense necessity that frequently in the case of our offenders cannot be supplied without complete change of environment.

Our failures largely include cases which have gone

back to an unchanged environment or to new conditions that have created further conflicts and consequent need for more repression. If a conflict has arisen in a child from suggestions of its own illegitimacy or banal parentage, for instance, and such suggestions recur, there is bound to be further trouble. The same is true, of course, if there are further observations of sex affairs; even suggestions thereof may arouse new complexes and conflicts. To guard against this would seem to be a matter of sheer common sense, and yet only too frequently individuals whose careers have been based upon mental conflicts are allowed to remain in an unfortunate environment where there is renewal of the ancient source of their difficulties.

The *prevention* of mental conflicts is a matter of far-reaching importance. Since the activities of the mind are controlled by mechanisms, it is the business of intelligent people to gain some practical knowledge of these mechanisms and to utilize the knowledge for furtherance of weal and prevention of woe. In the up-bringing of children there are a number of general measures which are well calculated to forfend the development of mental conflict. I know of hardly anything connected with home life and education that I would call attention to more strongly than the following points, which have to do with matters of early mental experiences and of relationship between the child and the other human beings who form the most essential part of its environment. The main ideas may seem obvious enough to those who are thoughtful about the mental lives of children; common-sense ideas of morality should be sufficient grounds for recognition of the validity of the points made, but very few seem aware of the more subtle and hidden troubles which develop

through unfortunate early experiences which might
well have been prevented.   Indeed, the prophylaxis
of mental conflicts should form the theme for many a
sermon.

I may first take up the matter of sex education,
talked about a good deal in these days, but hardly ever
appreciated in its relationship to forms of misdoing
other than sex offenses.   In going over our case-histories of misconduct due to mental conflict, those
given in this volume and many others which are not
given, no point stands out so strongly as the fact that
in these instances early sex knowledge and experiences
have been gained in a most unfortunate way, sometimes
leading to psychic shock, or trauma.   (Here I should
call attention to our knowledge of similar beginnings
in hundreds of other cases where the element of psychic
shock was absent, but where, perhaps, the habit of
masturbation and other sex difficulties have followed.)
Those who are of the opinion that early instruction of
children in anything pertaining to sex life is to be de-
plored, and who themselves on this account in their
own families withhold information, should realize that
nearly every boy and girl actually does gain early
knowledge of these things.   Under the congregate
conditions of modern life, the chances for even a young
child to learn about sex affairs from others, from newspapers, books, theatres, etc. is very great indeed.

It is certainly unfair to allow a child to get its first
inkling of sex life from sources that, through their
very nature, cast an unfortunate shadow over the
whole matter.   The incomplete and often incorrect
character of such information and the tone of its utterance miserably vitiates what should be pure and free
knowledge.   It is the implication of something socially

forbidden that precludes the child going for enlightenment to older members of the family, who should be the
informants. The secret knowledge is sometimes accompanied by a sense of guilt and shame, quite uncalled
for by the requirements of nature or of morality, but
which is soil upon which mental conflicts may readily
grow. There are many problems of sex education
which are not solved, but we may be certain of one great
point related to the development of mental conflicts:
The dissemination of early biological knowledge, which
may be suitable even for young children, will do much
to prevent sex information with more personal bearings
coming with unwarranted shock, or with implication
that it must be suppressed.

Analysts have spoken of the bad effects of conjugal
embraces being witnessed by children; functional
nervous ailments have been traced back to this as one
cause. We have some evidence of such affairs leading
to misconduct, but more often we have known of instances where witnessing or suspecting illicit sex relations on the part of a parent has led to an intensive
anti-social attitude and to various sorts of misbehavior.
After what we have learned, this seems to me a natural
result, and yet it is rarely recognized that such influences create misconduct tendencies in other than sexual
directions. Then, we have known of many cases of
conflict leading to misconduct arising from witnessing
illicit sex scenes elsewhere than in the home. All this
brings up again the importance of confidences between
parents and children; nothing will so guard against
harmful consequences from an experience of the type
just mentioned as being able to tell about it and talk it
over with some good older friend.

The basis for much prevention of mental conflicts

is to be found in close confidential relations between
parents and children. A great deal could be written
about the failure of adults to understand the mental
needs of young people. Very often their own childhood
points of view are entirely forgotten, and the results
of the conditions of modern child life are met with the
statement that they cannot understand them, that
nothing like that occurred in their own youth. To
inquire and to try to understand are, on the part of the
older person, the first requirements of effective confidences. On the part of the child, to tell and to talk
over with the right person all important experiences is
no sign of babyishness; indeed, it is a feature of behavior that may lead to strength and independence
of character. It seems trite to say that guardians of
children should have oversight of what children are
doing, whom they are meeting, what they are seeing and
hearing, and as much as possible of what they are
thinking, but we find that even in families supposed
to be well cared for there is often little or no knowledge
of these important matters which lead to the troubles
with which we are dealing. It is said by good observers
that under the conditions of modern life there is an
unfortunate and growing laxity in this regard.

Children of recognizable sensitive temperament,
whether the symptoms of the sensitiveness show themselves by nervous reactions or by the individual drawing back as into a shell, are ones to be handled with care
and with full appreciation of their capacity for the
development of mental conflicts. Such cases often
call in times of stress for the most delicate treatment
through private confidences with some one.

Lying and misrepresentation to children by older
people, even when undertaken from the standpoint of

supposed good for the child, are highly dangerous. I conceive this practice to have the most extensive ramifications, to have effects upon formation of character which cannot easily be measured. Why should this not be so if the props of certainty and reliance are knocked away when those from whom truth is naturally expected fail to live up to their part ? From the general moral issues of such failures on the part of adults we may turn to the specific point that misrepresentations to children about matters of vital interest sometimes do actually cause mental conflicts with serious results. Freud has rightfully emphasized this fact and added the observation that youngsters are vastly keener in their impressions and feelings about lying and double-dealing than ordinarily is recognized.

Another sin by parents that has relation to mental conflicts consists in the use of bad language, namely, forms of swearing that are suggestive, and obscenity itself. Of course, this only occurs in households where a parent is of callous moral nature, or where, as is often the case, the unfortunate words are used during intoxication. Very few would deliberately choose to poison a child's mind. Besides cases where psychic trauma and conflict arose from bad language, we have known several instances where conflict and resultant misconduct began through the insinuations by a parent or another under the influence of alcohol that the child was not a product of lawful wedlock.

Where there is an adopted child or an illegitimate child in the family, there should be the most well-balanced consideration of how the facts concerning parentage are to be best handled. It may be disastrous if the first intimation of the truth is learned from others than the supposed parents (*vide* Case 6), or from documents that have been secretly discovered. It is astonishing how easily leakage of the truth may take place; many a guardian has said to us, "How could he have learned that; nobody has told him." Repression in its most vigorous forms often takes place with even the slightest suspicion of anomalous parentage; then conflict ensues. Parental relationship is so vitally connected with the emotional life of childhood that suggestion of irregularity in it comes as a grave psychic shock. And the importance of any peculiarity pertaining to parentage is immensely added to in the individual's mind if there be any social derogation on account of it. Innuendos concerning parentage, even of little playmates who hardly know what they are talking about, cut deeper than almost anything else in the world, arouse conflicts, and induce definite anti-social attitudes and misconduct. There is no help for the situation when once the facts have spread about a neighborhood; there should be a complete change of environment for the sake of prevention of harm. To head off in the first place any secret and shock-producing information that almost surely will be imparted, the truth in some form must be declared. Most frequently there is a feeling in the given family circle that the facts should be concealed, but from our experience with the bad effects of such *sub rosa* treatment of the unfortunate situation in many cases, I am strongly inclined to believe that openness of statement never does as much harm as concealment.

The prophylaxis, in general, of mental conflicts can be readily seen to depend, in the first place, upon knowing what type of experiences do so unfortunately influence the young mind, and in the next place, guarding as much as possible against these experiences, and especially guarding sensitive types of individuals. Once the experiences have been encountered, the next thing is prevention of harmful effects by means of the methods we have outlined above. All this has to do especially with the treatment of the case by those who are near to the child, but there is another outlook upon this problem.

Once mental conflicts have become active, there is not only need for the exploration and re-education of which we have been speaking, but also for prevention of further development of complexes. Conditions such as initiated or permitted the first unfortunate experiences only too frequently persist in the offender's immediate world. All that I have said about methods of prevention of mental conflicts ever arising in a child's life is applicable here. Healthy, vigorous mental interests and confidential relationships more than ever should be fostered, for through these is the best chance of adequate sublimation.

And re-education, too, of parents (or other guardians or members of a household) we find has now to be contemplated. Our case-studies will show how important, as well as how impossible this sometimes may be. It is extremely difficult in very many instances to make parents appreciate what is meant by mental conflict as the source of misconduct, even when analysis has resulted in a great change for the better. Nor is this to be wondered at if we think of how little comprehension exists of even the laws of the visible world. The conception of mental mechanisms and laws is subtle and new and altogether far beyond ordinary ideas of things. Fortunately the practical bearings are occasionally grasped, and the case intelligently handled in a fashion which demonstrates for us the therapeutic

possibilities in family life. To get older people to be
more sympathetically confidential; to cultivate more
understanding of the vital problems of youth, to give
more of their own time to companionship is the task of
their re-education.

In juvenile court work, we look forward to better
control of all features of environment which contribute
to delinquency. If even through the insidious paths
of mental conflict conditions are active which make
for misconduct, they should be strenuously combated.
If adults themselves are not willing to live proper lives,
and their influences induce misbehavior on the part of
children, their conduct on this count alone is a social
menace and should be treated as such. In some cases
it may be absolutely essential to put the child, after
analysis of the difficulty, under some one outside of the
family who will undertake to get confidences and to
re-educate. Pastors who have made themselves acquainted with this field might be utilized to direct this
effort, and perhaps well-trained probation officers, or
other workers who have developed psychological
insight. If a conflict case is not recognized as such it
frequently means, as shown in our case-studies, a long
and expensive period of institutional treatment by the
State, frequently without betterment.

The fact that the genesis of delinquent careers so
often dates back to mental life of childhood makes it
imperative that the problems of childhood should more
than ever be the subject of study. No reader of our
case-histories can avoid this conclusion. Around the
original source may be deposited in mental life an immense amount of material in the form of memories and
effects of experiences, and the whole later picture
consequently be colored by many other elements than

those which represent the first springs of tendencies to misconduct. In measuring the possibility of practical results, no one who appreciates in the least the effect of the establishment of mental and social habits can doubt the great comparative value of beginning reconstructions before the reactions to mental conflict create undesirable habits of thought and action.

CHAPTER V

CONFLICTS ACCOMPANIED BY OBSESSIVE IMAGERY

OTHER mental manifestations besides the conflict may be dynamic features of the background in cases of misconduct. It has been deeply interesting to hear how forceful a part mental imagery plays in some instances, — accounts of the phenomena being given by the victims themselves. The clearness with which the imagery stands in relationship to the conflict, on the one hand, and to misconduct, on the other, is most instructive. Mental mechanisms in these cases, as in the following illustrations, come plainly into sight.

Case 1. Of very great interest is the following remarkable recurrence of impulse to misconduct, originating each time with ideas or imagery concerning another person who was the center of an excessively emotional experience. The case shows very distinct repression of certain parts of the experience, with outbursts of impulse traceably related to the repressed elements. The associative activities showed so clearly that the analyst felt as if privileged to witness and understand mental processes ordinarily unrevealed.

Melda B. was almost eleven when we saw her for the first time. We have known her intimately three years.

Physically, she has presented decidedly normal conditions, except for enlarged tonsils. Vision is slightly defective. She is a pleasant appearing girl of good color and regular features.

Mentally, she proved herself quite capable by tests, although she has been a little retarded educationally through frequent changing of schools. All along we, as well as others, have observed that Melda is a thoroughly straightforward girl and is evenly balanced on the emotional side.

Melda's pleasant and exceedingly affectionate parents were terribly worried about her outbreaks of stealing, and from the first were willing to coöperate in every way. They showed a receptive attitude towards the facts, such as we have often failed to find among much better educated people. It appeared that at home the girl was very well behaved and helpful. No troubles had arisen between her and the other children, two older brothers. Altogether there had been a background of pleasant and healthy home life and of good general environmental conditions.

Developmental history was negative except for a head injury at seven years, which, however, had been only a slight affair, and attacks of convulsions, one at two years, and again at three years of age. She had not had a single serious illness.

No others in the family on either side had suffered from convulsions or epilepsy, so far as known, nor could we ascertain any other facts that showed abnormality in heredity.

Melda had been taken by the police, when we first saw her, for stealing a pocketbook from a woman in a department store. There was no question about the matter; she had been observed in the act. The case

was studied by Doctor Augusta Bronner and myself;
a few interviews were sufficient for us to get at certain
vital features of the situation. In working our way
back to beginnings, we learned incidentally of much
other thieving. Indeed, even at the start, Melda
wanted to pour out her troubles and soon told us that
this last event was the culmination of three years of
impulse to steal. Her whole story, gradually developed,
may be given in short as follows:

Some three years previously the family lived in a
neighborhood where there were a number of bad boys
and girls. Not that Melda saw anything very bad
going on, but she heard about it. In particular there
was Annie. She was an older girl who went with
boys, "big boys, too", and often asked Melda to go
along with her. This girl used vicious language and
would say "the bad words over and over again. She
wrote them on the house too." Melda told us that
at first she did not know what these words meant,
although she knew they were improper and knew they
had reference to what Annie did that was wrong.
Melda still remembered those words, perhaps ten of
them. Melda had suffered no physical sex experience,
but everything she had learned of these matters stands
out very clearly in her mind.

Going back to the occasion when Melda first had
acquaintance with stealing, we found that the story
involved this same Annie. "Then I saw her steal; she
took a pocketbook, and she would take things from
any store. I saw her walk past a counter and take
something, that was from M.'s department store. I
can see her just as plain as if she was doing it. Once
she took me to a store, a 5 and 10 cent store, and told
me to take a bracelet and a bottle of perfume, and I

did. She said to wait until no one was watching and then put it in my handkerchief and slip it in my pocket. When we came out of the store she took the things." Melda tells us that at this period when she was being told about sex things by Annie and being also instructed in stealing, she used to take things from her mother. "Annie used to live in the same house with us. She lived in the basement. She swore something terrible; such words I can't tell them to you. I never think about them. Only what she told me comes in my mind, and *I can see all those three times I saw her stealing. They always come in my mind before I take things.* When I am busy it does not bother me, and sometimes when it comes in my mind, I take a book and read and it goes away. But sometimes it stays, and I can't think of what I am reading, and then I take things off my mother."

From the parents also we learned about Annie. She was the daughter of some disreputable people; for a time, unknown to them, Melda had gone with her. They became so concerned that they moved away from the neighborhood on account of this, and supposed long since that all the bad influence had disappeared. Annie had the reputation of both stealing and being immoral, they afterwards learned. They had made absolutely no inquiry concerning what Annie in any secret way might have taught their own little girl.

The details Melda gave of the stealing affair when she was arrested, and of what preceded it, were a graphic presentation of her impulses and their background. In the morning, on that Saturday, her mother sent her to market with her brother. "There I saw Annie, and she came up to me and asked me if

I still stole. I told her no. Then I ran away from
her, but that night when I went back to M.'s department store, it all came back into my mind about her.
Then they caught me, a detective did, and they took
me to the station. I was so scared I said just anything. I didn't know what I said."

M.'s store is the same place where Melda had first
seen Annie steal, and it was there Annie had herself
taken a pocketbook. "It was there just like I saw
her. It came in my mind what she did."

Melda all along made much more of Annie's bad-
ness in other directions than of her stealing. She
stated that Annie would never tell her the meaning
of the bad words which she said, but just repeated
them over and over. Melda had never asked her
mother about these things. The child told us in detail
of her visualizing powers. Without any suggestion on
our part, she explained how plainly she could see
things in her imagination. "When I am reading
stories, I see things just as plain as if they were real."
She vouchsafed this, apparently, in explanation of her
statement that she could almost see Annie standing
before her stealing things. She was not troubled by
other mental pictures, however, and, in particular,
what she saw at moving picture shows did not come
up in her mind.

We tried to make the mother understand the bearing on the possibilities of better conduct of what this
intelligent child told us of her mental life. We heard
no more of the case for a year and a half, when she
was brought into court once more.

This time Melda had been arrested in a department
store in another part of town with a stolen pocketbook, an undergarment, and a waist. Our attention

was again called to the case, and once more our interest was keenly aroused by the association processes actively at work producing misconduct. Before we saw her this time, Melda had already told the judge that it was her memory of what a girl had told her years ago that caused her to steal.

From the mother we heard that Melda had been a wonderfully good girl since her previous outbreak; she had not stolen a single thing until now. The nice-looking older brother corroborated this account, which was all the more believable, because the mother herself had wanted her brought to us originally and had reported all that she knew of her misconduct. Since that time Melda had stayed at home very closely and had proved unusually industrious. Frequently she had asked her mother for extra work to do. She wanted to wash dishes and scrub the floor; it seemed almost as if there was not enough for her to do, she worked so well. Her parents were generous about getting little things for her as she desired them, and everything went along most pleasantly. Her school record, too, was excellent. The only point that her mother had noticed was that Melda sometimes seemed to be staring off in the distance and, if spoken to, a minute later would say that she had not heard what her mother said. The parents stated that they were on the verge of suicide on account of this new disgrace. The father could not do his work properly, he was so affected. The mother had tried to ask Melda about Annie's influence, after we saw her, but, of course, could not go very far in analysis of the trouble. Again she did not dream that there was any inner mental difficulty.

The circumstances surrounding and preceding this

last stealing were clearly described to us by Melda, and on several of the points we were fortunately able to get some corroborative testimony. Melda was going to her cousin's, as the mother had planned, on a certain morning, and got off the car a couple of blocks before she reached her destination, and went to the grocery department of a department store to get some cookies. At the door she saw Annie for the first time in a year and a half. The older girl called, but Melda would not go and Annie, whistling, walked away with her companion. Instead of going out, Melda then loitered around in the store. "I was thinking about Annie, so I didn't hurry out." We attempted further analysis of Annie's influence.

"The only bad girl I ever knew was Annie. Ever since I saw her steal some scissors I have got it in my mind. I see her as if she was telling me what she was doing. *I see her standing right beside me. If I read a book and it is about a girl, I see her like a picture.* Those bad words she used to say, they would often come back in my mind, but the words do not come back any more."

"It is like she was standing in front of me; as if she was telling me what she does; just as if she was calling me to go along with her some place. *Sometimes it is so plain, I think it is her.* Then I don't know what to do, and I ask my mother to give me some work. When I get to washing dishes, then I quit thinking of her. *I see her when I read in the book. It is like she was standing in between the people in the pictures.* Once in a while at school when we are reading, then I ask my teacher if I can do something else. When I try not to think about it, I have to do some hard thing to stop thinking about her. I would be so glad not to think about her no more, because I don't want to make my mother that shame."

"When I think about her most and feel like stealing, it is when I see pictures of boys and girls on one page. She used to show me picture books she stole. Once she showed me a picture of a boy and girl kissing. She told me then about bad things, and now, when I see a picture with a boy and girl, I think about what she told me, and then I think of her and the stealing. This is the first time I saw her since I stole that last time. I think that I ought to stop looking at picture books, because it is pictures that makes me think of her. *Sometimes when I look at a map in school, it is like she was standing on it. She once showed me a map,* but I don't think of that so often. It is when I see pictures about little boys and girls in one picture, that is when it is the worst."

As far as we could ascertain, this girl was not a great visualizer in general. We asked her about remembering pictures of other subjects, such as those she saw in her geography, but it appeared it was only the pictures which suggested or were directly associated with her vivid experiences with Annie which presented themselves mentally in any strong fashion. We found that Melda was once with Annie when the latter took some picture books from a department store. It was extremely interesting, also, that Annie had stolen a book with maps in it, perhaps a geography, and in showing Melda this book had opened it for her to see the maps. Here was the basis of the obsessional imagery associating Annie with maps and also with picture books in general.

Melda, as well as her mother, assured us that during this period of a year and a half she had stolen nothing

at all. She said that she often got "a feeling of taking things", but did not do so. She had managed to
overcome this by reasoning with herself and by busy-
ing herself as much as possible. She said that it was
when she was trying to overcome the ideas and pictures which came up in her mind that she asked her
mother for hard work to do. It was clear that her
behavior had broken bounds again when her associations were powerfully renewed by actually seeing the
cause of her original emotional disturbance.

All through this second court experience Melda appeared as a thoroughly normal and terribly distressed
child. She showed the judge the book of good pictures
which had been given her a few days before, and said
that she was going to have these in her mind instead
of the old ones. We had a very encouraging interview with the mother and child together. Melda
promised always to go to her mother now about any
kind of temptations which she might have, and we
tried to impress the mother more than ever with the
need of gaining the girl's confidence.

For over a year and a half now there has been no
trouble whatever with Melda. She has been doing
very well in school and at home; she is in the eighth
grade. Her mother reports that the girl seems very
happy most of the time and has been unusually helpful.
Melda herself tells us that her old imagery has been
growing less and less; only on a couple of occasions
during the last six months has she been bothered, and
then she told her mother about it and began to work
very hard. In particular she has been reading the
book given to her and has been trying ardently to
image to herself one of the pictures which was suggested to her as being especially good. She has tried

this, she states, whenever the old pictures have started to appear in her mind; indeed, she has been carrying this book with her most of the time.

During the year two most unfortunate incidents have occurred which bear upon the general problem of reformation of offenders. Melda was waiting for a few minutes on a crowded corner in her old neighborhood when she saw a woman with her hand bag open. She went up to the woman and told her of this, and the latter closed it. A man standing by led her to a police officer on the corner, and he, knowing of her, took her to the station. The juvenile officer of the district, an unusually discerning man, immediately investigated the case and found there was nothing to it. The woman herself said that no one had attempted to take anything from her hand bag. The matter, of course, was not carried to court, but Melda was naturally much disturbed.

Still another incident occurred, showing how a bad reputation follows the offender. Melda came in to us to report that she had been sent home from school and told not to come back. The school people knew that she had been "locked up", and when a certain other girl in her room told the teacher that Melda was stealing again, they believed it. Now, as a matter of fact, it appears that this girl had tried to persuade Melda to go stealing with her, and Melda refused, whereupon this girl made the accusation. Melda came in to us with tears streaming down her cheeks, bringing a girl friend from the same room to testify to us about the other girl. This affair was soon adjusted, and Melda was returned to school. She is now very jealous, naturally, of her reputation, and assured us that recently she has had no temptations whatever to take things.

(After this long period of success, very disturbing events have, since the above writing, developed in the family life, involving delinquencies or even mental unbalance of one of Melda's parents. Again a most unfortunate sex affair has been thrust into the girl's immediate experience. It was a matter of great interest to us to find that she reacted once more by stealing. On account of this miserable family situation lately arisen, the outcome for Melda's behavior must now be considered precarious unless she is removed to a better mental and moral environment.)

Case 2. A wonderfully clear, direct account of mental imagery was obtained in the following instance. The search for causation of the delinquency was greatly aided by the intelligent and stalwart attitude of both the offender and his relatives. His introductory statement to us was that stealing gave him a very peculiar pleasure which he could not explain, but which he would like to have fathomed.

Armond B., a well developed boy of nearly sixteen, came most willingly to seek help for his troubles. He had not yet been taken into court, although he had repeatedly stolen. Both he and his family felt that the situation was getting desperate. An intelligent police officer referred them to us. His delinquencies up to the present had been settled to the satisfaction of the losers, but if he kept up his thieving, there was no telling how soon he would be held for trial.

Armond's personal qualities showed no peculiarities; one could quickly perceive him to be frank, pleasant, responsive, well-mannered, thoughtful, and truthful. His mental processes were notably simple and direct. Dealing as his story did with the subjective elements

of his life, he showed in relating it no particular ego-
centricism and no approach to hypochondria. He had
been well brought up in an unusually wholesome family
environment, where only moderate means were avail-
able for the high ideals of education which the young
people set themselves. There had been no deep confidences between him and his relatives, but there was
much affection and trust among them.

Armond was attending an educational institute of
high school grade, where he was an earnest and moderately good student. The mental tests he did for us
showed nothing abnormal; a moderate slowness of
wit indicated nothing special, except the fact that he
was not unusually bright. We were interested to note
the point that he himself made concerning his own
learning ability; he said he had to see things in order
to remember them well; he tried to remember his
lessons as he saw them on the page. The ingenuousness which Armond displayed with us was probably a
tribute to his upbringing in a simple-minded and
truthful family; it was more than we usually find with
adolescents who are physically matured beyond their
years, as he was.

Armond presented a very sound body for examination. Nothing out of the ordinary was found except
that he was an excessive nail biter, he had a slight
defect of vision in one eye, and he showed premature
sex characteristics. With his broad, mature face, he
looked the part of a thoroughly wholesome and honest
young fellow.

This boy came from a family on the upgrade in this
country; the parents had been immigrants. There
were a number of older brothers who had done well,
two of them were now religious workers in Y. M. C. A.

institutes. The only abnormal traits in the family on
either side were to be ascribed to alcoholism, — there
had been some of this on each side, but not in any
near relative. The father himself earlier had been a
hard drinker, but he had reformed; he was always
steady at his work. In general, the family may be
said to be unusually God-fearing and industrious
people.

Armond's physical development had been absolutely
normal in all ways; indeed, the whole family were
noted for their good health. Our boy had gone to
school regularly and always cared, in a slow-going
way, for his studies. I would again make the point
that he had been unusually well protected from immoral influences at home and in the private school to
which he went.

Armond said that he was more than willing to
thrash out with us, as his mother desired, the temptations which beset him. Out of his completed story,
we may construct the following account of the facts,
many of which were verifiable:

At about fourteen years Armond began going first
with a boy by the name of Emil. Until this time he
had thought hardly at all about sex affairs; he had
not been taught by bad companions about such things,
nor had he been instructed at all in these matters by
his parents. It was already known to the family that
Emil previously had cheated his mother out of some
money and was somewhat dishonest, but they supposed he had overcome these tendencies. Armond,
who was somewhat younger, learned at this age first
from Emil about girls as objects of sexual attraction
and first heard about masturbation. He also found
out that Emil was in the habit of stealing occasionally.

At this time the two boys were together attending meetings at church. Armond found a key in church, evidently belonging to a poor-offering box, and Emil suggested opening the box. It was this same day or very near it that Emil stopped Armond in front of an art store and showed him a well known, really most innocent picture of a young girl in the nude, and told him that it made him feel like masturbating. The boys did open the box repeatedly and take money from it and spent it together. They kept this up until Armond was caught in the act by a church attendant. In the meantime this picture and its association with the sex impulse seized upon Armond's mind. He told us that this was what was really the matter with him. The thought of this picture was what he wanted to get rid of, and then perhaps he would not steal. After talking a time with us, it thus seemed to stand out very clearly in his mind that there was much connection between the two ideas. We asked for further explanation. Armond told us that after hearing what Emil said about the picture, although this was just about the time when he heard the pastor warn a class of boys against the evils of bad sex habits, he began practising masturbation often in his study periods when alone in the daytime. It occurred directly in connection with his thought and imagery about this picture; in fact, *the picture became like a vision* to him, around which he centered his thoughts. It flashed up in his mind often when he was reading. He repeatedly prayed that he might be relieved of this imagery and temptation. It was the only picture that he had ever thought of in that way, and he had only seen it once, there in the shop window.

We were emphatically told, both by Armond and

his family, that there had been no stealing before this
time; he had never dreamt that it would be possible
for him to do such a thing.   After he was found taking
this money in church, he was closely guarded by his
family, and he wanted to be so guarded, but they knew
nothing of his awakened sex thoughts.   His older
brothers frequently walked to school with him and
came home with him, that he might be relieved of all
bad companionship.   But he began a lot of petty
stealing.   He took sheets of paper and pens at school,
things that he did not need at the time.   He was never
found out at this, he did it so slyly.   During the vacation, he worked for a few weeks in an office, but he
resisted all temptations to steal while there.   He took
small moneys from his father's pockets, however,
although his parents had told him always to ask and
he would never be refused spending money.   On another occasion he took some roller skates.   The last
experience in stealing was the one that led to his being
brought to us for study.   The analysis of this recent
event and the mental processes which went on before
it showed clearly the mental mechanisms we are discussing in this volume.

It was Sunday afternoon.   Armond had been reading
a story.   He had much temptation that day to allow
the picture to remain before his mind because he was
alone.   He resisted his sex impulses by ardent reading.
Several times his pernicious mental imagery recurred.
By evening he became intensely restless and went out
for a walk.   He came to a place where there was a
little alley back of a store.   He walked in there just
out of curiosity.   He had no idea of stealing, nor did
he go there for any other improper purposes; it was
just restlessness that led him.   He saw a window

partially open and a box inside within reaching distance. He managed to get hold of it and experienced great satisfaction in doing so. Soon afterwards, when it was in his possession, he felt alarmed, but had not enough courage to replace the box. Even after this he remembers he had some pleasure or satisfaction in thinking of what he had done, but this rapidly diminished. He retained the money that was in the box and threw the box away. (It was a day or two after this that his mother found the extra money in his pockets and made him confess and pay back to the grocery store what had been taken.)

The stealing of the roller skates occurred when he was on an errand after a period when he had been alone and had suffered temptations to which he had partially given in. When he entirely fights off his sex impulses, he has the feeling as if nothing could make him pleasant. He has never told his people about this, because he was afraid that his mother would worry over it. She is his best friend in the world; he does not feel near to his brothers. This last year, while he has had such temptations, he has not been doing well in his studies. The year before he was one of the three highest in his class. He knew himself, he said, that the main trouble with him was sex thoughts; his stealing he felt to be of secondary importance. After the analysis, which was readily carried out in a couple of prolonged interviews, Armond had clearly framed for us the connection between the two, and without any explanation on our part stated that he now saw it most distinctly. This was a tribute to the intelligence, good will, and naïveté of the boy. He really wanted to do better and bring to the surface all that led him into evil deeds.

The advice to be given was plain enough in this case. With the boy's permission we called in his most sympathetic brother. Through this brother, success has been achieved. Armond laid bare to him his troubles; for months afterwards he purposely kept close company with people before whom he would be ashamed to exhibit any sex tendencies; he placed his mind more arduously on his studies, and entered an institute with the idea of professionally rendering religious service, as two older brothers had done before him.

Later reports from Armond remain most satisfactory, with never a hint of more dishonesty; he says himself that a year and a half has gone by without his having stolen anything, and, while he does not deny sex temptations, he has reduced the pernicious imagery to a minimum and has learned how to fight it, as we suggested, by replacing it with better mental pictures. The outcome is most gratifying to all concerned.

Case 3. The obsessional and almost hallucinatory force of early improper acquaintance with partially understood vicious words is graphically shown in this instance:

A boy of ten years, from a very poor family, gave much trouble on account of smoking, remaining away from home nights, and stealing. Once he had stolen sufficient money from a neighbor to buy clothes and shoes. He engaged also in much lying and romancing. The boy showed fair ability, but had suffered many disadvantages on account of excessively poor vision. General development was normal. In the background there was defective heredity, the father having been a very sickly man long before this boy was born and a sufferer from lead poisoning, and others in the family were subject to many headaches. The boy himself had had many children's diseases and frequently complained of headaches.

This lad gave a convincing story of mental conflicts and informed us of more stealing escapades than the mother herself knew. We afterwards found out that these were true. Excerpts from our interviews will give some idea of his mental content. This boy told first of a former companion who tried to steal a purse and who had succeeded in getting a bag of pennies out of the pocket of a rag-man's coat. "That kid I was telling you about was the first I heard bad words from. He was one of the kids that was in the barn I was telling you about, where the rag-man was. I never told mamma about him. His family moved away now. He would tell bad words in the settlement house. I think of these; that's how it spoils me. I used to tell bad words, but not no more. When a kid gets to know these things, he feels like saying them out. I don't no more; it makes me sick. I sometimes feel like saying them, and that makes me feel bad. When I get right up to it and get ready to say them, I stop. . . . If I see a girl going to the store, I think about what they said about taking money away. I think of things. *It sounds it; it sounds it;* it would be words what he said, those bad words; I don't like to tell you about them, I'm ashamed. It makes me think like anything about bad, that does. It's bad words he said, and what he says about ladies. . . . Sure, it comes in my mind about robbing. When it first comes in my mind to take things, I get sort of scared, and then maybe I take it and put it down in my hand like this, or roll it up in my sweater sleeve. They don't like me in our house, my pa don't. The

boarders call me a bum.   The teachers say they don't
want me because I spoil the other boys.   My father
he don't want to have me near him. . . .   I didn't
know what it was to take things.   I started to get
bad then.   That boy used to say all kinds of dirty
stuff; I went away when he said them things.   I didn't
like to hear it and I walked away.   He was a nasty
boy."

From this poverty-stricken home, so poor in mental
interests and understanding, so lacking in management as well as in material things, there was nothing
to be hoped for.   This lad had to be sent for a long
period to an institution.

CHAPTER VI

CONFLICTS CAUSING IMPELLING IDEAS

THE fact that mental conflicts give rise to impelling ideas is the essential reason for mental analysis coming forward so strongly in the practice and writings of neurologists and psychiatrists. They developed their studies of cases symptomatically presenting impulsions, compulsions, and obsessions (including the inhibitive phenomena of hysteria, psychasthenia, etc.) long before attempt was made to study, by similar investigations of causations, impulsions towards what is termed social offense. Now, however, many evidential facts have been accumulated which show the same type of mental mechanisms operative in this other field.

There is no doubt that indirect sexual offenses show impulsions in the most virulent form, but, as I have before stated, on page 47, this class of cases need not be included in this discussion when so much has already been written on that topic.

Impelling ideas towards misconduct following upon mental conflict form a common element in all the cases cited, but the two given in this chapter are vivid illustrations of instances in which the offender apperceived the impelling ideas. The reader will find elsewhere among our case-histories much that bears on this point.

Case 4.   As offering a thoroughly ingenuous account
of the mental mechanisms which produce misconduct
from the raw materials of mental conflict, the following case is remarkable.   Here we have a graphic statement of impelling ideas immediately preceding an act
of misdoing, given by a young individual who knows
nothing of the psychological laws to which her mental
experiences are witness.   The case also illustrates the
fact that analysis alone is not enough; it does not
afford help sufficient to overcome habits formed.
But we here see wonderfully well how a considerable
career of stealing can be entirely checked through
utilizing discoveries to be made only by mental analysis.

Beulah T. had stolen very frequently during a period
of two years before we saw her first at eleven and one-
half years of age.   Although a most modest and
delicate appearing child, she had already become
notorious, in a small way, for her thieving.   She stole
from home, from school, from shops.   Once or twice
she had run away for all day following her stealing,
and she had, naturally, lied much about it.   In school
she had been the source of a great deal of annoyance.
It was found necessary to trace her thieving by the use
of marked money.   Much more important, however,
than enumerating her offenses, is our showing some
details of the mental mechanisms leading to the stealing.
We found a girl of fair general development and
nutrition, with strabismus and defective vision in one
eye; she was also suffering from a mild chronic otitis
media.   Examination and inquiry showed nothing
else of importance.
On the mental side Beulah did very well, indeed,
in spite of her handicaps.   Although immigrated with

her family only three years previously, she was in the usual grade for her age and stood well in her classes. We found her responsive, frank, and apparently quite normal in her emotions and in every other way. In the ensuing years she has steadily advanced with her classes.

Beulah's mother died just before they came to America; we obtained the child's history from her grandmother and her father. Concerning her development, it appeared that there was nothing of importance. She had never been seriously ill; the otitis media dated from a slight attack of scarlet fever the previous year. There was no reason to think that she had suffered in any way from defective antenatal conditions; birth was normal. She walked and talked early and always had appeared to be a bright child. Reports from school were always favorable concerning scholarship and general deportment. There had never been any complaints, except about her stealing, and this was quite beyond the understanding of her family, who could not see why such a quiet and delicate little child should be a thief.

About heredity there was little to relate. One grandfather had been a deserter of his family; beyond this we got no history whatever of mental defect or peculiarity in the family.

During the course of a number of interviews, we obtained from Beulah an account of her experiences and mental life which was partially verified. We had heard from the relatives that there had never been any stealing until they had gone to live at a certain place. We pursued our line of inquiry from this as a starting point. We learned from Beulah of a boy, Sam R., who went to the same school with her and who had met Beulah and talked to her repeatedly. (Sam's case was at once investigated by a probation officer who corroborated much that Beulah said about the boy. Although never reported to the police, he was notorious among the children of the neighborhood for the type of bad conduct that Beulah described.) Before knowing Sam, she insists, she had never had the slightest thought of stealing. "He said I should take things from the store and from teacher, and everything, and he said I should call people wicked names; I never did though. He told me what names to call them; I never say those names. Sometimes I think about them, then I forget them again. Sometimes I used to see him roller-skating, and sometimes when he went to the pasture in the prairie with the cow, with the girl next door, I would see him. She is a nice girl. She doesn't say bad words. Sam used to talk to her. I know he asked her to go out in the bushes, and everything like that. He only used to say that to her because he knew she was nicer than me, and he liked her better.

"He used to say bad words to me. I told grandma that he said bad words, and she said I should not listen to them. No, she never explained anything. I didn't understand them. He says to her, 'Come on out in the bushes with me.' She didn't go. I wondered what he meant. Girls never spoke to me about it. She says, 'I wonder what that means,' and that is all she said. He didn't say anything to me before that. He just told me to steal, and like that. He told me a lot of bad words." (Beulah whispered the "bad words" which this boy had told her, and they were, indeed, very bad.) "He didn't tell me what they meant. He used to say, 'Come with me,' and I said,

'No,' and he said all those words. I don't know where he wanted me to go.

"Sometimes I'd ask girls, and they would say, 'I don't know.' Sometimes I think about it, and I wonder what it means. When I am in school I think about it, when I'm studying. That was about a year and a half ago, that he asked me to go with him. That girl said that once he knocked her down and was going to take off her clothes. She told me that he never done anything bad to her. I don't know what he tried to do. I saw him about a week ago. He was all dressed up in a new suit, and he had roller skates, and everything. Once he ran away from home. He slept in a basement. I saw him one night when I went to the store to buy something for my papa. Once I ran away too. I stole twenty-five cents, and my pa said I should go to the reform school if I did it again, and I thought he said I should go then, and I ran away. I was gone about three hours in the evening. I was with some Italian people. I told them, and they said I could stay by them."

Beulah told us much, in her quiet way, concerning the astonishing effect which these words had upon her. The following is her response, verbatim, in reply to our inquiry about how the words came up in her mind: "Sam said he liked us best, and we wasn't to say anything to anybody else. He used to write on our sidewalk bad words. Sam did this with Lillie — that bad word. Sometimes, when I think about the bad word he said, I get a headache. Sometimes, when I think about the words, I feel as if I wanted to take things. I get a headache, and then I seem to have to take things."

At this point we made a very careful attempt to

analyze the last occasion of stealing, which had only
been a week or so previously. The whole events of
the afternoon at school were gone over, and finally
the following was obtained: "I was thinking about
those words when I took money from my teacher.
My teacher was putting on her hat; school was over;
there were just three girls with me. I had been thinking about those words. Sometimes, when I am eating,
I think about Sam, and I think I hear him saying
those words. It was in the afternoon, we was having
reading at three o'clock; we was reading about a little
boy, and it said 'Sam', and I thought of Sam R., and
the words he said, and the teacher's pocketbook was
lying right there when I walked past afterwards to go
out."

"My little brother Willie, he swears because Sam
learned him. When I saw Sam come, I closed my ears.
Since I slapped him, he never says a word to me now.
They are not dirty girls I play with; Helen, she is a
nice girl. I sometimes told my grandmother that Sam
said bad words."

"Sometimes I think about what Sam said, but I
never speak it. I never told nobody. I never thought
it had anything to do with babies. I don't know what
he meant by that word. I know what he tried to do
with Lillie, that's all I know. I don't know about
little babies. I have asked lots of people, and they
won't tell. I asked my auntie, both my aunts, I asked
my papa, I asked my grandmother, I asked the mid-
wife, and they won't tell me. I asked because my
aunt had a little baby nearly a year old, I asked her,
and she said, 'I won't tell you.' . . . I like it better
in the old country, there are not so many bad boys
around; but I like school here, they don't give you

whippings. I want to stay at home, I don't want to go in another home."

The attitude of this family towards Beulah's needs, as expressed by their lack of response to her repeated questioning, was significant of what was to be expected of them. They were totally incapable of understanding the situation and dealing with it along the lines we suggested, although they were good enough people in their way. Beulah did very well for a few weeks, and then the complaint was made that she was stealing again, so she was sent away from the scene of her old associations to a very good school for girls, where she remained for a year. Her conduct there was beyond reproach. It is almost five years since this last stealing on the part of Beulah, and not a further word of complaint has been brought against her. The report, even from the grandmother, who early found her so incorrigible, is that Beulah now gives no trouble in any way.

Case 5. The misconduct of a neuropathic little boy included a serious delinquency — he repeatedly drove off horses with vehicles left hitched on the street. This form of theft was his besetting temptation, although he experienced little pleasure and sometimes punishment in connection with it. The peculiar basis of his impulse became clear upon analysis.

Jeddy N., a little less than twelve years old, was much complained of by his mother and by the school people on account of his general mischievousness and uncontrollability. This behavior, however, was largely to be accounted for by his nervous conditions. A much more important event had brought him into the hands of the police. As his mother put it, "he had a mania for stealing horses and buggies." On several occasions he had driven away horses belonging to business men, causing much annoyance. He had been taken to the police station already four times on account of this, and the other times he either had not been caught or had been allowed to go home. Further details about these delinquencies appear later.

Jeddy had been suspended more than once from school on account of his restless, bad behavior. He was said to be mischievous in general and dishonest in several ways. Other boys could easily lead him. The nervous foundation for this was recognized by all, but because he disturbed others so much, he could not be tolerated in school. The same situation obtained at home, where the mother says he is a great torment and cannot be controlled unless she gives up all of her time to him; there is a large family, and this is quite impossible.

We found a poorly developed boy of twelve years, weighing only seventy-three pounds. Vision about half normal in one eye and normal in the other. Specialist's report: no glasses needed. Many carious teeth. Bites nails excessively. Thyroid slightly enlarged. Quick, jerky, and incoördinate movements of outstretched hands and tongue. At times these movements are seen extending to the shoulders and head; on other occasions we find the movements almost absent. Beginning bilateral inguinal hernia. Scar and evidence of bone involvement from injury in the occipital region. Examination otherwise negative. Extreme dolichocephalic type; circumference of head, 52.4 centimeters, length 19.5 centimeters, breadth 14 centimeters. Shape of the head, together with his prominent eyes, give the boy a most peculiar appearance.

On the mental side we soon saw that we had to do with a somewhat abnormal individual. This boy has been repeatedly studied by us, and our final diagnosis remains the same as at first, namely, that Jeddy is to be regarded as mildly aberrational, with some element of dullness, probably from physical causes. He may be suffering from the psychosis of chorea, but there are several elements in the case which make it difficult to be sure of this. His mental peculiarities are evidenced on tests as well as on general behavior. The Binet (1911 series) record gives but little suggestion of the trouble. He does all of the nine-year tests correctly; all of the ten-year, except that he fails on half of the second test; he does only the first two of the twelve-year tests.

This brings him quite to grade, for he is not yet twelve years old. On tests involving control, either mental or psychomotor, he does poorly, indeed. His reactions on the opposites test vary greatly. The tapping test shows his extreme difficulty in controlling his finer movements. He is easily fatigued; probably that is the reason he gives only forty-five words in three minutes in the Binet test. His performance on numerous other tests shows the same characteristics; where no prolonged effort is required of him, where no great amount of attention is brought into play, the boy can do fairly well. During any sitting he yawns frequently and shows his fatigue. While actually at work, he bites his finger nails nervously. His attitude and conversation are normal and intelligent. In going over his story with him on numerous occasions, we note coherency up .to the point that mental effort is required. If it is a question of putting his mind upon actual times and places difficult to remember, he fails, but about his general apperceptions of his own career being clear, there is no question. Fortunately for the scientific aspects of the case, we were able to get much corroboration of his story from the mother. During the last year there has been a tendency towards improvement, but all that should have been done for the boy was never done, and then there has arisen the problem of possible effect of bad habits. In a general way the case is easy of diagnosis. The boy shows psychotic tendencies, chiefly characterized by a great lack of control.

Developmental history runs as follows: The mother was well during this pregnancy; the family circumstances were fairly good and she was not troubled. Birth was at full term, but was very difficult. Child weighed twelve pounds and it was a dry birth. Earliest infancy fairly normal. At two years bronchitis and whooping cough. Walked and talked at about two years, but slower than the others in walking. For several years has been a restless child. Talks much in his sleep. Adenoids and tonsils removed a couple of years ago. Nervousness developed so that he was not only treated at home for his jerkings and twitchings, but was also sent to a hospital on account of this. There he remained for a week previous to our first seeing him. Diagnosis was that he had a mild case of chorea. The boy is said to have dropped things frequently. A few years ago he was struck by a street car on the back of the head, but came running home by himself, and it did not seem to affect him in any way; in fact, he has been in slight accidents two or three times. Started to school at the regular age, but on account of his nervousness has made little progress and was most of the time in a subnormal room and changed about a great deal. His mother helps him in his school work at home; he rattles off a page from memory, but does not seem to take in the sense of things. Only been to third grade successfully. Has been to several clinics. His mother reports that for years he has been the most difficult individual to manage; she may warn him and scold him, and yet in an hour he is found in more mischief. Seems to have considerable musical ability. Gets along pretty well with other members of his family. Is much teased on account of his peculiar looks, and yet others readily lead him.

Family history was given in sufficient fullness. There seem to have been no mental defect of importance on either side, and no cases of insanity or of nervous disease. Father is alcoholic to a certain extent, but is never abusive or quarrelsome; supports his family. There are seven children alive; two are dead, and there have been a number of miscarriages. The child next younger than Jeddy is small for her age and only in second grade at ten years. These are the only two that seem backward.

For scientific interest, it should be stated that the story about the mental conflict in this case came out of a clear sky. We were not expecting it, and, indeed, not looking for it particularly. At the time when we first saw Jeddy, our attention was entirely taken up with his physical and mental peculiarities, as ascertainable through the usual routine examinations. At that time we strongly advised that the boy be sent to live in the country on account of his general poor conditions. It was after this little fellow had been brought in on complaint of his mother, some four months later, that we heard of some curious sex behavior through other boys under detention. He had nearly stripped

one little boy of his clothes and evidently was about
to engage in some form of perversion with him. We
saw him in numerous interviews after this, when he
always met us in the friendly fashion that he had done
previously. Even in conversation he easily became
fatigued, and talked generally in short, jerky sentences.
His story was told as if he were about eight or nine
years old; it was never clear at first, but upon questioning, it gained coherency. We were utterly surprised to have him without equivocation connect sex
affairs with his stealing. It would be a long story to
tell all that he said that was to the point, but the following is the gist of it :

A year ago or more, it was in the summer, he was
looking at some pictures outside of a show, when a
man with a horse and buggy called from the opposite
side of the street for him to come over and go for a
ride. They rode some distance, as far as South Park.
This man put his hand on Jeddy in sexual fashion for
quite a long time in the buggy, but although he exposed
himself, Jeddy did nothing in return. Jeddy claims
never to have done anything of the sort before nor to
have known of such things. This was when he first
learned. He maintained, also, that he never even
attempted to engage in such practices with another
until the affair with the boy under detention. But the
experiences with the man made him feel like doing
things to himself, and he had been masturbating every
couple of days.

When Jeddy first told us of this man, we asked him
if he had ever stolen a horse previous to that experience.
In boyish fashion he told us that he guessed he had.
He had stolen a pony before that. But as the analysis
developed, he said that he wanted to change that state-

ment; long before the pony was taken, he rode in the buggy with the stranger. (Fortunately, we were able to get exact data from the mother on these points, and it came out clearly that the experience with the man preceded all stealing of horses.) Jeddy told us rather vaguely in our first interview about considerable stealing of horses. His mother knew all about that, he said, but she knew nothing about this man. He had never told anybody before.

After gaining the information about his acquaintance with the man in the buggy, we got Jeddy to give us as good a description as possible of his own mental attitude towards the stealing. It was a comparatively simple task in analysis to get the following:

"When I see a horse and buggy, then I think of that man. I used to sit down and think then, maybe. I'd be sort of nervous. . . . Sometimes I'd walk away, and I would walk straight home. I would say, 'Your mother told you not to steal no more.' . . . It would make me feel like doing what he did." This last sentence was in response to our inquiry as to how he felt when he saw a horse and buggy standing on the street. He then again insisted that the first time he had ever experienced sexual feelings was when he was in the buggy with the strange man.

Concerning what occurs when he is driving a horse and buggy after having stolen it: "I feel nervous." (Excited?) "Sure. Sometimes I'd drop the lines and think of something; think that maybe the man that owned it was coming, and then I'd get out. . . . Sure, I'd think of that man when I was driving. That man was the one who told me about stealing a horse and buggy. . . . He said he had got the rig west some place; said he had stole it; said he was going to take it away out somewhere; he said he was going to get another one and hitch on back of it." Jeddy's mind reverting to my former question about his feelings when he saw a rig unoccupied on the street, he said, "Sometimes I'd see a horse and buggy and I would start running."

Speaking about the time he was left in South Park, he tells us that it was at night, and that he was extremely nervous. "I was all in. I was tired, and the conductor gave me a ride home on the car." (Why so tired?) "Because he was monkeying with me. I was nervous in the buggy." The boy then reiterates that he is always nervous and excited when he drives off by himself. (There is great interest in the fact that before the mother knew of this, I asked her to describe his homecoming on this night, the first time he was ever away from home late, and she remembered how worn out and nervous and excited and peculiar he seemed. She could place the time of this affair together with that of his later stealing escapades very clearly for us, so that to a great extent there was corroboration of what the boy had told.)

Speaking further about his temptation, although he does not know what this word means, Jeddy tells us: "Sometimes I get crazy spells, and I go and get a horse and buggy. Sometimes it makes you feel like you ain't going to bring the horse and buggy back. Then sometimes I am going along when I see a horse and buggy, and I walk away. Maybe I think a while and say, 'Oh, no,' and walk away. Sometimes I think of that man when I see a horse and buggy."

Jeddy likes to drive a horse. There is a nice peddler, whom he sometimes goes with, who lets him drive his horse, and his father has sometimes taken him on his wagon, "so I would not be stealing." Crying in very normal fashion Jeddy says he wants to go home. "I think if I'd go home, I would never go stealing no more."

The police had caught Jeddy a number of times. With one exception, he always took the horse and buggy when he was alone. On the occasion when he was in the "X" Street Police Station, he had been with other boys. "I just was breaking myself of that stealing, and some other boy said something about it. The judge said he would put me away." But on other occasions Jeddy has driven for a time and then got out and left the rig. He told us about once driving a horse a large share of one day, and then he put it into an alley and went home. The next morning he sneaked around to see if it was there and, sure enough, it was, so he drove it that day also, and then finally left it without getting caught.

As we often do with young children, we had a final interview with the mother and the boy together; that was after she had given us her corroborative facts, which included certain times when the older brother had suspected this boy of engaging in bad sex habits. He came home looking so queer, with his eyes all bloodshot; they had asked him about it, but he had always denied it. Jeddy had never stolen anything before this affair with the man, except that in a childish way he had taken apples and other things to eat. Even as a little boy he had always been fond of horses. With us he told his mother that he had never felt like informing her about this man. He frankly went over the whole sex affair with no variation from what he had told us, and it became clear that the brother's suspicions were correct.

The relationship between the sex matter and this remarkable stealing was apparent even to the mother. No one could doubt the mental conflict and the mental repression that had gone on in this boy's mind, and that the strange impulse to a serious delinquency, such as any ordinary boy, to say nothing of this puny little fellow, would hesitate to indulge in, was developed on a strong emotional basis, namely, his first sex affair. Except for our exploration and enlisting the mother's better understandings of the problem, nothing more was now undertaken than had been done previously when the boy had been taken in by the police. Indeed, this time he did not go before any judge.

A year has elapsed, and there has been no further trouble with this boy stealing, but his nervous condition has excluded him from the schools, and there have not been sufficient funds in the family to get him properly placed. The educational and neurological outcome of the case is still problematic. Even our earliest recommendation, namely, that he live a quiet life in the country, was never carried out.

CHAPTER VII

CRIMINAL CAREERS DEVELOPED FROM CONFLICTS

IT can readily be shown what happens in some instances when conflicts which create misconduct tendencies are not faced with courage and discernment. For the valid reasons given at length in Chapter III, we have refrained from commencing studies of cases when careers of misdoing have been already carried beyond years of adolescence. The safer way for us, we felt, was to begin with younger people when we could obtain verification of facts incident to the beginning of mental conflict, and with this foundation of knowledge watch the future developments. Unfortunately, even after our early discovery of some special mental conflict, through family ineptitude or failure on the part of social agencies or of enterprises established under the law, the career in some instances was not checked. Two examples of such long continuance of tendency to misconduct are offered. (Case 12 may also be profitably read in this connection.) The lessons that these case-histories convey are obvious, particularly when they are compared with records of similar beginnings where tendencies already demonstrated and perhaps active over a considerable time have been completely arrested. (Suggestions of many practical points in this con-

nection are to be found in the accounts of successful
Cases 2, 9, 20, 22, 25, 30, 31.)

Case 6. A definite beginning of a long career of
delinquency is known in the following case to have
occurred with an event that had solely to do with the
inner mental life. Through our first study, which
was made shortly after this beginning, there is an
understanding of the case which, perhaps, never could
have been obtained, at least so clearly, in later years.

Royal M., when only twelve years of age, had
already been arrested twice, in two neighboring States.
Immediately after the last escapade, he was brought to
us by his father with the inquiry, "What in the world
can be the matter with my boy? He has been repeatedly stealing and running away from home."

Now, six years later, this boy's record includes a
long list of offenses and many remarkable incidents.
The most striking thing to me about Royal's career
is the amount of suffering which he has gone through
and the repetition of delinquency which has invariably
led to more suffering. Since his first two thefts, no
very serious stealing had been engaged in until recently, when, far from home and penniless, he, with
another young fellow, attempted to rob a store. He
was caught and sent to a reformatory in New York.
But during those intervening years he has repeatedly
run away from home, even in winter, and made his
way about the country as best he could. Earlier he
was an excessive truant. Through leading this kind
of life, he has, of course, indulged in much lying and
deception, and his people have been terribly worried
by his conduct.

From time to time, as we have seen him, we have

obtained clear evidences of intense turmoil going on within, only half framed in consciousness, but so deeply felt that it frequently impelled him to action. Even the slightest reflection would have made clear to him how inimical such action must inevitably be to his ultimate well-being and even to his immediate comfort.

At twelve years Royal was just fairly developed physically. A slightly lowered auditory acuity in one ear was the only evidence of sensory defect. Complete examination showed otherwise no abnormality. He was a bright, boyish, loose-jointed type, with a round face and a frank, open expression.

The general report was that Royal was a distinctly bright boy. What he accomplished on tests at any given time, we found depended very largely upon his mental attitude. He was clearly one of those cases where interpretation of test results requires taking into account the mood of the individual. The same was true about his school career after his delinquencies began; it was stated that the boy was bright when he wanted to be. Some employers have found him a good worker. The reformatory superintendent writes that he considers him a very gifted fellow in many respects. We have noted that tests done at different times vary somewhat, evidently according to his re-action to the individual giving the tests, or according to his mood of the day. Judged fairly by his best results on tests, there is no doubt that Royal can be classified as a boy of fair innate mental ability.

Concerning his development, we learned from the intelligent father that pregnancy was entirely normal. There was a prolonged labor, but no evidences of damage, and infancy was entirely healthy, notwithstanding some months of early artificial feeding. He began to walk and talk at an early age, and in all of his life, up to the time when we first saw him, he had no serious ailments. His functions in all ways were normally controlled; he has suffered from no accidents; he has indulged in no bad habits to any considerable extent. In the years characterized by his delinquent tendencies, Royal has suffered greatly from exposure, underfeeding, and illnesses which were the result of his penniless wanderings for weeks together.

There is no doubt that Royal comes from exceedingly good stock on his father's side, and that from his mother he may have derived certain peculiar mental traits. Hypersensitiveness, a tendency to jealousy, with some erratic conduct otherwise, seems to have characterized her family. Several members are said to have cordially hated each other, and many family quarrels occurred as the result of temperamental difficulties. All this comes out very strongly in such history of the family as is obtainable, although no one is known to have exhibited anything like the delinquent traits that Royal has shown. There is no doubt that Royal's mother was rather an exceptionally bright young woman, and his father has maintained a reputation for intelligence and ability.

Our main interest in this case centers around the facts pertaining to the mental and moral development of this boy. It is here clearly shown that important phases of the inner life may be affected by acquirement of emotion-producing knowledge, without any change having taken place in external conditions of life. To bear out this point, I must insist that the family environment all along has been decidedly good. The mother is a very good-natured woman, who has attempted

in a thoroughly rational way to be the right kind of
a mother to Royal; she was this before his delinquent career began, and she has made many kindly
efforts to meet his difficulties since that time. I
must also make it clear that up to a very definite
time, namely, when this boy was eleven and one-half
years old, his behavior was normal in every way. We
have repeatedly had this stated to us, and the boy
himself perceives that his character underwent a
change then; he has told us this many times.

In the good account which we received of his early
years, there was nothing that indicated him to be
out of the ordinary. He was prone to change his
interests rapidly from one thing to another, he was
playful in school instead of inclined to study, not
over affectionate, rather sensitive about the way he
was treated by other boys, who really did handle
him pretty roughly because he was not specially
athletic.

When we first saw him, complaints had been piling
up for a few months. "Something has come over
the boy," his parents stated. Not only had he lately
stolen on two occasions considerable amounts of
money — home savings — and run away to other
towns, but for some time he had seemed to have no
ambition to work, either in school or about the house;
he had appeared very greedy at the table, would
never say please; he could not be trusted with the
younger children because of his misbehavior toward
them; "he would seem to get mad and sore over
being scolded." They had found that he had told
boys in school, some days before he went, that he
was going to steal money and leave home. The
effect of punishment during these months had been

almost nil; the next day he would repeat the same offenses.

Somewhat later Royal became a confirmed truant and had twice to be sent to the school for truants. At one time he was found selling small articles about town, representing himself as an orphan. He also engaged in much lying and complaining about the way he was treated in general. This went on alternately with the spasmodic flights from home, which we have mentioned above, and which lasted for weeks or months at a time. On several occasions he was found in farming districts, or in small towns, having been picked up by the police as a vagrant. On more than one occasion we have seen him when he has been returned suffering greatly from lack of food and general exposure; once we saw him after he had been without food for three days, a miserable and pathetic specimen. From being out in all weathers, he had an acute attack of rheumatism. Just after he had been nursed back to health, he ran away again from his home. Through his father and by virtue of the good impression he makes, he obtained many jobs, but would stick to none of them for more than a few weeks at a time when he was living at home. Before his offense in New York State, his whereabouts had been unknown for several months.

The very fact of there being a special time when this boy began his delinquencies in such force made us suspect some experience that the parents knew nothing about. We found the boy very hard to deal with for a considerable period; he showed the same attitude to us that he did to his father, but one day he blurted out, "He's a liar, and she's a liar, and they are all liars, and I am going to be bad if I want to be."

This statement was what was needed to give us an opening clue; from this the boy by skillful guidance was led to analyze his motive and conduct. It appeared that several months previously a meddlesome neighbor had suddenly told him that the woman whom he had always thought to be his mother was not his mother; that the latter had died soon after he was born, and the younger children were not his brothers and sisters.

These facts later proved true. When the child was three months of age, a terrible accident occurred, in which his mother, standing near him, was instantly killed, but no harm was done the infant; the father, upon our inquiry, now stated that, needing some one to bring up his infant, he had soon married again a thoroughly good woman. For eight years or so they had had no children, but now there were others added to the household. Every evidence of Royal's real parentage had been destroyed in order that there might not be any friction about the stepmother; the father dreaded this and thought it best to let the lad grow up in total ignorance of the true facts, and it was really not until he was almost twelve that Royal had any suspicion regarding his parentage.

A most ingenuous account was given by the boy: "I was so sore that I got terribly red and hot. The next day I went to that woman's house again, and she started to tell me again, and I wouldn't go there no more. . . . I want to be a bad boy — I would rather live in a shed than there at home."

This boy, who, until a short time ago, had always been truthful, fond of home, and devoted to his supposed mother, had changed his social attitude entirely. With us at this time, and even later, he made intense complaints of duplicity and general bad treatment against both his father and stepmother; he was discriminated against in favor of the other children; he could see that this had long been the case; things in general were awry. Soon after he had heard the news which gave him this shock, news which he had kept to himself steadily all these months until the father brought him to us, he very deliberately began to plan an anti-social career. He read, he told us, whatever books he could lay his hands on which might offer suggestions of how to become a criminal. His stealing the family savings and fleeing to another State was in direct pursuance of these definite plans. He boasted to us of some little familiarity with jails in towns where he had been picked up as a homeless boy.

In the ensuing years we have seen Royal a number of times after various adventures. These have consisted for the most part, as previously stated, in running away from home. Very little stealing has been engaged in, but there has been at times a great deal of lying, deceitfulness, and misrepresentation, — a development of the very characteristics of which this boy so bitterly accused his own family at the time when he first became delinquent. We have several times had Royal go over with us the specific causes of his separate delinquencies, and on each occasion he has made statements quite similar in tone to those which first found such explosive utterance.

A year after his first running away, when talked to by a kindly official who wished to be a friend to him, Royal told a somewhat fanciful tale of his latest scrape, making it out to be much worse than it ever was. Here again he evidently desired to pose as a "bad man." At that same time, when he was asked what he wanted to be when grown up, he answered, "Nothing." He burst out laughing when his future was discussed; he went through some mental tests in a bored manner; he said, in a sarcastic way, that he was treated well enough at home, the trouble was that he did not want to go to school. All through he was trying to force the situation to appear something entirely different from the reality. It was about this time that his lying and deception grew to considerable proportions.

Most noteworthy, throughout our study of Royal's case, appears the fact that ever since the first development of his anti-social attitude, he has proceeded at times in a deliberate attempt to make himself out just as bad a person in a criminal way as he could. Even more striking, however, is the antithesis that he is thus frequently attempting something which is really foreign to his own nature; in facial aspect, in temperament, he is anything but the criminal. He makes no attempt to harm any one; his criminality is of minor degree, his delinquencies react mostly upon himself. It is all an expression of feelings which well up within him; his reactions are directed against the world of social relationships, against his position in his family. His wanting "to be bad" is, after all, not consistently carried out; in spite of his early reading he has developed no art of professional criminalism.

Something of the character and violence of Royal's inner feelings are witnessed to by his own statements from time to time. We have described his first reactions to the sudden information about his real parentage; his own ingenuous, boyish statement

shows the psychic shock.   At twelve years of age he
said, "I am wise to you all right, doctor; you're all
right, but you can't do anything for me.   I want to
be a bad boy."   A year later, while stating that his
home was good, and he was well treated, he insisted
that he would rather go to any kind of a place than
go back there.   We found him then tremendously
self-assertive, positive, and sarcastic.   Our inquiries
about his home were met at first by scornful laughter;
he complained about everything and raised his voice
petulantly and aggressively as he told of his troubles.
He had already been sent to the school for truants.
When he returned home and one day was alone, he
went rummaging inquisitively through the storeroom.
(He told this incident after he had vented in a couple
of interviews the scorn that was within him.)   There,
in a box, he found a picture on which was written,
"Mrs. M."   "It don't look like my stepmother at
all.   I didn't tell my father I saw it, because I didn't
want him to know. . . .   She always fools me, too.
I had some batteries, and she hid 'em on me; and I
had three pencils, and she put 'em away.   It's all like
that.   After that I made a little box down in the
basement, and I kept my things down there.   I wish
I had a little safe. . . .   The judge can say all he
wants to, he can say all day if he wants to, he'll find
out in a couple of days that I'm missing, and they'll
never hear any more from me. . . .   She hollers at
me because I get up so early.   At four o'clock I am
awake already; I can't sleep. . . .   I don't get along
with none of them. . . .   If I came back home after
a while, there would be more trouble.   Lots of times
I look in the paper for places away off where they're
looking for boys.   I don't want to go to no place

where there is a whole bunch of kids; I don't get along with kids very well."

Two years later Royal was once found by his father in a large city hospital where he had been for some time suffering acutely with the attack of rheumatism from exposure. He had then been away from home for many weeks and did not even let the hospital authorities know who he was. At periods during the intervening time he had done fairly well for as long as a couple of months. He had had several places of employment and been fairly satisfactory and brought home his wages. During one entire summer season the parents had lived with him out on a farm, purposely that he might have the country life he said he craved, but he did not take to farming, after all, and after six months or so the family circumstances made it necessary for them to return. The good stepmother had now reported to us that Royal had developed no bad habits; that at times he seemed to be pleasant enough; his biggest fault was in deceiving and misleading them; he seemed to have big ideas about little things, as, for instance, how far five dollars would go. But, as she expressed it, "he has something like a grudge back in his nature."

Some months later, after being returned by the police from another town, Royal talked more frankly than he ever had before about his own feelings. He said there really was no trouble at home; it was no different from other homes, but he was not comfortable there; he did not feel right there; with a queer little laugh and half averted face, he stated that he did not want to go home. We characterized him at that time as a peculiar personality, pathetic, lovable, but still curiously ill adjusted to the world.

A few months later Royal came back from another trip. He had not been able to make his own way in the country and had often gone hungry. He realized he was more of a city boy, but he thought he ought to live away from home. He would rather go his own way for a while longer, would rather eat in a restaurant. He thinks that after a couple of years he might get over it, but things at home still did not seem just right to him; he had no special complaint, but he could not stand it there. He knows he has been a bad boy, and he knows if it had been his own mother he would not have done these things. Another home was found for him, but Royal proved unstable at his place of employment, and thought he would like to try it with his family once more. After a few weeks he again suddenly left and was not heard from until he had long been in the eastern reformatory.

The reader will, naturally, ask what efforts at adjustment were made in this case. At the very start the father was told what the boy knew. He was tremendously astonished, but came back in a day or two with the corroborating information that the boy had been told of his parentage in the way stated. We urged the father then, and at later times, to make a complete confidant of the lad, — the father being an intelligent man, it seemed as if he could handle the situation. He did tell Royal that all that he had heard was true, but he went very little further; no deep confidences were ever established between them. It seemed impossible for the father to put himself in his boy's position, or to understand the very reactions of hypersensitiveness which he so well described to us as being a family trait. He believed that Royal should be told the facts of his birth, but after all, the boy had learned that much from outsiders. A couple of years after Royal had found his mother's picture in the storeroom, we learned that he carried it with him for a long time. When we told the father about it being taken, he looked for it in its old place and found it gone. This affair is some indication of the boy's inner state of mind. The father gave him a good home; he wanted a thoroughly good education for the boy; the stepmother was most kindly in a wholesome way. Once, on the very day when an unusually nice birthday celebration had been planned for Royal ,in the evening, and he knew something about this affair, he ran away to more suffering in most inclement weather.

Case 7. Among other things, this case shows that the effect of different types of enforced segregation must be the subject of intensive study if they are to be fairly evaluated. The social and economic import of the results is very great. The failure in any such case as this is due, of course, to several causes, but perhaps the greatest is the slight appreciation of the value of the application of scientific studies in general to the problems of misconduct.

Mack S., now twenty-three years old, is serving a one-year sentence. We have seen him in and out of jail during a period of seven years, and even before then he had been in institutions for delinquents several times. With one exception the charge has been stealing. He has been held, since he was twelve years old, nine separate times, for periods varying from a couple of weeks to almost three years, in five different institutions for delinquents. He has been thus detained eight years out of the last eleven, but his first ex-

perience with institutions began at six years, when
he was kept in an orphanage for three years. Then,
between the ages of nine and twelve, Mack was in a
training school for dependents — sent there because
difficulties had arisen about getting him to attend
school regularly, and, besides that, he had begun to
steal. His life in institutions, therefore, totals about
fourteen years. And yet Mack is anything but a
vicious character; he is intelligent and capable; he
has never stolen to the value of more than thirty-five
dollars at any one time; he has for considerable periods
held to some good ideals, and in several ways he has
proved himself particularly decent.

About his physical conditions we may say that
Mack is fairly strong and fairly well developed. At
seventeen he already weighed one hundred and twenty-
five pounds and was five feet six inches in height.
He has no organic disease. When he comes from an
institution he generally seems flabby, as might be
expected, but soon picks up strength. For years
he has shown a slight tremor of outstretched hands,
but that may be due to his smoking. The whole
torso is not developed in proportion to his size; in
this, and in the compressed and expressionless mouth,
he shows himself an institutional type. He has a
serious defect of vision (R Sph. –3, Cyl. –3.25; Axis
180. L Cyl. –4; Axis 180.) for which he has only intermittently had glasses. In the last few years, at least,
he has bitten his nails excessively. Complains of
frontal headaches at times. In attitude and expression
he is normal, but of a quiet type; he speaks in a
low and rather repressed voice; head well sized and
well shaped. Further examination is entirely negative.

We have had opportunity to test Mack at intervals,

years apart, and we know of his mental life from other sources. He can be readily classified as of fair mental ability, and he shows no aberrational tendencies. We have been interested always to watch for signs of mental deterioration, but there has been rather a steady progress upwards, until nowadays we find that he has learned a skilled trade, namely, that of operating a linotype machine, and is capable of earning good wages. The report from his employers during the last period when he was free, for some ten months or so, was that he was efficient and willing, but he was unable to find work at his trade for longer than a few months. He has recently shown his good mental ability by writing us a decidedly cogent, short autobiography. It is written in a good hand and with fair diction. Mack's other mental characteristics come out later in our account of him.

Our knowledge of his development and family history came from an unusually reliable source; they were given by his mother, who is a woman of sterling integrity and character. Mack is the second of three children; none dead, and only one miscarriage that came after his birth. The mother harks back to the time of her pregnancy with this boy; makes considerable of the fact that she was sickly part of the time; she lived in a town where the climate disagreed with her. Her husband was drinking then, and she particularly remembers being much provoked because he brought home some embroidered handkerchiefs which he said he had "swiped" from girls he had been with. She was also worried about their unsettled circumstances. But they were fairly well off, and her husband was good to her when he was not drinking. She remembers that she had a longing for things, but states that she never took anything that did not belong to her.

Birth was easy and rapid; infancy was normal until six months, when the child was accidentally pushed on a red-hot stove. His head was terribly burned, and it was about a year in healing, but no delirium or convulsions followed, and there was not known to be any involvement of the bone. The child had many ailments after that; he was not expected to live when he had cholera infantum at about one year of age. He walked and talked early, and there never seemed to be anything peculiar about him. He had scarlet fever and black diphtheria when he was seven; he had no enuresis after he was six years old. There were a number of minor accidents and his head was hurt several times, but they were never known to be severe, he was never rendered unconscious.

The father was an intelligent business man, but was a hard drinker and went off on sprees; he also consorted with other women. His father before him was a great drinker, but, in general, the family was composed of good people. One brother out of his many siblings was also alcoholic, but the others all did well and there is not known to be any outbreak of criminal tendencies, or any mental or nervous disease in the family. On the mother's side, a great-aunt of the boy was insane, and an uncle drank considerably at times. Otherwise the family history shows a group of fine, honest people. The mother herself is a strong, intelligent woman who has had to work very hard. Mack's older brother became a steady, honest fellow after one runaway escapade of his boyhood, and the younger brother is a remarkably able boy, with an apparently fine future ahead of him.

On account of the father's death when Mack was five years old, his mother sent him to an orphanage. He came home four years later and was found to be a problem; he was then sent away to a training school. The mother is not quite certain just when his truancy and stealing began; she is not nearly so clear on this point as is Mack himself, who places it very definitely. They both tell of his stealing as a little boy. The mother has tried hard to give us every detail, and Mack has engaged with us in analyzing his career at two series of interviews and has added items at other times. This earlier stealing certainly amounted to nothing more than taking cookies and apples, and perhaps a penny or two; nothing more than usual childish delinquencies. The mother went back to the boy's taking his father's watch when he was three years old, but that really merely amounted to his putting it into his own pocket while going about the house. The fact is that she did not know when the real stealing began, namely, when he returned from the orphanage and began petty thieving. She informs us of some of his later delinquencies, but all that she knows Mack told us, and much more besides. The poor mother has had occasion to learn of merely a few of his doings.

It is much to the point in this case to give in summary the characteristics of this young man as we know them from observation and from information derived from several sources. Mack is recognized by all to be neat, clean, and quiet. His mother states that he is kind, affectionate, and a "great home boy." The neighbors speak well of him. He has never shown bravado; on the other hand, he is often rather depressed and repressed. He is not a fighter, but

yet is not cowardly. On the whole, we should say
that he is notably a truth-teller; he is fairly frank,
but has to be thawed out. It is important to state
that the accounts of his early boyhood, which he himself gave twice in detail, two years apart, agree in
almost every respect. He is sure of himself in his
statements, which are never characterized by evasion.

His mother says that he is modest and never uses
bad language. He is recognized by girls as a distinctly
innocent type. He blushes readily. Just before his
latest trouble, a nice girl found herself interested in
him. His attitude towards women has been better
than that of perhaps the average young fellow, and
absolutely different from that of the young toughs
with whom, as a young criminal, he has had to be
classed. He does not care for drinking and can give
up smoking at will. He does not appear in the least
dissipated.

In the background Mack constantly keeps a store
of good intentions. He does not seem weak in other
ways than in succumbing to temptations which we
later give in detail. He has been a reader of good
books and has some ability in drawing. He has
demonstrated fair earning power. During his most
recent period of freedom he gave a large share of his
wages to his mother. The characteristics of his inner
mental life come out elsewhere. His rather immobile
features and the tight expression of his mouth indicate
something of his mental repression. He bites his
nails much. Most of his life he has been notable as
a boy who kept to himself a great deal, but he was
never of the "shut-in type" of which the psychiatrists
speak.

For this account of the development of Mack's

tendencies to delinquency I draw on many pages which form our transcripts of interviews with him and other people interested in him, and I shall also utilize the short autobiography which he has written. We have to confess to general feelings of skepticism about all such accounts, a skepticism which has been found largely unjustified, to be sure, but yet which is probably best to maintain. To satisfy our attitude of doubt, we have, particularly in this case, obtained whatever corroboration we could from other sources and have gone over the same ground at intervals, years apart.

There seems to be no doubt whatever that the real stealing in this case began when Mack first came out of the orphanage at nearly ten years of age. He found no father at home, no particular parental guidance, for his mother was out working every day. He "got in" with a gang of boys, who proceeded at once to instruct him in sex matters and in their arts of stealing. Over and over we have heard from him how vividly this now stands out in his mind when he thinks over his past. He does not remember that he had ever considered the matter of genesis before we first asked him to go over his career, but after our first period of analyzing, he always has seen these beginnings most clearly.

The boys took him down to the lake shore, and there they proceeded to mutual masturbation. He had no knowledge of such things before, he maintains. On the way to and from the lake shore, the boys stole whatever they could; particularly does he remember their taking pennies from news stands. After a short time he became truant in order to join these boys in their excursions. As the result of this truancy, he was sent away to the training school for dependents. There Mack began his solitary sex practices and started secret phantasies, which assumed no great proportions, however, until he was in other institutions later. He remained in this training school three years; his record must have been fairly good, or they would not have kept him.

He returned home again at twelve years and found conditions much as they were before; he began going out with boys of the same type. He now became recognized as a petty thief and was sent to a school for truants. After a few months he was tried on parole, but was a failure and was returned to this institution. He was once more sent home when he was about fourteen and soon got into trouble again. Once more he was tried at the training school where he had been up to the time he was twelve years old. This time they found him incorrigible. He stole repeatedly from the officers there, a most unusual thing for a boy to do, and he was sent back to court.

Mack looks back upon this period in his life as particularly black. His moderate talent for drawing he sometimes used at this time for making pictures which represented his ideas of sex affairs. He had already felt a distinct desire to steal, apart from any particular desired object. No older person had ever seriously offered him any sex knowledge or advice; the mother never brought herself to speak to him of these things. He believes that at this period he was probably putting up no fight at all against his temptations.

Brought back into court he was sent to an institution for delinquent boys, behind high walls and barred windows, where he remained fifteen months. His experiences here with other boys were worse, he insists, than anything he had known previously. For the first time others deliberately offered themselves as sexual objects. Mack states that this was something that he never could bring himself to do, and he warned them that he would spoil the life of no one. However, their talk aroused his own feelings, and he indulged liberally in masturbation. He thinks that by this time he was much worn out by his practices and ascribes to them his headaches and queer feelings in the eyes. (We, however, are quite as much inclined to believe that the cause of these troubles was his extremely defective vision, for which he had not been provided with glasses.) In his little autobiography Mack states that he remembers how he keenly wanted to steal while in this place, but there was nothing to steal.

Upon his release, at nearly sixteen years of age, a chance was found for him out of the city, and Mack went to live on a farm for some months. He was honest while there and satisfactory. His mother brought him back to town because she thought he was getting "too thick" with the stepdaughter in the household. She was sure that nothing irregular occurred up there, and the letters which the girl wrote to him later were of the nicest kind. Mack's own account of this affair throws a great deal of light upon his character. He states that one night when there was a terrific storm of thunder and lightning, and the others were away from the house, this girl came and crept into bed with him. He respected her thoroughly, and nothing bad in any way occurred. She grew to like his company and came back on several occasions; always he felt the same honorable way towards her, but his own feelings were much aroused, and he gave in to his old practices so much that farm work became burdensome. Coming back to town, this boy's conflicts started in full force.

In order to get valuable understanding of the mental mechanisms in this remarkable case, we have twice asked for a detailed account of certain times when Mack suddenly developed intense impulses to steal. We received, evidently, a very frank story of these events. For the understanding of this type of impulse and its cause, one must give each occasion and its antecedents in some detail.

Just after returning to the city, Mack was receiving letters from this girl on the farm and was thinking much about her. He had obtained employment delivering goods for a grocery store and was doing well. He was alternately fighting off his sex temptations and giving way to them. He states that he was somewhat tempted to steal and did take things in the grocery store when he could just as well have had them for the asking. One day he had collected thirty-three dollars, the most he had ever had in his hands, and he remembers his feelings of stress and restlessness that day as he rode about on the wagon. He left his wagon, went down-town, and spent the money on cheap shows, restaurants, and lodging houses for a few days, and then returned home. He was full of remorse and went to his employer and told him to take three dollars out of his wages every week until the money was refunded. He was a faithful worker, and for ten weeks paid up until there was only three dollars due.

Next door to the grocery store was a restaurant where a rather pretty waitress worked. She had taken a fancy to Mack and on several occasions had gone out with him for a stroll in the evening. One night she kissed him. The next day he saw her while he was driving by, and a great feeling of unrest came over him. He had just collected six dollars, and suddenly, after driving on a little way, he tied the horse and made for down-town all alone. This was when he had only three dollars more to pay up on account of his former delinquency. Again he spent the money on cheap shows and wandered about restlessly in penny arcades. He returned home the next day, but this time his employer refused to give him another chance, and Mack was sent once more to the institution for delinquents.

These two outbursts of the stealing impulse were connected with an intense feeling of restlessness and immediately followed much thought about girls. At this time Mack was engaging much more rarely in masturbation. He made no attempt to satisfy any sex feeling in spending the money. He says that he did not know what he wanted to do; he wandered about aimlessly far into the night, seeking first this little enjoyment and then another. He had no desire to be immoral with girls and wanted to take no advantage even of the one who kissed him.

Back in the institution conditions were the same. He speaks of again experiencing the desire for stealing, and by the time that he was released after nine months, he states that he had fully made up his mind to go into thieving as a business, but after he once was out he gave up this idea; it evidently was foreign to his nature.

Several events which follow soon after this seem worth relating. One of the jobs that he first found was peddling samples of shoe polish. When calling at doors, he met girls who were pretty free with him. His autobiographic letter states, "I used to see all kinds of pretty girls and would give them lots of samples for a kiss. They would set my mind a-whirling, and I could hardly work." He remembers that he indulged in masturbation again and also that he stole something from a house. In his earliest story he told us of the great feeling of "wildness" and "upset" which finally culminated in his fleeing his job under the impulse to go out for some kind of a good time; but he stole nothing that amounted to anything. He got other positions and gave way to more serious stealing. The story of the latter is most enlightening, but at this place we must relate some other significant behavior.

It was just about this time, when Mack was still considered to be under parole from the institution for delinquent boys, that his mother noted that he acted as if thoroughly discouraged, and one night, going into his room, she found a bottle of carbolic acid in one of his stockings and a dagger under the bed. He was never known to show any tendencies towards violence and did not deny that these objects were intended for his self-destruction. Some little time afterwards he turned on the gas in his room at night and almost succeeded in his suicidal design; he was resuscitated with great difficulty. Looking back on this period, Mack states that it was a time of great depression; he then felt the inadequacy of his attempts at fighting his own impulses. We note this is quite in contrast to the optimism which the young man has latterly shown, when he has been at least partially successful in combating his own tendencies.

The story of the two following events has special interest for us, because at one of our interviews, after we had found out that Mack remembered now that many of his stealing escapades were connected with an inner feeling of unrest and sex stimulation, he stated that at least an affair about a gun-metal watch had nothing to do with girls or sex matters. We carefully went into a deeper analysis of the event. This particular watch Mack stole from a man at a bathing beach. He could not remember at first why he had stolen it. One day we went into the details with the greatest of care. He gradually recollected the events preceding the stealing. He went to the bathing beach with a boy. He remembers now that he gave the gun-metal watch to this same boy the next day, after he had stolen a gold watch. "What had this boy to do with it?" "Well, nothing." "What happened with him at the beach?" Now Mack remembered. He and Mack were in their bathing suits and there was a girl there watching the swimmers. She seemed "like a pretty tough girl." As he remembers it, the other boy was a friend of hers; he started fooling with her, and she said that Mack was jealous. While they were dressing, the other boy said he was going right up to her house and have a good time with her, and he told Mack just what they were going to do together. Mack remembers he got excited about this, and when dressed he wandered out on the pier and there took this watch from the clothes of a man who was swimming, a stranger. He took it and ran away. Mack did not know that his boy companion had ever engaged in stealing.

That same night Mack took a girl to an amusement park. He had seen her only a couple of times before.

His pay for the week was in his pocket and he "showed
her a good time." She was not bold with him, he
merely kissed her. He took her home and was thinking much about her, and was again filled with unrest.
He stayed away from home that night and went to
a boarding house where a man lived whom he knew.
The next day he was still thinking about this girl
and about sex matters, and, going up to this friend's
room, saw his clothes hanging there. Mack took a
watch, a lady's gold watch. He did not look for
money or anything else. It seems to him he just had
a sudden notion he would like to have the watch.
In the account of the girl which he later wrote, he
says, "I said to myself, 'I'll give you a present of a
good watch and get you for my girl.'" He remembers
that after getting several blocks away from the house
he thought of taking the watch back, but was afraid
to do so because the man was probably already back
in his room. He met the boy companion of the
previous day and gave him the gun-metal watch.
Mack wandered around all that day and much of the
night. He was hungry and cold, and while trying
to steal something to eat from an ice-box on a back
porch, he was caught. The gold watch was found on
him, and as there had been a complaint handed to the
police about his stealing it — the owner knew him —
he was held to the Criminal Court. After some weeks
in jail he was given an indeterminate reformatory
sentence, one to ten years.

His autobiography concerning this time is pathetic;
it states, "I lost the girl. In the reformatory I thought
and thought of that girl and would dream of her."
He was incarcerated for thirty-one months. During
this period he sometimes would give way to his sexual

inclinations and would pick out passages in books and pictures in magazines that seemed suggestive. At other times he would, he says, come to himself and think what a fool he was making of himself, and "would brace up and quit that sort of thing for a while."

There were a few setbacks on account of not following all the rules of the institution, but he finally was released on parole. Then Mack soon got a position with a large mail-order firm, where he had to wrap small articles for delivery. Girls worked all about him. "I used to receive smiles and nods of encouragement and used to think of these girls continually while at work. I don't know what it was, but I had the desire to steal very strong in me, and steal I did. Every day I used to walk out of there with something in my pocket. It never amounted to much, but I used to take things regularly. One day one of the fellows working with me took something and they caught him at it and he told on me. I was arrested and, upon being assured I would not be prosecuted, gave back the things I took."

It was just after this that we first began analysis of Mack's tendencies to misconduct. It is true we had seen him some four years previously, but then, I have to confess, we were not at all awake to the psychological aspects of such a case as this. We were able to obtain, with great clearness, an account of the impulses which led to this last stealing, begun within a couple of weeks after he had been placed on parole. The articles taken included a flash-light, a box of cigars, a cigarette-lighter, a pearl-handled knife, another similar knife, a jar of shampoo, etc. When asked, a short time after he had taken them, whether

these articles had any special meaning or value for
him, he cannot imagine that they had in any way.
He just took a notion to them. He had a desire to
take things, and these came down the chute to be
wrapped up. As a matter of fact, the articles were
found at his home, some of them untouched; other
things he had taken one day and replaced a day or
two later. The girls at that place "talked fresh, but
they never said bad things and never did any bad
things." Mack at this time confessed that he was
having daydreams about sex affairs and was also
dwelling on such matters at night.

We attempted to diagnose his imagery, and it seemed
clear that it was of the mixed type. Tunes run through
his head, words come up in his mind, or perhaps some
bad song that he had heard; on the other hand, he
pictures to himself scenes and objects, particularly
girls as he has seen them half dressed in pictures.
He never really saw a girl under such circumstances.

I must emphasize at this point several peculiar
features of Mack's case: First, he has never stolen
with other boys since the time when he came out of
the orphanage. This marks the case as peculiar, because such a large proportion of the thieves that one
studies are gregarious in their habits. He has already
stolen at least a hundred times, he tells us, but he
has never been engaged in a burglary or in any really
serious affair. He insists that he has had temptations to steal on numerous occasions when he has not
succumbed to them; indeed he thinks this has occurred
more often than when he has stolen. He has frequently
during his life replaced things that he had previously
stolen. We had ample proof that for many articles
which he had taken he had no use. He also never

sold stolen property. He worries sometimes at night about what he has taken, but never bothers himself much about the danger of stealing.

Up to this time he had never tried to think out his career as an entirety. He shows this by his early statements to us that nobody had taught him to steal, and that some of his thieving was not connected with sex affairs, when on later analysis it proved to be. In fact, his very first declaration was that his stealing had nothing whatever to do with girls or sex affairs, as far as he knew. He had then never thought of the relationship, but he was already certain that his bad sex habits and his dwelling on sex affairs have blackened his whole career through weakening his body and will power. In many interviews it came out that Mack had repeatedly made a good fight for a time against these undesirable tendencies, but then again had weakened and given way until his last great improvement, beginning when he was twenty or twenty-one years old.

Most striking was what we learned about Mack's attitude towards women. This, in some ways, was nothing less than chivalrous. He said that the last thing he wanted was to do harm to any one, and there is no doubt that in spite of all his temptations and bad associations he had never been immoral with a girl until he was over twenty-one years of age. This, of course, is most remarkable and unusual among criminals.

We were able to make enough of an analysis of this case at the time when he had just been stealing so soon after coming out of the reformatory to be able to see plainly where Mack's trouble lay. We advised with him and the Association which had his parole in charge, but in spite of our urging the necessity for an entirely different adjustment of the case, with a new understanding derived from our exploration, only the same sort of treatment was given. After working in a shop for a time where an opportunity was given him as a matter of charity, Mack was found a place in a dry-goods establishment. No attention had been given to our advice and prognosis, and he found himself at work in the immediate contiguity of a group of unusually forward girls. They made much fun of him, calling him innocent and saying to each other, "watch him blush." He stood this for a little while and then suddenly left the place in the middle of a morning's work.

Mack now got into further trouble through idleness and seeking association with acquaintances he had made in the reformatory, and he was returned there for violation of parole. The circumstances and Mack's state of mind during the period after he suddenly left his work, we have some knowledge of from several investigators and from a visitor to the reformatory, who interviewed Mack without his knowing that it was done at our request. When he got out again, after serving fifteen more months, we had a further chance to get the exact details of his previous failure. They run as follows:

Mack was intensely disturbed by the bantering of these flippant girls at the dry-goods establishment. They told him he was a nice-looking fellow and continually tried to "make up" with him, but he rejected their advances. "They got pretty friendly with me, but never hinted at anything intimate. Their smiles and flirtations aroused me, so I quit." This boy, that morning, wandered over in the neighborhood of a certain park where he thought some fellows might be "hanging around" whom he had met in the reformatory. They were there, and began telling him what a good time they had had recently, particularly with girls. They introduced him to a girl who at once took up with him. "She and I were very much infatuated with each other. I used to stay with her every day, and she liked me very much. Then I got mixed up with that bunch of fellows, and we were going to hold up a cigar store. I was not afraid to tackle anything then. I went over to the store and looked the place over and told the fellows it was all right, but they got cold feet and backed out. I gave them my gun. The landlady saw them with the guns and called for a detective. He arrested three of the fellows, but could not get me, as I didn't go up to the room any more. I went and stayed with the girl. A couple of weeks after that they caught me just as I was going into her house. She cried and tried to take me from them. They told her if she did not go home, they would take her also. She said, 'I don't care, take me too', but they sent her home, and I went back to the reformatory for violation of the parole."

There seems very little doubt that this was really the first time that Mack, now about twenty-two years old, had ever been immoral with a girl, and this girl was in love with him. It seems also true that this is the first time that he ever even thought of a bold robbery or joined in with other companions.

Returned to the reformatory, Mack evidently resolved this time to brace up as never before. "I started to control myself. I read good books and kept away from evil pictures and stories. It was hard to do it at first, but I did it, and I am glad I did now, because all desire to steal was taken out of me and all desire to debase myself left me. When I came out again, I determined to live straight." We note from the reformatory record that Mack was changed for the better in many respects; he worked hard to learn a trade, and when he came out it was stated that he could earn twenty-five dollars a week as a linotype operator.

After being released once more, everything went very well for ten months. Mack worked earnestly, lived at home, stayed there evenings, and gave his mother most of his wages, and all were happy. His printing work failed him and he changed to another occupation in which he also proved industrious and a fair earner. The men with whom he worked frequented saloons. He got to drinking a little beer, but it did not affect his behavior. He began keeping company with a very good looking and modest girl, who evidently was fond of having him come to see her, — a girl of entirely good reputation. There was not the least hint of dishonesty. Twice during this period he confesses he went to sporting houses, but felt himself conquering his desires and thought he was a much better fellow. His employer got into financial difficulties and was unable to pay his wages for a couple of weeks, so Mack left and was unemployed. A little prior to that time he had decided that he had better stop drinking beer and did so. This ten months was the best period of his life. We learned from several sources that he was well regarded everywhere.

After a few days of unemployment, a little girl, who was accustomed to play about his house, came up there and in a childish, affectionate way, sat on his lap and played there. Mack allowed himself to touch her body in an improper way, making not the slightest attempt, however, at anything like rape. He apparently thought nothing serious of this and remained at home as usual. The child told her parents, and they, in turn, consulted the police, but later made it very clear that they did not wish to prosecute, because they knew Mack as a neighbor to be a very decent young fellow, and their physician said no harm had been done. The little girl was interviewed at great length by the authorities, and Mack, who was, of course, known to be a repeater, was once more thrown into jail. After ten or eleven weeks of incarceration, he was brought to trial and pleaded guilty to taking improper liberties with the child and received a sentence of one year.

Seen in the jail this last time, Mack had no particular excuse to offer. He said that he certainly did wrong, but that he meant no harm to the child and that he had been extremely weak in allowing his feelings, even to that extent, to be aroused. What he regretted more than anything was this further break in his endeavors. He carried in his pocket the picture of the modest and nice looking girl who had recently been his friend. "All the time I was out this last time, I didn't steal or abuse myself. I was living straight. I was arrested that night when I was just coming home from visiting the girl I was going with." Seen in the jail, Mack says that he was not smoking even there, where there is so much temptation to excess in using tobacco. He spent his time walking up and down the corridors, thinking a good deal about himself. "I think now that every time I ever got into trouble it was on account of a girl. I always got in with a girl, and I would steal and get arrested." This was in response to one of our last questions as to why, in general, he now thought he had had so much trouble in life. It was after this that Mack wrote out for us his thoughtful story of his own life, which tallied, as we have stated before, so accurately with accounts given to us at intervals during previous years.

(I have been asked what treatment I would have advised early in this case and what I did advise later. The several factors that have entered into the making of Mack's career have been set forth with care; what the disposition of the case with these special needs in mind should have been is quite obvious. From the first appearance of his delinquencies he was certainly not an institutional case, or at least should not have gone to any institution which accepts boys without special study of their qualities. His conflict at that time could have been readily analyzed, and there is no reason whatever why he should not have succeeded, with personal help, in overcoming his tendencies. I have elsewhere in this volume cited instances where just such cases, or even worse ones, have readily reformed.

To continue to commit him so many times to institutions without consideration of the fact of previous failure, or even of deterioration, through institutional treatment was, of course, nothing short of stupidity. The supervision and vocational placing through parole agencies was likewise notably unadapted to his needs and even contrary to advice which we then had the chance to give. Clearly it was unwise ever to have allowed Mack to work where he handled articles which might tempt him to steal, or where he was frequently thrown in association with girls. He just as well might have worked at a trade with men, or in the country on a farm, where he would have earlier gained the physical vigor that he lacked.

Added to all the previous want of understanding that has surrounded this case, his last treatment under the law was almost as faulty. His misdemeanor, prosecution for which was not desired, was punished in the light of his long record of unwise commitments. Mack's career is very largely a product of social blunderings.)

CHAPTER VIII

CASES READILY ANALYZED

THE directness and clearness with which the relationship between mental conflict and misconduct stands out as a main causative fact varies greatly in different cases. It is only to be expected, as has been suggested in a foregoing chapter, that with older offenders the underlying causes will prove to be more covered up and harder to get at, less readily perceived either by the investigator or the misdoer. Easily ascertainable relationships will be found more often among young people who, however, may already have a considerable record of delinquency. Then, too, we find that certain types of causal experiences are easier to uncover than others. For example, conflicts about parentage are usually more deeply hidden than emotion-producing contacts with sex affairs. Some of our least difficult cases for exploration are presented in this chapter.

Case 8. This case illustrates how vital may be the facts elicited during the investigation of a single half day, if requirements are favorable. A very young boy had been repeatedly stealing for about a year, in spite of pleading, punishment, and change of environment. His mother, a fine type of working woman, was able to corroborate much that the analysis brought

out. It was learned that there were marked mental
conflicts and repressions, and curious physical dis-
comforts following directly upon the repressions.

A little boy of just eight years, Arba T., was the
object of much complaint by several people, including
his mother. We found a very normal and pleasant
boy to deal with. Outside of moderately defective
vision his physical status was decidedly good. His
expression was lively, responsive, and merry at times;
his features were well formed; he was unembarrassed
and fairly talkative, but showed no disposition to
make much of his own case. Altogether the lad presented decidedly normal attributes.

His general apperceptions, as indicated by his behavior and coherent conversation, would have indicated
his good mental powers, but in confirmation we may
say that mental tests were done by him quite up to
his age-level. As one finds in children no older than
he, there was some little uncertainty manifested about
memory of events occurring a couple of years earlier,
but fortunately all of the points which we needed
were given with enough detail so that for verification
they could be compared readily with what his mother
knew. We found some little self-contradiction at
first, which later disappeared, evidently as the boy
made clear to himself the development of his own
tendencies. In this way it was a very interesting
exhibition of how an individual may, upon questioning, clarify what before was confused in his mind or
not at all consciously thought of. From our standpoint, of course, the value of his statements increased
greatly when we were able to corroborate them by
the mother's independent assertions.

This good mother had suffered much from his steal-ing. She had moved from the old neighborhood on account of it, then placed him in an orphanage, and recently tried him at home again. She had felt her-self bound to pay for some of his thieving. Taking it altogether, it was a case of excessive stealing of small money from neighbors, from pocketbooks that might be found in teachers' desks or elsewhere, and of articles that would seem to have little or no value for him, all continued for more than a year.

After sympathetic general questioning about his troubles, this little lad began to volunteer information about various bad boys; not so much concerning stealing as other things that he had been taught. Several of them had told him very bad things, he said, and "there is one little boy who does bad things to girls and even to a grown up lady." The story was told rather indefinitely, implicating several boys. When asked if the things that he has heard bother him, he says, "It goes right to here, in my head, and goes all around in here, and gets me dizzy. It is what they told me, you know, what I told you before." The boy denied ever having seen any bad pictures, and when asked to describe more in detail how he is affected said, "I try to go to sleep, and it hurts me. I sleep a little, and then it starts up again. I think about what they told me, about that stuff, and some-times it goes right up to my eyes." Asked if he means that it is words that bother him, he insists that it is, but neither now, nor at any time later, nor when interviewing him with his mother, would he say what these words were. He has heard bad words, but does not now know what they are. "I don't know that word now; I can't remember it." It was very curious when the boy repeatedly pointed to the back of his head and said that the word hurt him there when it came up in his mind. According to his mother, he had once complained to her that a word bothered him, and she insisted that he get it out of his mind; she also stated that he often spoke of pain and queer feelings in the back of his head, but had not told her before what was the cause.

Arba also confessed that he touched himself sexually in bed at night when he thought of what this boy had told him, and that his mother knew of this habit. It came out later that the mother had been aware of this and had tried to prevent it, but there was no evidence that he was masturbating to an injurious extent; indeed, his good physical condition showed the contrary. Whenever the subject of stealing was approached, the boy began talking about what he had learned concerning sex affairs. He stated that he dreams the things that he has learned from a certain boy, that this other lad takes girls into basements, and that "When he says, 'Go ahead and steal', it hurts me awfully in my head." While telling us of this, the boy seemed very serious and sighed often. A long story was related about boys with whom he had stolen, or to whom he had given things that he had taken, and in each case he volunteered the information that these were boys with whom he had talked about sex affairs or who had done such things.

When we tried to get at the very beginnings, we came to a remarkable statement: Arba told us that at one time, which the mother was able to place at about a year previous, when he was in a moving-picture show, a man approached him and said he would buy some candy for him, and then this man took him to a

shanty and played with him sexually, but did not hurt
him.   The mother remembers the time very well,
because the boy had the candy and told her that a
man had bought it for him, and she had thought no
more of the matter.   The connection with the impulse
to steal, the boy assures us, dates from this time,
because the man told him that since he, Arba, did
not have any money, he ought to go out and steal
things, particularly money.   Arba is sure that this is
the first time that he ever knew anything about sex
affairs or about stealing.   The mother, now placing
this event with some accuracy, was certain that the
first theft, which was of money from a neighbor's
kitchen, occurred very soon after this.   There positively
had been no stealing before.

Going later into the matter with the mother and the
boy together, the probability of the truth of all this
became for me much increased.   The nervousness
which she had before told us the boy had shown for
the last year and the bad habits which he had begun
and the complaint of headache and the repression of
words, which even now he would not utter to the
mother or to me, all went back to this experience
with the man, which he had never told his mother
about, but which had so deeply impressed him.   From
that time, delinquency, particularly truancy and stealing and sex affairs of several kinds, all entered his
mind as possibilities of behavior.   He had been once
taken by the police while with another boy in a house
where he had gone to steal, but this had not acted as
a deterrent, any more than sending him to an orphanage on account of his bad behavior, or punishment
by his mother for stealing and also for masturbation.   No reprimand counted for much while the real

nature of his trouble was undiscovered, while he suffered impulsions the background of which was not known.

Arba is an only child; the parents were married very young. The father died when the boy was two years old, and the mother was obliged to earn her own living at once after the father's death. On account of poverty and the mother being away at work, there had been lack of parental control, and normal home interests were not built up as they otherwise might have been. Heredity was evidently entirely negative on both sides; in neither family had there been mental trouble or tendencies to misconduct. Developmental history was also negative. On account of the good sense of the mother, we were inclined to believe that she should try once more with the boy at home. She was willing to meet the situation by going further into his special troubles, and Arba was anxious to take them up with her, but we felt that time only would show whether or not under her circumstances she could be successful.

(Reports and one further study of the boy carry us to about a year later. The mother's unfortunate circumstances continued to lead to failure during the several months when she again tried to manage him at home. She had no time or strength to watch him, nor could she afford to live in a better neighborhood. He ceased stealing, according to her account, but he himself told us that everything was just the same with regard to this and his sex temptations. Companionship with bad boys continued. His headaches ceased, but evidently bad sex habits increased. The failure being apparent to every one, he was now placed through private funds in a country home, and from there, after four months' trial, comes the report that the boy is doing wonderfully well.)

Case 9. An exceedingly important case, proving the immediate therapeutic effects of exploration when this is followed by intelligent measures for mental readjustment, may be given in a few words, since I have reported it previously.[1] For six years now there has been complete freedom from the misconduct which was the original cause of complaint.

This little girl of ten years, notable for unusual modesty and refinement, had for two years engaged in an astonishing amount of stealing. She had taken money and other things, not only from her parents on repeated occasions, but also money and jewelry from neighbors, and various things from school. She had already stolen in two schools and been expelled. In spite of much threatening of police and reform school, and some whipping, and having been given money regularly to spend, there had been no improvement. She was said to be strong-willed, but not quick-tempered, and to lie only about the matter of stealing. The story of delinquency seemed astounding when one met the girl, so pleasantly bright and affectionate. When we sought to analyze the case, we were soon frankly met by her statement that she was continually fighting against certain thoughts. Although the mother regarded her as so exceptionally modest, there were "bad words" which continually came up in her mind. She suffered from headaches sometimes. "These things come up in my mind often. Well, when I am in school and have that headache

---

[1] Case 65 in "The Individual Delinquent", Healy.

I told you about, and sometimes at night, and then I get all mixed up. . . . When these things come up, I forget all I am doing and get upset, and then sometimes I take things. . . . These things come up to me when I am in school, and I cannot study well. I got all mixed up at the P. school, too." (This was one of the schools where she stole and from which she was expelled.)

In this case the parents proved themselves highly intelligent and thoroughly able to cope with the situation. They entirely won her confidence and explained such sex affairs to her as she had already been running over in her mind, and, as I recommended, went further than I did in learning the details of the early associations which formed the genesis of her impulses to steal. From certain incidents related by the girl, they were able to corroborate much of her story. Two or three years previously, when they were on a vacation in a country town, she had often played with a boy, who, they themselves heard later, was accustomed to steal. He had told her about stealing, but, above all things, he had also given her her first knowledge of sex life and taught her words which she had never heard before. She knew they were words to be ashamed of, so she repressed them and the whole incident itself; but the words and thoughts came back and back to her with the strength of an obsession. Her impulses to steal were derived directly from this conflict. The parents made the connections between all this clear to themselves and to the girl, and intelligently developed as many new interests for her as possible. The result has been admirable; the tendency to steal disappeared as if by magic. A recent report, six years since we analyzed this case, is that she has never been delinquent again upon any occasion. Her progress in school and in every other way has been entirely normal.

Case 10. No case illustrates more clearly the relationship between mental conflict, as cause, and delinquency, as result, than the following instance of a young boy whose night wandering caused his family much anxiety.

We first heard of John B. through a policeman who had been asked by a street-car conductor to "pick up" the little boy because he had been riding for hours on the cars in the middle of the night. An investigating officer was told by the school people and by John's mother that there must be something wrong with him; they judged so on account of his habit of night riding and certain other strange actions; all were anxious to have his case studied.

We found a frail, plaintive boy of eleven and one-half years, weight, seventy-one pounds, possessing a rather well-shaped head and delicate features. His face looked tired, with rings about his eyes. When younger he suffered from tubercular skin disease and enlargement of the cervical glands, and had been operated upon for these. There were some scars of head injuries, which, however, had not been serious.

On mental tests the boy did not do very well, but he was studied at a period of great stress for him. We felt it would be necessary to re-examine him to know his real mental ability. He gave many indications of having good apperceptive powers. On the Binet tests he showed just one year of retardation, but yet, as in the test which requires sixty words to be given in three minutes, we felt that he might easily

have done better if he had been in a more settled
frame of mind. His chief trouble seemed to be lack
of power to command his mental resources. School
work was equivalent to the fourth grade. There was
no intimation from anybody that the boy was subnormal, merely that he had been behaving rather
queerly at home of late, and that his attention was
poor in school. We had a chance to study this boy
again eight months later, at which time we found
physical conditions still poor, but he showed a decided
gain on mental tests.

From the healthy-minded and sensible mother we
learned that John has always been regarded as a
delicate boy. At his birth there was some trouble
resuscitating him, and he was small in size. In early
childhood he had various illnesses which held him
back. There had been pneumonia a couple of times,
measles, and scarlet fever, and the tubercular trouble
of the glands and skin. For some time now he had
seemed to his mother unduly restless and wild; she
hesitated to leave him with the younger children because of his wild shouting and jumping about. However, he had had no definite nervous ailment, and no
one had observed bad habits. From his various
illnesses he always made a slow recovery, and all
along had been a rather puny child, although coming
from a family where the others are stout and healthy.
John's intelligent mother stated that there was nothing of significance in the family history, no mental
trouble and no nervous disease, and he "takes after"
no one in his delinquent tendencies.

Two years previously John had been truant for a
short time. The family had thought this a matter
to be taken in hand immediately and had sent the

boy away to a private school for a year. He returned home some nine months prior to the time when we saw him. There had been no particular trouble again with him at home, or in school, until two months ago, when he started staying away from home all night. After his first adventure, they watched him closely and did not allow him out in the evening, but later he repeatedly stayed away from home altogether instead of returning from school, and did not come back until the next day. He thus was away all night eight or ten times, apparently not having slept on these occasions. At least four times the police had found him on the street cars early in the morning and had returned him home. What seemed more strange was that he was out on some of the very coldest nights, when he could have been anything but comfortable. There had been no trouble at all at home to account for his staying away. We were witness to the great affection in which the mother and boy held each other. John repeatedly said that the trouble which he had caused his family was all his own fault. His mother had been well-nigh distracted during his absences.

The keynote to the situation was found with remarkable ease in this case, when, after the first establishment of friendliness, John was asked to tell about what was worrying him. This simple invitation seemed to loosen all that held back his story from his parents. He gave us at once the outlines of his experiences, which later we were able to prove in many particulars. It may be of interest to note that at a second interview, when more detail and more exact dates were asked for, with a response characteristic of the testimony of young children,

John filled in some hiatuses with additions which proved untrue. However, later he denied these and returned, with full ingenuousness, to his original and important story. Other aspects of the case developed later. They were also important, and with the mother we were enabled to get at all the main facts of what John said had been bothering him.

John told us that he always went on his strange excursions alone. Where had he heard about that sort of thing? How did he get the idea into his head? "A lady my mother knows was talking to my mother about a boy who stays out nights." Following this simple clue, we gradually obtained the connections, step by step, of this woman's conversation with his delinquency. We heard that the boy of whom she spoke was known to him, although he had not seen him to speak to for several months and had never gone out at night with him. He was a bad boy whom he had known for years, who said "bad words", who had "bad pictures." "He said bad words, and I never listened to him. He said bad about girls. He had bad pictures. He had a camera; he was taking pictures, and it showed where girls was naked, at the swimming pool. He was standing on the steps there, and there was a window there. He told me how he took the pictures when he showed them to me. It was last summer. He told me about doing it with girls when he showed me that. He said he was going to do it. I told him, 'No, I wouldn't.'"

An astonishingly plaintive look came over this boy's face when we asked him if this was what was bothering him. "It's mostly in my mind, those pictures. It's hard to forget. Every time I think of it, I don't like it."

At other interviews we obtained a detailed account
of the boy's delinquencies.   It seems that the impulse
to ride on the street cars at night and to stay away
from home came to him directly after hearing this
neighbor tell his mother that Bill T. had stayed out
nights riding on the cars.   John became possessed of
the idea and started very quickly afterwards doing
this himself. He would either slip off from home,
after hiding his hat and coat so that he could secretly
get them, or he would stay away from home altogether
after school was out.   Sometimes he did not return
home after he had been sent out in the late afternoon
on an errand.   Two or three times he had begged a
quarter from a friend; once he had taken some money
which his mother had given him to buy biscuits.
Other times he had told stories to the conductors on
the night cars about being homeless or losing his way.
Once at the police station he had alleged that he was
a half orphan and that his mother had badly mis-
treated him.   He rode back and forth on long trips
between the outlying districts and the center of the
city, and more than once had met some farmer in the
early morning who had given him a ride in from a
suburb.   The idea of doing all this, he many times
asserted, arose from the thought of how Bill T. went
on the cars at night, and Bill T. had been so often in
his mind because he could not forget those pictures.
"They always come in my mind. Sometimes at
night. When I am in bed. I told him I wouldn't
do that to girls. I told him it was too dirty. I
haven't seen him since last summer. It was in the
alley.   He tried to do the same thing he did to girls,
and I wouldn't leave him do it. . . . Lots of times
they come up in my mind, those pictures. In school

I would be talking to boys; it would start and I would be thinking of it. . . . No, he doesn't go to our school. . . . I saw some other bad things. I was hiding. I saw through a place; it was a barn. There was three men and three ladies. There was a saloon in front. They were doing the same thing that Bill T. was talking about."

John was never able to tell exactly his object in staying away all night. He remembered very distinctly how the idea came into his mind, but he could not say just what led him to go riding, even on those coldest nights, in street cars, when he could have been warm and comfortable at home. He could not describe any pleasure that he derived from his trips, nor, indeed, did he even allege that there was any pleasure or any idea of pleasure in taking them. He could only tell of the impulse and when it first arose. Among other details, he recounted how he had waited sometimes in a hallway across the street from his home until the late car came — about eleven o'clock, on its way down-town — on which there was a conductor who didn't pay much attention to him, and who had let him ride on and on when he was out a previous night.

In the old days when he and Bill went to the same school they were truant together a few times, and it was hearing about his truancy that led John's mother to send him away to the private school. In those days Bill had no bad pictures and never talked about such things; it was only last summer, after John had returned from the private school. John absolutely denied any bad sex habits. Other boys have told him about these things, but he thinks it is wrong. His mother has warned him about it. He frequently

showed to us his disapprobation of all that is connected with illicit sex affairs.

We worked with the mother on this case, and together we were able to get very certainly at the details.
She had never known who this Bill T. was until a
couple of months ago, when this neighbor told her,
as John said, about his being a boy who smoked and
used bad words and stayed away from home riding
on the cars at night. She was not aware that he had
ever been truant with her boy. She had not inquired
with whom John was associating in those days, just
before she sent him to the private school. She knew
nothing of any bad pictures that John had seen, nor
of his witnessing a drunken orgy. It was clear that
he had always stayed away alone and was not influenced by any recent bad companionship. From
her we heard the details of an affair about which
John seemed to have little recollection. He told us
vaguely about some other sex experience, but it seems
that when he was quite small a man had used him
in some peculiar way as a sexual object, but had done
him no harm and not forced him in any violent way.
The man was sentenced to jail on account of indecent
liberties. It was not known to her that this had left
any deep impression upon John, and indeed, the boy
told us, when questioned by his mother, that it was
not this that ever bothered him at all. As a matter
of fact, it was a rather superficial affair, and perhaps
the significance of it had not sunk in at all upon the
little fellow. John reiterated to his mother most emphatically how he was worried by what Bill had told
him and shown him, and how these things kept coming
up in his mind. He also restated once more in her
presence that his whole idea of staying out at night

came from hearing that Bill had done this, — a form of delinquency which was evidently possible for him, John, as a clean boy, to indulge in without great self-disapprobation.

(During eight months that have elapsed, John has not repeated his peculiar conduct. To be sure, there has been trouble on account of sudden poverty in the family. At first the boy was sent away for a little time to a school from which he readily could have run away. He did not make any effort to do so. He lately has turned to selling papers at night as well as before school to help in the family situation. This led to his sleeping away from home a couple of nights, but in no delinquent way.)

Case 11. An exceedingly difficult school problem and its causation was clearly explicable after a short time spent in analysis of the following case.

Billy M. at ten years of age had already been suspended from several different schools. From the parents and school authorities we heard that the trouble was mischief, malicious mischief, but there had been no stealing or running away from home and very little truancy. In the schoolroom Billy insists on humming and singing and annoying others. As he pretends to read, he simply seems to be concocting schemes for making disorder; he sticks pins in the children. At home he continually plays with matches and once in a most malicious way tried to burn his brother with a hot poker. He started a fire in the house, perhaps accidentally, and has given much trouble in other ways. At Sunday school they simply will not tolerate him. His parents punish him and deprive him of various privileges; the boy ever promises

to do better, but his misbehavior speedily recurs. It
seems as if he is almost possessed with the idea of
pestering others.

We found a bright-eyed and open-faced boy in
very good general physical condition and with no
sensory defects. Mentally he graded well up to his
years and could be readily characterized as a bright,
well-spoken, and intelligent boy. His record in school
for scholarship was as good as he permitted it to be.

We heard in great detail about the family and developmental history; there was nothing that seemed
to bear positively upon this case. In the home circle
there was one element that might have affected this
boy's behavior, — an older cousin who lived there
was an impertinent and difficult girl to get along with.
However, everything else faded into insignificance in
comparison with the data which we obtained from
the boy himself.

Billy met us in a thoroughly frank way. He seemed
to be anything but the little villain that he was por-
trayed. When we asked for his troubles and the
beginnings of them, he told us about his behavior in
school and gradually, under our leading, went on to
discuss companions that he had several years before.
Out of the long tale which was told us, the main point
was that older boys had long ago told him about
bad sex affairs and their masturbatory practices.
"It comes back, and I can't forget it." What he
could not forget appeared to be some of the words and
ideas which he had been told; that is, he had tried
to repress them, but they insistently reappeared in
his mind. Billy's story that he absolutely did not
indulge in any bad sex habits and had not for a long
time we should feel inclined to believe from his robust

appearance, but he did complain of local irritation either prior to or connected with his thoughts about sex affairs, particularly in school. This was the part of his life that he was repressing and fighting. Billy complained that sometimes he had headaches, and that he felt extremely nervous, that he had definitely to reject temptations to indulge in masturbation. He objected strongly to some careless words about sex affairs uttered by his girl cousin and resented what other boys said in this way, evidently feeling it keenly through what he himself was attempting to conquer. It was all a very graphic account of an inner life that was being repressed as much as possible, and of desires for activities which were finding outlet only in reactions of nervousness and mischief.

When definitely asked about this matter the parents said, oh, yes, they knew that long ago a fellow about twenty years old and mentally subnormal had told Billy bad things and probably had done them to him. The mother at first asked him a little about it, but never made any detailed inquiries. She always thought it was best to let such things alone. The father never uttered a word on this subject to the boy or went into his life at all with him. They were very much astonished to know that he had ever dwelled on sex subjects.

The parents frankly felt themselves incompetent to handle this matter when they had taken the boy home, and, after thinking it over, they placed him with an exceptionally capable woman friend. She reported that it was clear to her there never had been the right kind of affection and confidence between the parents and the boy. She treated him as one of her own children and talked with him about the nature of his troubles. Not only this, but when the parents came to see the boy, she took great pains to educate them concerning their proper attitude towards him. With her he did very well. Then Billy went home; after a time there was some renewal of his truancy and perhaps of his sex habits. A good physician now got hold of the boy and saw him repeatedly, once a week. The results of these efforts have been admirable. The boy's record for over two years has been very good. His parents report his behavior as being entirely different. He shows no more evidences of meanness towards children and apparently has never tried to communicate bad ideas to them. Even the school principal who earlier complained so bitterly about the boy states that he is causing absolutely no trouble.

CHAPTER IX

DIFFICULT CASES

THE chief difficulties in successful treatment of a case of misconduct having its genesis in mental conflict are three: (*a*) Difficulty in approaching the problem with the misdoer. This may amount to complete inaccessibility. (*b*) Difficulty in getting proper environmental adjustments after exploration has been adequate. This may be experienced even when parents are anxious to help and have been informed of the real nature of the trouble; they sometimes are quite unable to grasp the significance of the facts. (*c*) Difficulty in breaking habits of delinquency which have been formed. The illustrative cases in this chapter show these points clearly.

Case 12. The steady development of a remarkable career of misconduct, showing a definite set towards criminalism, is illustrated in the following instance. From the failure in this case there is much to learn. In spite of very friendly help given this boy by court officials and others, he has obstinately pursued his own path. It is a good example of everything being done except to discover the basis of impulse to misconduct, and that could be discovered by no ordinary method. During many years this young man's record of delinquency has been piling up. It has seemed as if something, not himself, was forcefully urging him into criminality. One of the striking features of the case all along has been the fellow's own attitude towards his conduct; this has rendered him absolutely inaccessible so far as really sounding his depths is concerned.

The career of William G., now nineteen years of age, we have ourselves observed for several years, and the accounts we have received of him from relatives and others cover a much longer period. This boy began stealing from home when he was eight years old. About this time and later he was a truant occasionally. He could hardly be said to have run away from home, however; rarely has he been away for a few days and nights at a time. His early delinquencies were committed with other boys; later he has engaged in them entirely alone. After the first years, during which his stealing was of a petty variety from home and other places, he began in larger measure to take from stores; he became a sneak thief of pocketbooks and other articles, and he went from one delinquency to another in the most deliberate fashion. Before he was seventeen he engaged in burglaries, embezzlement, and an extensive scheme of forgery. A resourceful fellow, he has tried his hand at many types of dishonesty, although there has been no attempt as yet to follow any one particular line in professional fashion. We have been impressed by the fact that mixed in with his major transactions there has been stealing of small articles which would seem to have little value for him, and these were often taken in foolish ways that put him in more immediate jeopardy than the larger affairs. William has been arrested many times; he has been before courts at least ten or twelve times; he has been sent already three times to institutions for delinquents, and besides this, he has often been put on probation, has had positions found for him, and has been specially befriended by a judge and his assistants who have tried to reform him. Thoroughly well-intentioned attempts have thus been made in many ways to help the young man.

There are no great peculiarities in the physical make-up of this young fellow. He is of ordinary size and steadily growing. Our record shows many teeth in poor condition; tonsils large; eyes rather swollen and sleepy looking; head high, rounded, with a broad forehead. Significant for any student of physiognomy would be the boy's mouth, so peculiarly hard and firmly closed, in contrast to a proportionately small and weak type of chin. Many have commented on the fact that he appears obstinate and self-contained. At twelve years of age he had already been smoking a little for a couple of years, and he was in the habit of drinking three cups of coffee a day; however, there were almost no signs of nervousness. We many times noted that he was a great biter of his finger nails. As we have seen him, he has generally appeared serious and depressed in a normal way under the conditions of being held as a delinquent, at other times normally buoyant and active, but on all occasions inscrutable beyond the point of superficial friendliness.

We have many evidences that William is a very capable fellow. He advanced rapidly through the grammar school, graduating at twelve years in spite of occasional truancy, and he had done well in as much of the high-school course as his delinquencies permitted him to attend. By all he has been regarded as bright and by some as precocious. On tests of all sorts which we gave him he did very well, and he enjoyed problems that demanded mental effort.

However, there is much more to set down concerning his mental and moral characteristics than can be given in the enumeration of test results or what one found by conversation with him. When he was only twelve years old he had already impressed experienced probation officers as "a thoroughly bad chap, one who will be back again in court." At that age we ourselves also recognized his peculiarities; they were particularly brought out by his stealing a valuable article which was of no use to him from a woman who was at that very time attempting to befriend him. His mother stated that for three or four years previously he had been "wild and spunky" at times, and then again would cry and promise to do better. She herself brought him first to our attention, stating that she could not understand what was the matter with him.

The history which the undoubtedly honest mother gave us included nothing that seemed to account for his tendencies. Birth was natural, and the pregnancy had been normal. He had been a large baby and walked and talked early. With the exception of bronchitis and measles, spasms on one occasion, and the development of a rupture in infancy, which was cured by a truss, there seemed to be little the matter with him. The only thing she could think of was rare complaint of headache and catching cold easily in his throat, but both she and his teachers had noted that something seemed to come over the boy at times in the last few years, when he did not seem to be paying attention and did not look well. For long he had been in the habit of biting his nails excessively. The father was unsympathetic, occasionally a drinking man, who gave this boy very little consideration. The other children, all older, have done well in every way, but have never been close companions to William. Honesty is a watchword in the family life. With the exception of a maternal uncle who was insane, no defect in the family history could be ascertained. In the mother's pleadings with William she never could get anything out of him, except that he had temptations to steal; he would always promise to do better.

We began our studies upon the basis of the outlines given us by the mother, and since then we have seen the boy on numerous occasions. We have been able to carry out all that an ordinary schedule of study of the individual might call for, but we soon found that we had to deal with a boy who would be neither ingenuous with us nor frank with himself when it came to investigation of the deeper problems of his inner life. On many occasions he has presented to us, as well as to others, his characteristic impenetrability. As compared with other delinquents, he has been most unusual in this respect. He meets any attempt at deep inquiry with a little toss of his head or shrug of his shoulder. No one has ever persuaded him candidly to face his own situation. Once he became friendly enough with us to assert that many times he had temptations to steal to which he did not succumb, and that his thieving had begun with a bad crowd which had influenced him when he was about eight years old. This was at one of our earlier interviews with him; as time has gone on, William has become more and more inscrutable. After arrest and in court, he takes on almost a mask-like expression; this being quite in contrast to his ordinary facial mobility. A diagnosis was presented in court from a physician who had seen him, the statement being that he was "a highly nervous boy and a thorough kleptomaniac"; but, of course, that explained nothing and helped not at all.

After much work early on this case, we were totally unable to find out what was in the background, although we were convinced that there was a great deal that was significant in this boy's mental life. We recommended probation several times in the hope that his trend towards delinquency would be checked. The boy was found very good positions, and in them he did well, but in the midst of his successes he would again have outbreaks of delinquency; in fact, his worst delinquencies occurred when he had the best opportunities. He gradually developed a more hardened attitude; he tried to defend himself by ruthlessly making misrepresentations about a probation officer who had done much for him; he insistently lied to the judge and to others, and demonstrated a typical professional attitude by his attempt to "bluff" court proceedings.

William has thus grown obstinate and hard. One cannot say that he is exactly defiant, but he assumes the most peculiar lack of concern about his misdeeds and demonstrates an extraordinary trend towards criminality. He is thoroughly anti-social in his general attitude, although he displays no grudge against particular individuals or against society. In this he differs from some other cases cited, where a feeling of grudge is clearly exhibited. Even the last time he was seen by us he appeared friendly enough to all, but one felt the superficiality of his very friendliness. The danger of such a bright boy turning so definitely toward criminality was all along felt, and this was one of the reasons why such great efforts were made to give him the best chances.

Not only were many advantages given him, but also short punishments were tried; in fact, everything was done except to penetrate his reserve and find out what was back of his delinquent tendencies. The resistance to exploration was always too strong for us to break down. Some early suggestion of possible bad sex habits arose from his appearance, which, however, improved as time went on. We felt it significant that from the first William utterly refused to discuss sex affairs with either his mother or with us. As for his father, he never gave the slightest attention to the boy, except alternately to defend him from kindly probation officers or to berate him; he occasionally varied the last by beating William. The mother was incapable of going far enough or keeping long enough at the task of winning the boy's confidence. We ourselves were always met at the important points by complete silence. Much as we suspected the deep influences of early companionship, nothing definite about this was ever found out. The boy's own extreme reticence concerning it was in itself remarkable. Still more suggestive was the fact that once, when he was searched under arrest, a little collection of obscene pictures was found in his pockets.

Possibly if all had worked together in this case, if there had been a really intelligent attitude toward the boy at home, the underlying trouble might have been discovered, and the extraordinary career of misconduct checked. There can be little doubt that it was built upon a basis of mental conflict. That this career has not been headed off is a deeply regrettable fact, both for society and for the young man himself.

(I can now add to the above history an account
of recent occurrences which further illustrate various
points already made in regard to the case. The young
man was sent to an institution with the idea that
perhaps prolonged separation from society would
reform him. From this place he readily escaped on
several occasions, but took no pains to go farther away
than his own home and so was speedily returned. He
escaped for the fifth time and obtained a good position,
working, however, under a false surname. His opportunities now were exceedingly good, for his abilities
were recognized, and within a few days he was given
a place of trust. His old impulses, however, seized
him, and he forged checks and cashed them in his old
method. It needed no very clever detective work to
trace the uttered checks to William — his physiognomy
is so unusual that he is very easily identified. Considering William's intelligence, this transaction can only
be regarded as utterly foolish. It was the result of
impulse; no skillful planning was undertaken, nor did
he attempt to avoid his ordinary whereabouts. We
chanced to see William before the trial for this last
offense. We found the old superficial friendliness and
the old inscrutability. At the preliminary hearing he
chose to make silly denials in the face of complete
evidence against him. Again here, as always, William
could not, even in his own best interests, bring himself
to face reality.)

Case 13. Misconduct that was frankly acknowledged
to be beyond the understanding of the parents, the
interested pastor, and the girl's teacher, appeared quite
clear in its relationship to mental conflict as a cause,
when a rational approach of thorough inquiry was

undertaken, but on account of unchanged environmental conditions, the case was long a failure.

A pastor of fine spirit from a country town came to make an appointment for some members of his congregation. The father of Ada M., a little girl, nine years of age, had read some articles in the newspapers concerning psychopathic studies, and he wondered if they could be of any help in his child's case. Medical and especially surgical attention had been given her, but proved of no avail. Ada had been stealing very frequently for a couple of years at least. She was in the habit of taking money from home whenever she could, and candy and fruit from children at school, and in other ways had shown a marked tendency toward petty stealing. The father thought that perhaps a period of detention might do the girl good. An older boy who used to run away from home improved greatly after punishment of this sort.

Sometime previously a surgeon had performed *a rectal operation "to cure kleptomania"*, but Ada had only been at home from the hospital a week when she began stealing again. Her developmental history was as follows: Pregnancy was normal and birth natural. She walked and talked early, and with the exception of having some children's diseases lightly and a severe attack of whooping cough, had never been seriously ill until an attack of appendicitis a few months prior to the time when we saw her. She was operated on then and again made a speedy recovery. Ada showed certain nervous signs at home; she was said to have attacks of excitement, when she clenched her fists and cried and yelled with bad temper. Her school work was satisfactory, she readily kept up to grade; indeed, she was regarded as being decidedly bright in her studies.

The family belonged to a good, hard-working type, and the children had whatever advantages could be afforded. We could learn of nothing in the family history that bore upon the problem of Ada's conduct. The other boy, who was for a time delinquent, was not known to have influenced her; however, later we learned more concerning this boy and his relationship to the sister. The mother was a nervous, sickly woman, who freely acknowledged her own incapacity for controlling her children.

From Ada herself we gained the fullest enlightenment concerning the details of her continued delinquency. Her parents did not know to what extent she had been involved. About three years previously the family had moved to the town where they now lived. Prior to this, Ada knew nothing whatever about stealing. In her room at school at present there is a boy named John, quite a bit older and not very smart. She had become acquainted with him upon entering school in this town. It was he who told her first about stealing, and she maintained that many of the things which she had taken she had given to him. Now, there was also a boy in the room by the name of Sam, and he and John went much together. Sam, in particular, was bad with girls and had been known to try to engage in sex affairs with them. In fact, he had tried with her and had told her about such things. The trouble with John was that she was afraid of him because of his threats. She had never told her mother about any of this or talked about it to any one. She stated that she had had very definite temptations to steal ever since she had known these boys. After the operation for appendicitis she had been taken from school and felt that she was better able to resist her temptations than formerly, although she had not been able to stop stealing altogether.

We found her such a bright and straightforward little girl who appeared desirous of helping herself, and the nature of her trouble seemed so obvious, that we went no further in the case than to acquaint the mother and the pastor — who again came to us — with the gist of the situation. They felt they could ask the coöperation of a teacher who was much interested in the child and of whom Ada was very fond.

About a year later we were again consulted about this case from a new source. Ada had been stealing excessively, and the school authorities now had complained about the matter to the court in the district. The parents maintained that Ada had kept on thieving ever since we saw her last. She might stop for a week or two, but she would begin again. She took pencils, handkerchiefs, candy, money, and sometimes articles for which she had no use, things which she would then leave lying around the house. She was still showing attacks of bad temper, in which she would seem to get rigid, and she would even swear. The parents once more stated that Ada was completely a truth-teller concerning everything except her denials of theft. The mother had noticed that Ada was sleeping poorly. Our inquiry brought out that absolutely nothing had been done to help this child after our previous study of the case. The pastor had left the town; the teacher whose aid was to be sought felt that she did not understand the problem sufficiently to give help; the mother said she just never could go into the sex question with the girl.

We found from Ada that she still was going to the same school, and John was still in her room, but Sam had been placed in another part of the school building; however, she sometimes saw him outside. Sam still endeavored to meet little girls in the basement, although this had been reported to the teacher. Ada recounted in the same clear-cut way her early troubles. John used to tell her to steal, and she used to give him things. He used to threaten her and would particularly tell her that he would get Sam after her. She thought much about this and of what Sam might do. The words these boys said came up in her mind and at night time she didn't sleep well on account of thoughts about them and about her own stealing. She claimed never to have known anything about the practice of sex habits. Ada told how badly she felt after she had stolen and how she wanted to stop thieving, but it was just a temptation — she saw things and took them. Sometimes she took things that she did not care for. She thought if the family could move away, and she didn't ever see these boys, she could forget about the things which they had told her and about stealing too. Over and over she brought up the idea that stealing and these sex ideas were connected in her mind, but she did not know how.

As we attempted to trace the situation back still farther, Ada now told us about another boy, who had himself been the teacher of Sam. This boy had lived next door to Ada, and he was the one who used worst words of all. He had offered Ada money if she would go somewhere with him, and she told us the bad sex word which he had used. She informed her mother about this boy earlier, but she had not told her the words which he and Sam and John used and which came up in her mind. Then there was the delinquent brother; he had once come to her bed and she had screamed, and her father had come and caught him. (This seemed to be very likely done under the influence of this other boy next door.) At any rate, sex affairs and stealing were most intricately mixed in this girl's experiences and in her mental content. She gave a vivid idea of how she had been endeavoring to repress all of the sex thoughts, and how she hoped to be able to conquer her impulsion to steal.

The parents gave confirmation of these two events, upon which they had laid little stress, namely, the bad invitation by the boy next door, which Ada had told them about, and the earlier affair with Ada's brother. Neither of these matters apparently had amounted to anything, and the parents had dismissed the incidents from their minds. That their daughter had ever been dwelling on these things, or that she was having a mental and moral fight, did not seem to be possible for them to understand, excellent people though they were.

Another year passed, and comparatively unsatisfactory results still were forthcoming. An intelligent person now took hold of the case, following our last study of it, and gave Ada much help. She was placed in another home for a few weeks, and while there engaged in no stealing whatever, but when she returned to her home, many of the old conditions recurred. During the following year the boy who had originally suggested bad things to Ada still lived next door, and John was still going to the same school, although he no longer plagued her. The report on Ada for this period states that she would do well for a time, and she no longer stole anything at school, but her temptations

still existed, and she did give way to them sometimes.
She occasionally not only takes a little change from
home, but she steals small articles that have no particular value for her.   She, then, has only partly overcome her tendencies.

The point which, in spite of all that we had said to
the parents and to others interested, does not seem
to have been grasped in this case, is that previously
exhibited conduct tendencies stand a great chance of
being renewed by stimulating old association processes
in the mind.   That Ada ever had to see at all these boys
who started her original impulsions was unfortunate
indeed.   From our experience with others, and from
our knowledge that old impulsions are renewed through
seeing former companions, as in instances cited elsewhere in this book, we felt that in this case essential
re-educative measures demanded, first of all, a complete change of environmental conditions.

Case 14.   The following case offers an illustration of
several points.   Left under the old conditions this boy
continued to be a moral failure, because his father could
not or would not face the underlying problem, and
because there had been a gradual development of
mental habits leading to delinquency, and because
only rarely is any first exploration of mental conflicts
effective without re-education.

Anton B. at fourteen years was a nice looking, attractive boy, rather undersized, but with no physical
defect save that of vision, which was corrected by
glasses.

Mentally we readily found him to belong in the class
of those who are quite up to the ordinary in ability.
He was almost through the grammar grades and did

very good work on the several rather difficult tests which we gave him.

Anton was bitterly complained of for truancy, an excessive amount of petty stealing, and running away from home, even as far as to another State. The boy was characterized by his relatives as being "slick, sly, and clever." He was said to be an excessive liar. When caught he confessed, but showed no remorse. He had few friends and had never been connected with any gangs. He is a great reader, often losing sleep in order to read. He began his delinquencies when he was about eleven years old, then taking small sums of money and keeping back change. From neighbors he had taken a number of articles, for some of which it would be difficult to explain his desire.

The boy's health had been good except for typhoid, when he was about seven years old. His birth and early development were normal. The family knew that he engaged in masturbation at seven years and much effort was made to cure the habit. Presumably this was accomplished. The father acknowledged, however, that he had established no confidences with the boy.

We were astonished to find a lad who was entirely frank when properly approached. The story of beginnings came out very clearly. When he was about seven years of age he went with a crowd of boys who taught him both to steal and to masturbate. His parents' efforts to break him of the habit were not altogether successful. He had not indulged, he said, with any one else, nor by himself to any extent, but these things repeatedly came to his mind, especially in the form of certain words. He naïvely stated that when he fights off the coming of these words into his mind, he grows uneasy and then will steal the nearest thing at hand. His father knew early about his habits, but he did not know anything about the words which so disturbed him. Anton has wondered a great deal about sex things, but has never asked any questions. At first when he thought of these things, he used to have a very "funny feeling inside of him", and then he would steal. Now sometimes he thinks that he takes things without sex affairs coming up in his mind first, at least it seems so to him. Stealing has, he believes, grown to be a definite habit with him, so that when he wants money he is tempted to take it and plans how he can do so. He has not been associating for long with any bad boys and has no other troubles. His home is happy.

A couple of months later it was reported that this boy again had been stealing everything that he could lay his hands on and had run away, taking another boy with him. The father came in to see us about it and stated that he had been unable to approach this boy on the matter that we outlined to him. Again the boy acknowledged to us the troubles with his inner mental life. He gave us many evidences of being an unusually bright boy with many wholesome interests; for instance, when he had run away the last time, he had taken with him some painting materials, saying that while he was away he thought he would paint some pictures of the country. Intelligent though the family seemed, it was evident that no efficient treatment was to be expected in the home circle. They made no more effort to utilize the good interests which the boy had than to gain with him full knowledge of his inner difficulties. The boy was sent away to a private school; the principal reported six months later that the boy had done well there from the start.

CHAPTER X

CONFLICT ARISING FROM SEX EXPERIENCES

We have seen many instances where early sex experiences led to excessive misconduct, quite non-sexual, through producing an active mental conflict. The following cases will serve to show how the tendencies to misdoing evolve. The same type of experiences will be found also in still other of our cases used to illustrate the special topics of other chapters.

Case 15. This is the case of a severely delinquent boy whom his vigorous parents found absolutely impossible to handle by their methods, which included no attempt whatever at understanding of causes.

Otto R. was left in the old country with relatives when his father and mother came to this country with the other children. He was three years old when they came; when we saw him at eleven years old, he had been here eight months; his parents went back on a visit and brought him over. When they arrived in this country the father outfitted him very nicely in American fashion, but within a few days Otto began a career of stealing which had been excessive during these eight months. He had found ways of disposing of valuable articles, such as automobile tires, to second-hand dealers, and he had stolen from other boys, from

183

home, and had even been caught burglarizing a house.
He took things which seemed of very little use to him
and sold them perhaps for a trifling amount, or hid
them away.   Once he tried to rob the pocket of a sleepy
fruit vender.   His delinquencies of this order already
mounted up into the dozens.   He had also been truant,
several times had come home in the middle of the
night, and finally had run away from home for several
days.

The father and mother were unusually strong people,
who had rapidly become prosperous in this country.
Their measures of reward and punishment were coarse;
if their children pleased them there was liberal spending
of money; if the children did not do well there were
harshness and severe beatings.   This boy had been
very roughly treated, without any improvement in
his conduct.   Complaints had already come in from
neighbors who objected to the boy's depredations.

We were informed that Otto had been a remarkably
healthy child.   In his developmental history there had
been in no way any peculiarity or anything to set
him back.   In looking him over physically we found
fair development and nutrition.   The teeth showed
some areas of defective enamel that, however, were
not typical of lues.   Vision was extremely defective,
not more than $\frac{20}{80}$ in each eye; there were strabismus
and complaint of frequent headaches.

In the mental examination Otto passed tests well
enough so that he could be graded as of fair ability.   His
school attendance in this country had been so irregular
that he had made little advance.   Concerning heredity,
we were assured that there was nothing of significance.

These parents, who so bitterly complained of Otto's
conduct and who had punished him so severely, had not

made the slightest inquiry into any possible causes, either by patiently inquiring from the boy himself, or by corresponding with those who knew him and his companions in the old country. They did know that on account of illness of the relatives he had received poor attention for a time over there, and that there had been complaint of his behavior. On the other hand, the teacher in the school here stated to the father that Otto was the best boy in the room, and that she could not believe that he was so much of a thief. The father was nothing short of vindictive about the affair; he was of an aggressive type and had made such a good reputation and such success that he disliked greatly suddenly to have this trouble and burden thrown upon him. That conditions might be bettered by a different point of view toward the boy had certainly never entered into his mind.

Since Otto began stealing within a few days after he had arrived in America, it seemed most natural to inquire whether or not he had developed impulses in that direction before he came. We found no trouble in getting at the history of his school and other companionships, and the boy gave us a typical story. He told us that some things did bother and worry him, some things that seemed very much worse than his stealing, of which he seemed inclined to make little, so far as his feelings towards it were concerned. The worst were the things that he had seen and heard about when he was six years old. Both boys and girls had talked to him of sex affairs; he had seen them "do things together" over in that small town in Europe; there was one girl who talked to him about it; boys also taught him masturbation.

These were the things which really bothered him.

The account which Otto gave us of his early experiences and how they led up to his stealing so excessively was most straightforward. Many things were revealed of which his parents knew nothing. A man over there who had associated with the boys, some one whom Otto had recognized instinctively as not being a good man, although he did not know exactly what evil things he did, said, "If you haven't enough money for what you want, go and steal it." These boys over there did steal, although Otto made little of this compared to their talk about sex affairs. He insisted that he had never engaged in anything of the kind, and he would not do it, but ideas about it often appeared in his mind, although he did not want them there. He fought against these things coming in his mind, he ingenuously told us, but he could not always succeed in keeping them down.

Otto seemed to feel positive that even entertaining the idea of these things was much worse than stealing. When asked in this reasonable manner about his transgressions he showed none of the characteristics of which his father had complained, namely, that he would not utter a word about them. With us he talked freely and pathetically about his inner troubles.

This was another case where the ignorance and attitude of the parents was an absolute barrier towards constructive measures being undertaken. The boy was tried at home again, but the father made no efforts to get a real insight into the situation, and the boy soon began stealing again and running away. One time we saw him after he had been arrested; he was then pale and dirty and woebegone, really suffering greatly on account of his own delinquencies. The father had not even procured the boy any glasses. He attempted to

treat him by nothing other than by increased severity.
It was necessary then to send Otto to an institution.

Case 16.   The tragic life history of this boy brings out
powerfully his mental conflicts derived in typical
fashion from sex experiences, and shows his struggles
against impulses originating from conflicts.

Abner B. was first brought to us by his mother when
he was twelve years old.   Two years later he ended the
difficulties of his career by taking his own life.   We
may at once acknowledge and deprecate the fact that
there never was a thorough analysis of his mental conflicts ;   family conditions prevented this and also the
utilization of what we early ascertained to be the trouble
in his case.   It was plain from the start that continua-
tion of his former environmental conditions would tend
to increase his mental struggles.

Almost the first word that we were told, both by an
officer who had investigated the case and by the mother,
was that Abner would steal "everything he could lay
his hands on."   Just before we saw him he brought
home opera glasses and a purse and said that he had
found them.   He had frequently stolen money, both
from home and elsewhere.   He took things which he
wanted and things for which it would seem he had no
use.   His mother stated that he began stealing when he
was six years of age.   Summarizing his now closed
career of delinquency, we may say that it included
petty stealing on many occasions, from home, from
school, from places where he was sent on errands, and
from shops down-town.   On one occasion the stepfather wrote a letter to the court, stating that he
objected to his home being made a storage place for
stolen goods.   Besides this, during his last two years

in school, Abner became at times very disobedient and
truant; in fact, he was once sent away to the special
school for truants. He occasionally behaved badly
at home, and several times stayed away all night.   Once
he was away from home for two or three days.

Of great interest to any thoughtful student of delinquency is the attitude which this boy assumed
towards his own misconduct. His mother stated that
he never admitted his stealing unless he was faced
with the proof, but we ourselves experienced no difficulty in getting him to enumerate a considerable number of occasions upon which he had taken things. She
had used every form of punishment with him, and his
denials, undoubtedly, were in self-defense. Outside of
this, however, she had observed that he often seemed
to be tremendously sorry over his stealing, but he did
not seem to be able to stop it, and even to her it appeared as an uncontrollable impulse.

A short time before we first saw him, Abner had come
home with a bottle of holy water which he had obtained
from a priest. They were not Roman Catholics, and
yet he had been to a priest in the hope of getting something which would make him good. After that he
commenced to read his grandmother's Bible — apparently making a very definite effort to reform. A
little later the boy wrote a letter to the person in charge
of his case, stating that he had come to realize how
wrong it was to steal, and that he would never do it
again. None of these things, however, influenced him
for long. Only a couple of weeks after he wrote voluntarily this letter descriptive of his self-examination
and good intention, he stole ten dollars from his mother.
This was in school vacation; he speedily obtained work
and paid her back the ten dollars.

His own feelings toward his delinquency Abner expressed in the most vivid fashion. This little fellow of twelve years stated to us that he had times when he wanted things, when "a sort of wave" came over him so that he could not help taking things. About the opera glasses, for instance : he told us they were in a room where he had been on an errand, and he had looked at them; then, in his own words, "I said to myself, 'No, I won't do it,' and I got a block away, and something seemed to drive me to go back and get them." He thinks he has no special use for many things that he takes.

From the physical standpoint we found nothing of great significance. The boy was a trifle small for his age; he had slightly enlarged tonsils and crowded teeth, but there was no sensory defect, nor were there symptoms of any nervous disorder; his head was well shaped and of good size; his eyes fairly bright, and his features pleasant and normally boyish.

Our mental examination showed Abner to have fair ability, but he was unquestionably inclined to be shiftless. He showed no mental energy; to think through any task at all difficult was a great effort, and yet the boy worked quietly and thoughtfully. Once he laid his head on the table and complained of being tired — an unusual action for a boy. He was given a considerable number of tests; the results on them showed him to be a rapid and careless worker on school tasks, yet with other things which interested him more he did proportionately better. As far as tests for age-level were concerned, he graded a trifle below his age.

We were informed that Abner had never suffered from any severe illness. Sore throat in the winter, and measles and bronchitis were his only ailments. There had been no convulsions, nor any serious accidents. Although the mother was only fifteen years old when he was born, the pregnancy with him had been normal, and there had been no special trouble at birth. The father's family were very little known to the mother; she could tell us almost nothing of significance about them, except that a number of them were hard drinkers. Abner's father, who was twenty-four years of age when the child was born, himself was alcoholic, and Abner's mother had been soon separated from him. She herself was a runaway from home and preferred, as a young girl, an irregular life. Her father was at one time alcoholic. We noted that she seemed to be a woman of good moral impulses but was distinctly careless. She was a delicate type, fairly intelligent and apparently a very hard worker. Her home had been much broken up during Abner's boyhood; she had tried two other men in marriage.

We were enabled at the start to partially analyze this case, with very definite results. Unfortunately, our beginnings were never followed up, and our recommendations never carried out. We found Abner, for such a little fellow, very well oriented in regard to his past. All along there had been much self-realization and unusually good apperceptions; he said that he remembered stealing a little box of paints when he was four years of age, but this was very vague in his mind. His mother had reminded him of it so frequently in evidence of the early beginning of his delinquent career, that he felt that he remembered it.

Further exploration brought us to the period when he was about six years old, when he had stolen a number of articles. The mother went over all this with us later, and there seemed little doubt that this was the

real beginning of Abner's delinquent tendencies. The
mother had already informed us that she caught Abner
masturbating when a little boy and had whipped him
for it. To us, at first, he vigorously denied knowledge
of anything of this sort. After he told us the story of
his stealing, he entirely changed his tune and revealed
a great deal of inner mental life which had long been
centered on sex affairs. It appeared that when he was
about six years old, — and we were able to get verification of names, etc., from the mother — a girl, considerably older, gave him sex information and entered
into bad practices with him. From this as a starting
point, Abner told us about further sex experiences
and about his early thoughts concerning these things.
"I don't understand about it yet. I was always
wondering about it. I think about it when I am
sleeping; I mean I dream about it. I dream that
girls always want me to do it." Abner was very
sure that his experiences at six years started his masturbation, and by checking up dates we found that it
was soon after this that his mother caught him at it
and punished him severely. Thenceforth the boy
suffered frequently from temptation, but insisted
that he never had given way very much. A boy caught
him at it when he was about ten years old and warned
him what would happen. Occasional enuresis, which
the mother had told us about, was the result of the
sexual dreams, the boy informed us.

Abner's mother remembered Ella, whom the boy
now named. She had not been aware that Ella had
ever influenced him, but she knew Ella certainly was a
very bad girl, notorious in the neighborhood. At these
first interviews Abner was never able to dig up specific
memories regarding whether or not Ella taught him

stealing as well as bad sex habits. She used to "hang" about a certain small candy store with another girl, and they used to "swear and say bad words." Abner was hazy about everything except the special events, mentioned above, which made such a deep impression upon his mind. However, there could be no doubt, both from his story and his mother's account, that this was exactly the period when he first definitely began stealing. Never in our incomplete analysis did we ascertain any direct correlation between his "waves" of impulse to steal and periods of special sex temptation, as we have in so many other cases. If we may judge by other cases, however, it is more than likely that there was causal connection between the two.

There were other elements in this case which we would not minimize. On account of the breaks in family life, the boy had been at one time in an institution, and thoroughly confidential relations had never been established with his mother or either of his stepfathers. After it was discovered that he was engaged in bad sex habits, and he was once punished for it, his mother never approached him again on the subject. She said she felt that she just could not do it, and her new husband felt the same. It was perfectly evident to us that although the boy made no special complaint against his family, he felt no respect whatever for his present stepfather; towards his mother he evinced some affection. One of the stepfathers had been a man of loose talk and of somewhat loose reputation, and from this source, at least, there had been renewal of the boy's ideas concerning sex affairs.

Whatever family affection may or may not have been shown to Abner, his peculiar experiences and needs had never in the least been understood, nor was there, even after we saw him, any fundamental effort made to adjust the case. There was further stealing on his part, more running away, some miserable suggestions of illicit sex affairs arising in his home life, and more striving to get hold of himself, with frequent failures.

A reliable account of this boy during his last two years states that at times he showed a most excellent disposition, but then again he would fall back into misconduct. Much quarreling, particularly on his account, developed at home. When he was found positions he failed to hold them. He finally sought to meet the world upon its own terms, and at fourteen years of age started housekeeping for himself in a little basement room near his mother's home. His rent he paid out of his small earnings. After a short trial of this he evidently found the burden of further strife against his own impulses and against an unkind world too great to bear; one night he turned on the gas and removed the jet. He never awakened.

CHAPTER XI

CONFLICTS ARISING FROM SECRET SEX KNOWLEDGE

THE effect of illicit sex knowledge acquired very early in life may be to produce a severe mental conflict, with vicarious reactions following in the form of misconduct. The cases given below demonstrate that secret sex knowledge in early childhood may constitute an unfortunate "mental complex", quite as severe in its effects as when the original experience has been physical.

Case 17. As shown in this case, even intelligent teachers in institutions and private schools working specially with young people as problem cases, cannot offer the re-education and constructive measures that are necessary in cases of mental conflict, unless there is clear understanding of what secret sex knowledge may mean for the production of conduct.

A boy of eleven years, just fairly developed physically and above the average in ability and intelligence, was complained of for disobedience at home, petty stealing from home and shops and neighbors, running away, and bad temper.

We found an intelligent and healthy-minded father, and a frank, non-suggestible boy. The former went

194

over several points which he thought might account for the breaking out of delinquent tendencies in his boy. There was a stepmother, although she had tried to do everything possible for the boy; there had been some fault-finding and working at cross purposes with his first wife's family; perhaps the boy together with the family had gone to motion picture shows too frequently; possibly the ideas of stealing had been obtained through the interfering suggestion of neighbors, who said the boy ought to go to certain relatives and take from them a watch belonging to his mother; other members of the family in the past had lived rather loosely, and the father wondered if this meant something defective in heredity, etc., etc.

The boy, on his part, soon showed that there was a great deal on his mind that he had never spoken of to his good father. There was no trouble at home of which he complained. After thinking it over at length, the boy could tell us just about how his misbehavior began and about certain things that had been bothering him. He had been stealing for a couple of years; there was an older boy who lived in the neighborhood who had first introduced him to the art of thieving. Furthermore, the older fellow told him other things which had worried him much, among them words which persistently came up in his mind. Then there was a girl friend of his sister; he had heard the boys say that she went to the park with them at night. Those are the things that bothered him more than anything else. What this boy said to him "is hard to forget", it "makes me feel like doing bad things." He heard about stealing and about sex affairs at the same time. He had been much discouraged about himself; he felt badly sometimes about all this. He had never given way to bad habits, but he heard the boys talk about them, and it made him feel like doing that as well. When he was scolded for taking a watch, there was so much on his mind that he felt like dying, and he really did get carbolic acid to kill himself, but he was afraid when it burnt his tongue. (This was an attempt at suicide that his father had told us about.) Later on he felt better, but continued to steal and to be troubled about much that he had kept back and of which he would not let himself think.

The story of this boy was wonderfully convincing. As already stated, he was distinctly not a suggestible lad; he stated what he clearly felt, and he repeated it to his father and to us without equivocation.

The father, good man though he was, found himself unable to meet the needs of the situation, and the boy was packed off to a good private school. The régime there, which has proven successful with scores of other boys, did nothing for this lad, and he ran away from the school several times and got into further trouble. His ideas of stealing flooded back upon him, and on one of his expeditions he committed a major burglary. Because no better solution of the case offered itself, he was finally sent away to a state industrial school.

Case 18. The following case is that of a very bright and vivacious little girl, brought to us at such a tender age that we could hardly allow ourselves to believe that so young an individual had stolen so much. The story of her mental conflict rang as true as if she were a thoroughly self-conscious adult; the essentials of her experiences were verified.

Nima H. was six and one-half years old. On the physical side in every way she appeared quite normal. She looked very well and was strong and active. She readily did mental tests for her age and showed good ability in many ways. Regarding other characteristics, she showed herself to be voluble, self-confident, and a tremendous little falsifier.

Developmental history was entirely negative. It had been good in every way. Of heredity we cannot say so much. The mother was a high-strung and confessedly neurotic author — a brilliant woman, who kept herself going largely by the stimulation of coffee and tea. The father of Nima had died when she was very young and then, on account of the mother's nervousness, the child had lived in some four or five households, one after another, until the mother's marriage again two years previous. The mother herself had lost her own parents early and undoubtedly was, as she herself said, a spoiled child. Nima's father had been a thoroughly healthy man, and the child was said to resemble him in complexion, manner, etc. From this most intelligent family we heard nothing else of significance pertaining to heredity. It was hinted that a paternal aunt had been accustomed to take things that didn't belong to her, but there were no substantial data on this point.

Much more important, it seemed to us, was the fact that Nima had lived about in different households where she had largely been spoiled. The mother frankly acknowledged that she was much to blame for the lack of discipline. When she had the care of Nima she had been too indulgent with her, and even nowadays interfered with attempted correction by the stepfather. She could not stand his punishing the child any more than she could attempt it herself. Of course, this had not started Nima on her career of stealing, and yet it certainly must have interfered with the proper management of the case. The parents were really desperate

about the situation since it had taken on such large
proportions.   They wanted to know what could be the
matter with this little girl that she should show such
definitely delinquent tendencies.

The specific account of Nima's misconduct included
the fact that she had been stealing for over a year, and
that she had taken many scores of articles.   She had
taken things at home and from other houses; she had
taken things and hidden them — things that she could
not possibly use.   The mother stated that no doubt
the things taken were for the most part attractive;
even two umbrellas that Nima recently had stolen
were perhaps more or less desired.   Nima liked parasols,
but because she often tripped and hurt herself she had
not been allowed to have one lately, and perhaps that
was the reason why she took a child's umbrella from
school, brought it home, and hid it under the porch.
But then she took it with her to Sunday school on a
sunshiny day and brought still another one home and
hid them both under the porch.   The next day she took
one umbrella to school and left it there.   The teacher
later in the week put it on the piano and asked whose
umbrella it was.   Nima stated that it was hers, that
she had forgotten it, and her papa said she must bring it
home.   Nima had taken pennies from newspaper stands,
pencils, medicines, powder bags from satchels, pocketbooks, money from neighbors' houses, etc.   She had repeatedly opened pocketbooks when she had the chance;
she had often stolen things from other pupils.   She
had made it a business, also, to arouse the sympathy
of strangers; she had obtained money from them by
telling them that her parents were very poor.   She
would go to the window and call out "you hurt me",
even when no one was in the room with her.   She had

told friends that her parents fed her on bread and water and that she was whipped continually. Nima blamed bruises, which she had received in other ways, to the bad treatment of her stepfather. She was distinctly secretive in her feelings and ideas. She had been found, both by her teachers and her parents, to be a great liar. With the exception of evidences of her being spoiled, all the above excessive misbehavior had appeared in the last year. (This was an important point for us, but it had not seemed to occur to the parents that this might be the fact about which a study of the genesis of her delinquency might center.)

The following is a short account of the results of the first interview. Nima, of course, knew that she was brought to us to have her case studied, and she showed the "nerve" that her parents said she always displayed; she was afraid of nothing.

"They got to taking things; they got to doing it and that made me do it. They did it before I did. Jim and Amy one day went in our barn, Jimmy's grandmother's barn; he gave the horses too much hay. He went and hid and hit and spit and kicked. There was a hole, and he played with glass and threw it and cut her finger, and threw her down in there. Her mother's name was Mrs. K." (etc.) . . . "They were inside Amy's yard; she had a little play-house, there was cans and glass in front " (etc., etc. Nima is most voluble). . . . "He touched her and asked her to touch him. She did it, she touched his arm." At this point Nima very evidently began to back out of the story she had started to tell us and became evasive. After a little time we urged her to be more confidential. We came to know later that this was a method that Nima pursued in regard to most of her delinquencies;

she would tell a little and then back down on it. Her
natural inclination, thus, was to be frank, but she
quickly censored her statements. In a few minutes
Nima gave the following:

"She took off his cap and then his rompers, and then
he asked her to take off his other clothes, and they
went inside the play-house, and she took all his clothes
off, and that is all I saw them do. He took off her
clothes. Then they laid down on the little couches they
had there; both on one couch. I was in there. Yes,
he took off my clothes too, and we three laid down.
Then Minnie and Roland came along, and they had to
take off their clothes. Jim and Amy, they did it; I
think they kept doing it every day. Jimmy's mother
was hunting for him, and she came and saw him all
undressed, all bare, and she gave him a scolding, and
she put him to bed in the house. They didn't get any
chance to do it to me more than once. Jim was the one
who tried to do it."

To appreciate the force of the above story it should
be known that all of it was in response to our question,
"How long have you been taking things?" We had
not the slightest previous clue to the other incidents
involved. Coming back gently to the same question
later, we obtained the following:

"Jimmy took Amy's toys and he hided them in his
old shed and went and hid them. He took some of his
mother's powder, that's all I know of. He didn't tell
me, but he took me out there and played with the
things which he took."

We then asked Nima about her own mental life, what
she thought about, and whether these things came up
much in her mind. As before, we got a voluble response:

"Think about it? Yes, I think about it every day — all day. Yes, last night. I don't think about Jim and Amy, but about myself and about my being good. Yes, I think about the play-house. I don't know what they meant — about their taking off their clothes — I didn't ask what they meant. Yes, I think about it, yes, for a minute in the night. I think about Jim and Amy, about what they steal, and everything, and besides after that I forgot; I mean I forgot to be not stealing. They touch themselves. They went and took — well — they went and took some of their clothes off. I wonder, but I don't know. I am worrying because sometimes I think I forget, and then I wonder. It comes in my head to take things when I forget."

We asked Nima to tell us about those umbrellas. "I forgot and stoled them. I forgot about stealing. I took two umbrellas, two umbrellas because I thought I could play one day that I had a little sister and had one belonging to her and one to me. The teacher said that I didn't need it, and I said, 'Please give me my umbrella.' I told her my papa told me to be sure and bring it home."

By this time we had received confirmation of some of the above statements from the parents, who knew the corroborating circumstances which are recounted below. Going on further with the matter and the situation, as suggested by her parents, in her present neighborhood — for all of the above had happened where she had previously lived in the South — Nima continued:

"Nobody talked to me about it. I never told mama and papa about this — about Jim and Amy. They did those things two times when I was with them. Jim

touched me; Amy did it too. Jim put his body near
me when he didn't have any clothes on. I didn't have
any on. Yes, I think about it every day. Are my
mama and papa here now? I thought they went home."
(Nima laughs merrily.) "Jim used to say, 'Oh, you
nasty kid.' Well, I've forgotten just what he did say.
They said to — to — they wanted to lay down — they
was tired. I've forgotten what they said, to — to —
so they could play — they wanted to play undressed.
Yes, I think about that word, but I don't know what it
was, I've forgotten — I'm trying to think — undressing
— and, and — they wanted to rest. Sounded to me
like they said they was tired. Jim said he wanted me
to undress and then lay on the couch and then we —
we would go to sleep. He said he would put me on the
couch and then he would undress me — after he would
undress me he said we would play. He showed me how
to play. Then we both went to sleep. He called it
being — he thought it was being naughty — yes, that's
the word." ("Then you sometimes think about the
word.") "Not very often. I thought about it two
weeks ago, but I've forgotten. He called it being,
being, being — . . . They taught me stealing —
that's the bad word."

We tried still later to get Nima to tell us, or to tell
her mother, or any one, what the words were that came
up in her mind. But all we got from her was that
they did use "the bad word." "They called it nasty,
just that."

Going again into the question of stealing with her:
Jim was certainly the first person she knew who stole.
"He took one of Amy's baby dolls, and she played
with him and the doll in his barn." This was before
the event of the play-house. Asked again about her

thoughts : "Yes, I think about those things every day. I can't forget them. I think of them mornings and nights and afternoons — sometimes in school."

From the parents we obtained a most accurate account of this child's former life with the dates and events that were needed to justify us in giving credence to Nima's story. They knew in a vague way that she had affairs of this sort in her head. She had told her step-father that a little boy here in Chicago had undressed in front of her and what an awful thing it was. The parents had worried about it at the time and then later found out that it had not happened at all. In regard to the earlier incidents, we now heard that Nima had had very few playmates until she was over four years of age. From then until a year ago she had associated much with Amy and Jim. The parents at that time heard reports that Amy had stolen some things and asked Nima to do so. They also knew that Jim and Amy were caught doing sex things, and at that time fearing that Nima might learn something of the sort, they kept her away. From what they heard of these two other children, both of whom came from exceptionally good families, they surmised that sex affairs between Jim and Amy had been going on for some time before Nima associated with them. But, of course, it had never entered the head of these elders that Nima knew anything of the sort.

Further analysis of the situation was attempted by the clever mother, and more verification was obtained. A verbatim report of her conferences with the child was rendered to us, and, as the mother states, it shows that Nima feints verbally with almost the skill of an adult. It was this way about all of her confessions; at first there was some little acknowledgment and then, continuing, a denial and finally more acknowledgment.

The neurotic mother proved herself incapable of building upon the foundations which we had prepared. She interfered at every point with the work of the step-father. A further record of Nima's stealing, which was begun again in short order, reads like extracts from the stock list of a department store. In her school desk were found five bottles of paste, scissors, letters; she had hidden a child's fur tippet in the sleeve of her coat. She had stolen some valuable jewelry, entering a neighbor's house for the purpose; she took a gold pin belonging to her mother, a chain and locket, a bracelet, and a ring; she took money whenever she could, and on account of this she was expelled from a second school for continuous stealing from the teacher's table and from the children's pocketbooks.

No rational punishment, no discipline, no re-education whatever was carried out in this case up to the time that I last heard of the family, when they left this part of the country. A complete analysis, that might have been so easy, was thus never finished, and sound treatment of the offender never took place. The impossible attitude of the child's own parents continually stood in the way and offered a psychic environment that remained disastrous.

Case 19. A few months of extreme delinquency (as the result of mental conflict based upon disturbing sex knowledge) was followed by exploration of the causes and entire cessation of the bad conduct.

Delia B., eleven and one-half years old, was reported on account of her dramatic stealing escapades. After some investigation we were able to fix the time of the beginning very clearly, at some five months previously.

She had been stealing from her own home and lately had, in amateur burglar fashion, broken into several houses and taken money and, in one place, a watch. Also, from one woman, whom the family knew well, she had repeatedly stolen amounts ranging up to one dollar at a time and bought candy and clothes and a pocketbook. She had been suspected of having entered a neighbor's house, partly because she had so vividly described a man whom she had claimed to have seen go in there. When she was accused later of this, she went into a sort of hysterical attack, became rigid and speechless, and that night stayed away from home until she was at a late hour found shivering under a porch. On another occasion she remained out until nearly midnight and told a long story of having been kidnapped by a man who had locked her into a room and of how she got away by jumping out of the window. Once more she stayed away half the night, and it was never known where she was.

She secured work for herself after school at a stranger's house, who really did not want her, but pitied her, and Delia explained her coming there by stating that her mother abused her terribly and did not give her enough to eat. When Delia's mother was away from home, she took all of her belongings and went over to this woman's house to live. When her mother traced her, she screamed and said she would kill herself if she had to go back. During this period Delia was truant a few days from school.

The case was taken up by experienced social workers, who ultimately saved the situation. The mother came to us and proved to be an exceptionally strong character. From her we learned that the father was an excessively alcoholic and immoral man, who had been arrested

over and over again for non-support, and who finally
deserted the family about five years previously. The
mother, in great contrast, was a neat, refined, and
honest woman. She had long ago secured a position
and had worked steadily for her family. On neither
side was there any mental abnormality known. The
father came from a decidedly good family, as did the
mother also. An older boy was backward in school,
largely on account of very bad physical conditions;
when tested by us he proved to be normal mentally,
and since then, as his circumstances have been bettered,
he has done well.

The developmental history included a story of great
privation during the period of the pregnancy with
Delia, when the father was drinking to excess and
abused his wife; indeed, the mother suggested that
conception took place during intoxication. However,
development after birth was fairly normal. There was
never a serious illness. She walked and talked early
and never suffered from convulsions.

In regard to her companionships, the mother told us
of an older girl who lived in the neighborhood who was
known to be bad in sex ways, but the mother insisted
that Delia was never upset by this or by boys saying
bad things to her or by their making advances. "All
the neighbors say you can judge by her actions that
there is no fear of her getting spoiled."

At our different interviews with Delia she always
reiterated that she had never stolen until she saw some
pictures about stealing and burglaries at the moving
picture shows. She told us that this was the summer
previously and that when she was at home alone much,
as she had to be on account of her mother being away
working, the idea of stealing came up a great deal in her

mind. "It always comes up when I am thinking about things. I don't see anything like pictures in my mind; no, I don't hear anything, but when it comes up in my mind I thought I'd steal."

(Delia's mother had suspected that the picture shows might be affecting her badly, and so for several months before we saw her she had not been allowed to go to them.)

When we tried to go farther into this story, we at once found a very great deal of repression about the affairs of last summer and what Delia had been thinking about mostly then. Next we turned to more recent events and inquired about the circumstances of this amateur burglary, when eighteen or twenty dollars was said to have been taken. Delia said that she was with a girl in the house that was robbed on the day previous to the robbery, and this girl had talked to her about bad things with boys. They were down in the basement, and Delia saw a key there and took it. About that time Delia's mother came by, and nothing more was said. The girl told Delia that she did bad things in the basement, but didn't exactly say what. It was the next day when the people of the house were all away that Delia used the key to get in. She seemed much more concerned to get the substance of this girl's conversation off her mind than to deal with the circumstances of the stealing.

After some time we were able to learn about the previous summer. It seemed that there was a period then when she was undergoing a great deal of mental stress. Her older brother had talked to her about sex affairs and perhaps had done even more, but we were never able to ascertain just what this was, although later the brother himself said that something had gone on between them. We learned from Delia's mother that a man had exposed himself to the little girl during the previous winter at a certain spot under the elevated railroad. The fellow was found to be given to this sort of thing, and he was heavily sentenced upon the testimony of Delia and some one else, but the affair did not seem to bother Delia at all. From the brother we ascertained that during the summer, when she was walking with him under the elevated, she asked him about how babies were born, etc., and it was perhaps just after that, when the two were together at home, that something occurred. We were never able to exactly fit this to a day with the period when she saw the pictures of the burglaries, but there was no doubt that it was about the same time.

Delia showed conclusively, in our later interviews, that sex affairs were what was really on her mind, but she had entirely repressed them within herself. The affair with the other girl in the basement and what it led to was typical of her reactions toward these repressed matters.

We asked in this case that the highly sensible mother and a most intelligent social worker go into the subject of sex affairs with Delia and attempt re-education. This was done, and it was all that was done. The outcome has been most gratifying. It is now three years since Delia's period of stealing, and the girl has progressed well in school and has never stolen another object, so far as known by her mother or any one else. She nowadays is reported as being a particularly businesslike little girl, who takes great care of the two younger children, gets her mother her lunch, and who is most ambitious for further advantages in education.

Case 20. It sometimes happens among intelligent people that every sort of study is given to a case of delinquency except analysis of the mental life. This was so in the following instance:

Tom S. we saw first when he was fourteen years of age, an active, responsive boy. His delinquencies had lasted over a period of about five years and had been exceedingly numerous. He had stolen much, in many sorts of ways; he had even snatched a pocketbook on a crowded street. Tom had often been truant, and he had also run away from home, taking trips to other towns. He had evolved a shrewd method of getting goods by misrepresentation, having them delivered to an address and telephoning to the place, stating that it was an error and a boy was coming for the goods. The intelligent father and mother were desperate about the case.

We found Tom only fairly developed for his age. He was a mouth breather from occluded nasal passages; his facial expression was typical. Together with this, we noted a poorly developed and somewhat asymmetrical chest. No sensory defect. Many carious teeth, although he had received considerable dental care. In spite of these conditions, he was an active boy of fair strength. His nose had been operated on just previously, and in many ways the care which had been given him was admirable.

On the mental side he was easily to be diagnosed as of fair ability, with no essential peculiarities. He did many tests well. His backwardness in school was accounted for quite ingenuously by the boy, who stated that he found other things more interesting. He was a frank, attractive, and well-oriented lad. We feel

it highly significant that the boy himself stated that he
wanted to break away from his habits of delinquency
and attain a new moral status.

A very intelligent and detailed history was forthcoming from his parents.   We could learn of no points
of significance in the family history.   The father had
made a considerable study of this lad and his traits,
and had taken him to physicians to get whatever light
they could throw upon the case.   Several other children
were all reported normal and were giving no trouble.
The family life, we heard, was pleasant; the father
insisted that this boy had been given many healthy
amusements; on the other hand, he had been punished
and whipped severely at times.   Tom was regarded as
the healthiest of all the children, since he could stand
hardship extremely well.   He walked and talked early,
and developed normally in every way, except for the
trouble caused by his nasal occlusion, which the parents
had allowed to go on year after year without seeing a
specialist.   One doctor finally said the boy's weak will
was caused by his nose being in bad condition.   A phre-
nologist had said that he lacked will and concentration.
The father insisted the trouble was "with the boy's
reflective faculties", and he was also "poor in powers
of restraint."   "He does not seem to know what fear
is, or ever to think of results."

Neither the parents nor the school people thought
that the fact that Tom was only in the sixth grade signified anything but his stubbornness; he seemed normal
in every way.   He was said to be full of ideas, to have
ready conceptions, but not to advance far with them.
The parents stated that "when the boy is by himself
his mind seems to be off on something."   It was known
that he had been with bad companions, but their

specific influence upon him in any deep sense was not investigated.

Tom readily acknowledged all the delinquencies that his parents and the officers told us about. He said that years ago, before he was ten, his companions had started him in little ways of stealing. He and another boy used to go out "junking", — they would pick up things in alleys at first and then take things from yards to sell. "This was the way it started and then they could never check me. F. used to follow meat wagons, and once he stole a cash box from one. He wanted me to steal and go in with him and then he would get the benefit." Then the boy went on to tell us about the companions of those early days. "It all comes up in my mind all the time; that was all I thought of in school, and I couldn't study, and that's what I got sent away from school for. It would be always, what am I going to do this afternoon, and am I going to steal something, and what am I going to get, and all about girls, and like that. I can see it right in my mind. My mother says I will make an artist. . . . I never read much about stealing, only what I saw in the papers. I don't get that on my mind. Once in a while I have seen robbing pictures in the shows, but I don't remember them; I always forget them. Even a cowboy round-up — I forget that. Have had some books from the library about boys that run away from home, but I don't like reading much now. Have seen pictures of bad girls, the R. boy had them. Only once in a while they come up in my mind."

From this he proceeded to tell most elaborately about sex affairs, which he had either witnessed or heard about in this same early companionship. "All the kids around there talked about that, and most of them did these things. Didn't hear anything else from them. It bothered me some. I think about it some. . . . I wouldn't study — I had something else on my mind. I think of that all the time in school, about stealing and about those other things. I want to go out to a reformatory and get those things out of my head. . . . I've been treated too good at home. . . . That F. fellow is in jail right now.''

Further inquiry showed pretty conclusively that this boy had never been sexually immoral or engaged to any extent in bad habits. He had, then, effectively repressed actions of this sort, but it was most clearly evident that he had replaced the impulse to sex affairs with those of stealing, and had gone much farther into thieving than these boys who were so immoral in other ways. The father looked up his companions and found this to be the case; he also heard that they had been teachers of other boys in these evil sex affairs. The parents had known nothing of this before, nor had their study of the boy, nor any examination, brought out this essential fact, namely, that the boy had much in the mental life that was constantly being repressed.

Tom's own attitude towards himself was most interesting. He not only showed that he was above the average in introspective ability, but his desire for a different mental life, when the temptations to delinquency might be removed with the cause, was most uncommon. After our exploration he willingly discussed the matter with his intelligent father. The boy was sent away to a private school, where he won an admirable record. He since has proven himself stable and intelligent in employment.

CHAPTER XII

CONFLICTS CONCERNING PARENTAGE OR OTHER MATTERS

WE have observed mental conflicts about parentage at the root of various forms of misconduct. Emotions are bound to be stirred by finding out unsuspected facts concerning the identity of one's parents, and repression in children following such a discovery is prone to give rise to outbreaks of misdoing. I could give, by way of illustration, many cases in detail (Cases 6 and 33 also have the problem of parentage in the background), but short surveys of a few will be all that is here necessary to demonstrate the main point for diagnosis and treatment.

I have earlier stated that mental conflicts are not necessarily centered on ideas or experiences of directly personal sex import. The main determining factor is arousal of emotion, and if this occurs in relation to something other than sex matters, and there is repression, a complex is established and conflict made possible. Some indication of what other factors may be active in producing conflicts is given by the last three cases in this chapter. But even in these instances the reader will note that my endeavor to find cases of mental conflict altogether free from emotional disturbance about sex affairs has not been completely successful.

Case 21. A small colored boy for five years has
been a great truant and runaway from home and a
petty thief. He has been held in institutions several
times, but whenever he returns to his home, which is
a good one, there is always renewal of the same type
of anti-social conduct. It is specially notable that the
boy suffers much as the result of this behavior; he
sleeps wherever he can, sometimes without bedding
on cold nights, and he frequently goes hungry.

We saw him first after he had been acting in this
strange fashion for a year or so, and then he was only
ten years old. The supposed father was a big, soft-
hearted colored man, who was making a good living.
The mother was a nagging, high-tempered woman,
who kept an immaculate home. We found the boy
poorly developed, but physically otherwise normal;
mentally, he demonstrated a very active mind. Even
a short observation proved his unsociability. When
he ran away he did not care for other human beings,
children or grown-up people. Beyond this he showed
great determination and exceedingly little fear, for a
small boy.

From the lad we obtained a story of dissatisfaction
with home life, but that seemed in no way to justify
his seeking far greater hardships. It was only after
several interviews that he told us that some other
people had suggested to him that this man and woman,
on account of their deeper color, could not possibly
be his parents. He brooded over this for long. To
us he said, "That black man is not my father."

The boy and his informant were right. A colored
woman who was a servant in a home of wealth became pregnant by the young man of the family. She
gave up the baby to these foster parents, who were

to pose as his real parents. Such was the history as given by the good foster father.

For this boy, with his active mind and sensitive temperament, the world has been all wrong ever since he has found this out. The lame explanations of these good foster parents have never established a right parental relationship for him. The big, kindly colored man loves the boy above everything; he has no other children, but he never can give the boy what he wants.

Various officials and institutions and social organizations have taken a hand in trying to modify this boy's conduct during the last four years. Each time when he returns home after detention elsewhere he apparently finds the old ideas unbearable. He does not react by vicious conduct at home or even by any demonstration of scorn; he finds expression for his feelings by again running away. Our latest reports still state that the home itself is unusually good. It has been impossible in this case even to suggest means for checking this boy's impelling ideas without unjustifiably severing the family relationships. A state industrial school has now finally taken charge of this lad for a long period.[1]

Case 22. An astonishing situation was found to be underlying the six months or so of violent delinquency of a boy of sixteen whom we studied. He had suddenly discovered — mostly from her own unguarded hints in anger — that his supposed older sister was really his mother. This boy's reactions as expressed in delinquency were most remarkable and violent. His mother herself, fearing that this knowledge might be the force that was raging within him, came to us

[1] See footnote on page 225.

after his arrest and begged us to explain the facts to the boy. It was as she had suspected. He had said nothing, he had tried to down his feelings of resentment, he had tried to avoid facing the facts. He had given way to an astonishing amount of vicious conduct which caused his arrest on several occasions. After this analysis with us and a short period of further unsettled behavior, the young man was able to readjust himself and check the impulse to misconduct.

This case may sound too extraordinary to seem of much worth for our general thesis, but it is a fact that we have known of an exactly parallel instance.

Case 23. A good-looking, delicate-featured, remarkably bright and well-educated colored girl of seventeen caused no end of trouble by running away from home and stealing. This girl was reported as never being in any trouble until her outbreak a year previously.

When we studied this girl we found her quite as clever as she was reputed. Going into the genesis of her troubles we heard from her, also, that up to a year previously she had been quite non-delinquent. Since this time she had been much troubled on account of knowledge which came as a great shock to her. A woman who had long known the family told her that the people with whom she had grown up were not her parents; that her father was a white man and her mother lived in another city. Almost immediately after the girl learned these facts, she ran away and obtained work as a maid. When she was found, she refused to go back home, but, unfortunately, associated with bad companions and was tempted into stealing from shops. After a time she was returned to her home by officials, who knew nothing of the true inwardness of the situation.   After trying it for a few weeks she again ran away, and this time went to see her own mother.   The foster parents by now had made a bare acknowledgment of the true facts, trying to persuade the young woman to live with them.   In spite of all they had done for her, she said that she felt indifferently toward them, and they, in turn, had no confidence in her.   After coming from her trip to see her mother, again she tried to live with her foster parents on the basis of the old adjustment.   This ended by her running away once more and stealing a considerable sum of money for her own up-keep while living in a hotel.   She was then sent, *upon her own request,* to a home for delinquent girls.

Case 24.   One of the most tragic lives we have ever known — now ended, and perhaps happily, with the death of the girl at twenty years of age — was that ensuing from unusually mixed parentage.   An intelligent, English-speaking Chinaman married an American woman of no mean ability.   One of their children was a girl, who developed splendidly both physically and mentally.   She was an exceptionally bright girl, who at fourteen had already commenced a delinquent career which only ended with her death.   No doubt adolescent instability and temperament were largely at fault, and perhaps had she lived she might have recovered herself morally.   But beginning certainly as early as twelve years, she had been a victim of inner conflict concerning her parental relationships, particularly to this man who had bequeathed her his oriental features.   The fact that she was different, so obviously different, from other girls attending the public and private schools to which she went, and that

there were many little whisperings about her, served
greatly to accentuate her inner distress. Her capabilities and ambitions were great, but how was she to
satisfy them? As a matter of fact, neither the mother
nor I could ever find out that any great social discom-
forts came to this girl; the struggle was all within.
She behaved most extravagantly as a direct reaction
to her own feelings, of the depth of which she had rarely
given any intimation at home. With us she essayed
to remember and to reveal all that had gone on in
her mind for years back: How could her mother
have married this man? Was she really this woman's
child? To what could she attain with this sort of
stigma upon her? Did she not properly belong to a
free-living stratum of society?

This girl wandered and wavered. She tried religion, and she tried running away from home and living with other people; she assumed a Japanese alias
and tried to make a new circle of acquaintances for
herself. She knew of her father's dissolute habits;
this knowledge she long kept to herself, but it, too,
had its influence upon her. She was early immoral.
Her life for the last five or six years was one constant
turmoil of repressed ideas and attempts at readjustment.

Case 25. In this remarkable instance a certain
early experience with the father proved most influ-
ential upon behavior. The mother of this little boy
was not aware until our study of the case that he had
knowledge of an event which, as a matter of fact, he
witnessed years before.

Giving this case history in the briefest form, we may
say that Jamesie T. was brought to us at eight and

one-half years of age, with the statement that he exhibited the most extravagant tendencies towards thieving. This misconduct had begun when he was only six years of age. Enumeration of his thefts would cover pages; they ranged from taking pennies from newspaper stands to amateur burglary, as when he crawled through a window into a neighbor's house and stole a purse. He had stolen so often at school that he had been expelled; he had taken a gold watch and money from the pockets of different people. For considerable periods stealing was practically a daily affair with him.

We found the boy in very good general physical condition, without discoverable defect or ailment of any kind. On the mental side Jamesie proved himself to be what the school people said he was — almost brilliant. Although so mischievous he was regarded as the brightest boy in his class. On tests with us he passed considerably above his age.

The mother's main thought was that this boy showed evidences of criminalistic inheritance. His father came from a family of delinquents and was himself, as she found after she married him, a thoroughly bad man. She had not lived with him since the boy was about five years of age; at that time her husband deserted her after taking from her a considerable sum of money.

We quickly found an important point in connection with this case, of which, however, the mother already knew. Jamesie had been placed in a boarding school and there Martin, a mentally defective boy, had attempted sex perversions with him and talked to him much about taking things from the village store; in fact, Jamesie had seen this older boy stealing. When we asked him what came in his mind when he thought of stealing, Jamesie promptly answered that Martin did. He got to thinking about Martin, and that would start the idea of stealing. He told his mother, it seems, about Martin's bad conduct, and she removed him from the school, but he did not tell her that he himself had there begun masturbation. The boy, during our interviews with him, gave many evidences of the usual inhibitory phenomena. "I always think of Martin, and I start in doing these things, taking things. He told me about some words, what he did to me. I forget what he called that, I forget that word."

The mother later called our attention to the fact, however, that unfortunate though this experience was, she really had sent Jamesie to this boarding school because he already had been stealing, and she thought that there he might learn better things. Analyzing with this bright and frank lad his earlier experiences, we came to something of importance which antedated altogether his own stealing. Asked who was the first person he saw stealing or who had made him think of such things, he answered, "I saw my father away back go and take my mother's money. I never forget that I saw him do it. It was my mother's money; I saw him take the money out of a drawer. I remember his taking it; I don't forget it, I always know that."

From his mother we found that the boy gave us an account of a true incident. Her husband had stolen her money when she was out of the room and then left, never to return. There was a great deal of excitement, undoubtedly, at the time; the boy had repressed altogether his natural reactions to the affair. The emotional background of this experience must have been very strong; a complex was established, and a conflict ensued. The second experience of importance with the boy who instructed him in sex matters and in stealing added fuel to flames already started. For the understanding of the case, it must be emphasized that according to both the boy's frank story and the mother, who watched over him very carefully, the practice of masturbation was entirely repressed after he returned home. Then it was that he renewed with violence his habit of stealing.

The outcome of this case, which at first seemed so difficult, so far has been most gratifying. The mother was intelligent enough to perceive the necessity for re-education. The boy had frankly explored his inner troubles, but we felt that his established habits would be hard for him to conquer, just as habits. He was placed in an entirely new environment, in a private home. He is regarded there as a very dear little fellow. Close observation shows cessation of bad sex habits. He has not stolen anything at all for many months.

Case 26. Here is illustrated the disturbing effect of knowledge or belief that older members of the immediate family are secretly engaging in misconduct. This case also shows that stubbornness and obstinacy sometimes may be extreme enough to be considered during childhood and adolescence as definite delinquencies. We have found, over and over again, that too much stress in explanation of this may be laid upon temperamental qualities; underlying features of mental content and of mental conflict are often overlooked.

James H. was complained of in court because of his desperate stubbornness. At fourteen years of age he was a fairly developed and altogether normal boy from the physical standpoint, with the exception of slight imperfections of the teeth which indicated defective early development. Mentally the boy proved himself of decidedly good capacity, a firm-minded youngster, who had evolved quite a philosophy of life.

We first saw this boy after he had been refusing to obey his parents and had been showing great obstinacy, both at school and at home, for several months. To be sure, he had once had trouble in the school a couple of years previously, but then, as we found out definitely, the boy was well within his rights. He made this point to us at the very first, and his school record showed it to be correct. We saw nothing to the case except that the boy seemed to have conceived a dislike for his high-school course and wanted to go to work; he seemed a manly, independent boy, without bad habits. His stubbornness was easily perceived, for at first he would say nothing at all to the court officials or to his parents in the presence of others. For whole hours he absolutely refused to speak, although his emotions could be observed as tears rolled down his cheeks. To our mind he demonstrated a certain strength of character, even though it was misdirected.

The parents were apparently very decent people, mindful of the boy's best interests. We learned of nothing in the developmental history or heredity that bore on the case, but we did observe the father to be himself a very strong-minded type of man. It was particularly stated that the boy's spells of stubbornness came in streaks and showed mostly at home, when he would absolutely refuse to obey his people. There has been no trouble with the behavior of the other children. We advised that the boy be allowed to follow his inclinations and go to work, since it was evident that he might readily develop a strong anti-social feeling, such as we have observed others of his kind do under like circumstances.

About three months later this case had to be reviewed. The boy had done well for a time at his employment and then had shown signs of his old recalcitrancy; this time he stayed away from home and slept out in a yard for two or three nights. By the officer who took charge of him and by others he was observed again to be one of the most stubborn and obstinate boys ever seen. For hours he would speak to no one; no impress could be made upon him at these times. It was after this that we were once more asked to see him, and the parents again recounted their troubles with the boy. They could not understand him any more than others could. For a time he would do well in every way, and suddenly his demeanor might change.

This time we were astonished to meet a different response. The boy evidently now appreciated our inquiring point of view, and after a time told us that previously he had lied to us about the causes of his difficulties. The trouble had not been with his school, as he had said; that was merely an explanation that he had given to throw us off the track. He hesitated to tell us by what his distress had been caused, but wished us to understand that there was something wrong which all along had been deeply afflicting him. "I could tell if I wanted to and make a lot of trouble." His father, whom we called in consultation, decided that it was best to have this trouble unearthed, whatever it was, if the boy thereby could be helped. After deliberation that lasted some days, this thoughtful lad decided that he would tell, first writing down the information in a few words and asking us to speak to his father about it. This method was evidently dictated more by his own natural feelings in the matter than by any sense of the dramatic, for the affair he had to tell was of very serious import. In the home lived several grown-up relatives, involving whom the boy made a charge of immorality that shook the family to its depths. He had inadvertently heard something at home during the last year that made him suspicious, and subsequent attention to evidences led him to feel positive as to the facts. This was what he had been repressing for many months; this was the knowledge that he had hardly let himself think about, that reacted in this strange taciturnity and obstinacy.

The mechanisms and behavior in this case are not altogether easy to understand, but yet we may assume that in a boy of his temperament, long before recognized as egocentric, self-assertive, and anything but weak, the reaction would be towards further growth of his strong characteristics. He perceived the value of silence, he felt the undesirability of breaking up the family; his obstinacy reflected well his scorn for the immorality that he believed to be going on. Measuring it all in terms of what the boy was and what he believed, one could hardly feel that his behavior was, after all, anything but rational. His repression of what came to him as a shock made it necessary for emotion to find an outlet somehow. The case in this light became plain enough, and family readjustmenrs speedily ensued after exploration of the real causes of this boy's months of misconduct.

Unfortunately, James' father felt himself unable

to meet by open declaration in the family circle the immoral conditions which the boy believed to exist, although he did readjust the family situation so that further immorality would be impossible. This conservative procedure led to the strongest feelings of scorn on the part of his son. It was clear from what we heard that James sometimes vented his feelings in glances of derision and disgust while at home. Not only did the father fail to declare himself openly, but as time went on, he rather doubted the truth of what the boy had said, especially as James himself did not behave any better. Good positions were found for the boy, but he failed to keep them and became more self-assertive and more curiously dogmatic than ever. He acted without regard for his own welfare and, finally, after many things were done for him, the boy had to be sent to an institution for delinquents.

NOTE TO CASE 21, PAGE 215: We have heard remarkable news of this case after the final proof of this book had been corrected. The boy has committed murder. He escaped from the industrial school after a short time, wandered about in other states, then was held and did well for several months in a reformatory for boys. He grew rapidly at this time and seemed quite normal. Returned home, he worked and seemed happy except for outbursts of feeling, as, for instance, when a watch he purchased was criticized as being too expensive, he instantly threw it on the floor and broke it. His foster father tells us that now and in earlier years the boy occasionally approached the subject of his own parentage, but was always put off without direct answer: "He is only fourteen, he's too young to be worrying about such things." This statement was made in spite of the fact that long before we had counseled frankness in the matter.

After a few months and in midwinter he left home once more. Next he was heard of in a western city. One bitter night he entered a watchman's shanty and when the man returned hit him on the head with an iron implement and robbed him. Being speedily caught, he readily confessed to this and said that he was cold and hungry and needed money; this was how he became a murderer at fourteen years of age.

CHAPTER XIII

CONFLICTS IN ABNORMAL MENTAL TYPES

WITH all the analyses that medicopsychologists have offered us of cases of mental abnormality, there has been little suggestion of the specific relation of mental conflict to misconduct in these cases, even when the misconduct has been a large part of the picture. The problem here is not to present the study of any psychoneurosis, as such, but rather to show the causation of special types of misbehavior when they occur in these cases of mental disorder, as the result of mental conflict. Mental conflicts evidently may be occasionally active in producing misconduct in the mentally abnormal, as well as in the normal. The hysteric may or may not be involved in misconduct, and when involved, the misconduct may or may not be due to the same cause as the disease, *e.g.*, mental conflict.

Three histories are reviewed in this chapter (Case 5 also illustrates the subject) to give some hint of how mental mechanisms of conflict may be active in producing delinquency in a variety of instances where mentality is not normal. I have selected mental troubles of the less profound types; a psychoneurosis, hysteria; feeble-mindedness of the moron grade; an example of a mild, ill-defined psychosis — and Case 5 presents mental disturbance correlated with chorea.

Case 27. This case presents a type of neurosis which neurologists know full well. Added, however, to the functional nervous disorder, hysteria, there was much troublesome misconduct on the girl's part. The main interest lies in the fact that by persistent social work, based upon professional analysis and diagnosis of her mental conflict, what is evidently a thorough cure has been effected.

Celia B. we saw first when she was seventeen years of age. From several sources there came reports of much misconduct extending over at least two years. Her delinquencies ran as follows: Although her family was exceedingly poor, she had been quite unwilling to work at suitable positions which had been found for her. On the other hand, she had engaged in begging on the streets or from house to house, and she had concocted several letters of misrepresentation which netted fair returns. When tried at various places of employment, she had showed herself extremely erratic and had always quickly given up the work. At one time she was reported for being out late on the streets at night and exhibiting much ill temper at home. At that period she was very untruthful and untrustworthy with money given to aid the family. Just before we saw her, the delinquencies had culminated in a series of thefts; a number of sums of money were taken by her from a building to which she had access; and she had also purloined some jewelry. Then she disappeared altogether from home for a few days and refused to state where she had been. Some of the money was found curiously hidden in several places.

In the mid-period of her delinquency, Celia had

undergone a spectacular conversion. She had attended church for years with considerable regularity, and it was well recognized that she thoroughly enjoyed religious excitement.

At our first examination certain typical conditions were found : Celia was an under-nourished girl of poor color ; weight one hundred and two pounds. No sensory defects. Physiognomy characteristic ; sharp, weak type of features ; eyes watery and weak looking, unpleasant expression about her small mouth. Laughs occasionally in a rather foolish fashion and often hesitates in answering a question, as if she had not heard it at first. Deep reflexes normal. Sensation of pain distinctly diminished. Complaint of numbness in her fingers. No tremors ; strength rather good ; co-ordination normal. Fairly well-marked dermographism on upper chest and shoulders. Slouchy carriage. Diminished palatal reflex. Skin muddy. Complaint of headaches and "it hurts when the hair is combed." No contraction of field of vision by rough test. Does not bite finger nails.

Mental tests showed this girl to have good intelligence. She did well on a wide range of tests, with one exception, — the tapping test for psychomotor control was an unusually poor performance. However, we had reason later to learn that she could be very deft with her fingers ; she made exquisite embroidery. Much more important were the facts we found concerning her mental attitude. She showed no sorrow at her misconduct ; indeed, she appeared indignant at the world for interfering with her life. There was much complaint about her physical troubles, very little of which was justified. At one time we knew her not to eat anything for two days. When interviewed by various people who wished to help her, there was much hysterical giggling or excitement with crying; she often stated that she wished she "were dead", that she "hated herself." Altogether, she showed so much peculiarity that one had to regard her as almost a border-line mental case; the diagnosis of hysteria seemed from both physical and mental findings thoroughly justified.

Celia was the eldest of several children who lived under atrociously bad home conditions. The father had been dead for several years; he had been an artisan and probably more than slightly addicted to alcohol. The mother had been mentally disturbed for years, but never so badly that it seemed imperative that she be sent to a hospital for the insane. The diagnosis of insanity in her case had been made by some physicians; a competent psychiatrist had stated that she presented "a terrifically bad case of hysteria." We have no further trustworthy information about heredity. At least one of the other children had convulsions in infancy. They appeared bright enough in their school work, but showed several signs of instability, perhaps largely because of their extremely defective home discipline. The family had been the despair of numerous agencies which had tried to help them. The home was reported as dirty and disorganized, and it seemed impossible to better it because of the extremely erratic behavior of the mother.

Much faithful professional and social work has been done in the case of Celia. Doctor Clara Schmitt studied her with me. After several interviews, it was found possible to get at the real trouble which induced Celia's general behavior and mental attitude.

A very short summary of our long studies I will give
as follows :

After a short period of intense depression, Celia
freely stated that she had much on her mind. It was
nothing that she had been accused of, nothing that
she was detained for; those things seemed to her
slight delinquencies, or not delinquencies at all. Prior
to her revelation of the full nature of her difficulties,
it was interesting to us to note that she complained
bitterly about having to associate during detention
with girls who were "not nice", who said "bad words."
"I don't know of anything that is more horrible; they
are certainly in a sad way."

She endeavored to make it clear to us that their
outspoken expressions of their sex knowledge were
utterly repugnant to her. This seemed all the more
curious, because later we came to know that Celia
had developed, perhaps involuntarily, some extreme
and obsessive forms of mental imagery about sex life.
She had been a chronic masturbator since she was
four years old, and her fantasies concerning sex affairs
had grown so that they were a part of her most vivid
dream life and were suggested, to her great discomfort,
during the daytime by the presence of men and boys.
When recounting her dreams and half-visions concerning these things, Celia gave much vent to her
feeling about the horribleness of it all. She would go
just so far and then begin to sob and wring her hands.
It made her "hate herself", she said; it made her
want to tear away the sex portion of her body. That
there was any experience in which the idea of sex
affairs and of stealing had originally entered Celia's
mind at anything like the same time, we could not
discover, — there had been so many untoward events

in her life that there was little chance of getting any particular experience definitely corroborated.

One point stood out very clearly in Celia's case; her whole misbehavior rested upon a foundation that had not been heretofore suspected. The girl was most unhappy and very willing, after a time, to try to help herself. She confided to two good women the extensive and unpleasant details of her dreams and the nature of her waking obsessive imageries which amounted almost to hallucinations. This required considerable time and effort for, as stated above, when first seen she set up a defensory reaction of insisting that she could not even mention the vulgar words which other girls had used in her presence.

After this exploratory proceeding, the reports from this girl straightway began to improve, and her dreams and troublesome thoughts rapidly ceased, according to her own account. We may be convinced that this is true, for she showed no more times of heavy depression. Years have passed, and she has never been known to steal another thing.

Not long after our exploration of her case, Celia began to work hard for more education; she took a commercial course at night school and did well at it. She has now long held a good position, having charge of others in a manufacturing establishment. The change in her has not at all been brought about by lessening economic pressure, for less aid has been given the family than formerly. The mother herself is no better, and the children are still troublesome, but Celia's personal relief, through exploration of her mental life, has been so great that she has withstood all this and become, in truth, the valiant little mother and the steady wage earner of the family. Observers have been deeply impressed by the change that has come over her.

Case 28. The question has arisen with us concerning the possibility of mental conflicts developing in those who are feeble-minded. We are convinced from several experiences that this is possible, and sometimes with disastrous effects upon conduct. No doubt the conflicts are simple in nature, corresponding to the general quality of the mental life, but still they must be understood and fairly met if there is to be improvement in conduct. A short summary of a case bearing on this point will serve to show something of what may occasionally be found:

John N. was a boy of nearly fifteen when we first saw him. He had been stealing for two or three years and was consistently a thief upon almost any opportunity. In spite of being sent to an institution for the feeble-minded a couple of times, his career had not been checked. He had run away from the institution when he felt so inclined and finally, convicted of the charge of burglary, he is now, at nineteen, serving a long sentence in a reformatory.

On the physical side we found nothing of great significance. He had enlarged tonsils, and although there was no obstruction of the nose, he was by habit a mouth breather. There was no sensory defect. His features were mainly characterized by a good forehead, well-shaped head, and a decidedly weak chin.

We have examined the boy mentally on several different occasions and given him many tests. He is undoubtedly feeble-minded, according to the ordinary definition. On the Binet scale, 1911 series, at fifteen and one-half years of age, he passed the nine-year tests, with four higher ones to his credit. This would not grade him more than ten years at the most. On other tests he did relatively as poorly, but he had learned to write a good hand. We were particularly interested to note that, in spite of his low grading, he had considerable apperception of the causes of his delinquencies. He seemed to feel his own weakness of will; when asked to express himself concerning what he thought was back of his misconduct, we found that he had a comparatively good insight into the initiatory forces of his temptations.

About the family and developmental history we are none too sure, and yet the very unreliability of the account given by the mother shows definitely that she too is at least somewhat subnormal. It seems that this boy was always regarded as a dunce, while it is certain that several of the other children of the large family have done well. These people were immigrants, and there was little chance to know more definitely about any hereditary factors for John's defective mentality.

Our interest is particularly in John's own self-analysis of his mental life. We know that the boy has often proved himself a liar about the details of his delinquencies, more than most boys who so often falsify in self-defense, but he could hardly have invented a story about mental conflicts and repressions. Let me give his account in his own words — he spoke coherently enough:

"Began stealing? That was when I was about twelve years old. We lived over on W. Street. There was a boy by the name of S. He was the first that ever told me, he was a big fellow. He was sent after that to the band house. I knew him about two years. He held up a lady with a revolver; he took her watch and chain. It was him that used to tell me to take things and sell them. I used to take iron and stuff out of wagons, and whips; I would sell them. He said if I see a man on a wagon without a whip, I should run up and sell him one. He saw me and thought I was a good looking kid to go stealing with him. He made friends with me and made me go around stealing with him. My folks knew him, but didn't know he was stealing. He was afraid to go in stores and steal. He cheats too, he takes pennies and polishes them up; he has some kind of white polish. Then he goes into a store where there is a poor man making a living and says 'Give me nine cents in change.' I used to sell the stuff in junk shops — would get about a dime or a nickel. I had the skates that time, but he took them away from me because he wanted them for himself. He is the only kid I went stealing with."

"Then afterwards I was thinking of the time about what he said about stealing, and so I went through alleys stealing and selling iron, lead pipe, like that. That kid S., he took little girls, when he sees them on the street, at ten or eleven at night, in the alleys, and he does things in front of girls. Well, he was going to touch me once, but I wouldn't let him. He goes to teach me, but I push him away. Every kid around there is sore at him for doing things to girls. My brother was sore at him and would not speak to him. I wouldn't do these things he was talking about; I would do something else instead of doing such a thing."

(The reader should be informed that the above naïve account was not given in response to any leading questions; John was merely told to go ahead with his story, and occasionally a general interrogation was made by way of stimulation.)

"I stay around and help my mother and read a book by the stove and go to bed and forget about these things, and then the next day I do it again. When I read, I forget about these things, and then when I am through reading, I do think of stealing. There was a friend of mine, Simon, he steals; he snatched teacher's pocketbook. He was sent away. Then he made up his mind he would not steal again, and now he is a good kid and is working."

"I think it was about three years when that kid S. was sent away. I think about what he told me about stealing. That stuff about girls, that don't come up in my head. He told me all what he does to girls, and I says I don't want to hear no more about it. Sure, I used to think about it at first; I used to think about girls and do those things, but now I forgot all about girls."

It is the naïveté of this recital which argues its validity. I need not go on with the other points that came out concerning John's repeated stealing and his confession of occasional masturbation. It was evident from his appearance and good physical condition that he has never been excessively engaged in this habit. The feature in this case that I would bring out most strongly is that this boy, while not having mentality enough to analyze clearly the nature of his mental processes, gave us unmistakable evidences of the activity of mental conflict and repressions. He originally had experiences of sex affairs associated with stealing. He repressed part of the complex, but could not successfully fight against the impulse to steal.

John gradually developed some little cunning in the attempt to emulate, probably, the type of stealing done by his more clever comrades, but he never succeeded in the ordinary professional way, and he was repeatedly arrested during the times when he was not in the school for the feeble-minded. When we originally saw him, he had already engaged in one or two amateur burglaries, and these became more serious as time went on. In his neighborhood he was regarded as a nuisance. The habit of delinquency grew steadily upon him, unquestionably from the beginnings which he so clearly revealed to us.

Case 29. The girl whose case is next summarized was considered for two or three years to be perhaps mentally abnormal. The main problem with her was delinquency; she was at one time thought to be insane, and at another time feeble-minded, and finally it was decided that she would best be treated by disciplinary methods. The largest factor in this case, we found, was that of mental conflict.

Verna L. we first studied when she was about fifteen. For three years there had been great complaint about her bad behavior; all who knew the girl insisted that her misconduct was extreme. She had first been reported to a social agency, which, hearing of her peculiar actions, had turned her over to a dispensary clinic, where she was seen by an eminent neurologist who at first registered the opinion that she might be suffering from a psychosis, but after further observation stated that she was a case for discipline. She was later again studied by psychiatrists in a hospital, as well as by us.

Verna had given way to several forms of misbehavior.

At home she was extremely disobedient and violent. At times she cried and screamed so that the neighbors complained; she was mean to the children and particularly vindictive towards her mother. As a visitor put it, Verna frequently indulged in "free fights" at home. Dishes were broken by her; she threw kindling wood at her mother; she locked both parents out of their rooms at times; she once tried to pour boiling water on her mother and spat in her coffee cup; at one time the mother was found black and blue from having been struck by Verna. She bothered her family greatly; one curious way of doing it was by persisting in unnecessary scrubbing. Her threats to kill the family perhaps were of no great significance. On several occasions Verna engaged in thieving from shops down-town. After that she stole on a number of occasions. She took a ring from her mother, money from the pocketbook of a working woman, jewelry from some distant relatives, and a watch from a cousin, who will be mentioned later. Her family considered it a serious delinquency when she ran out from the bathroom totally naked before some company assembled in the house.

Verna was well developed and well nourished. Professional observation showed that at twelve years of age she was prematurely developed in sex characteristics; she had already menstruated. Vision was decidedly defective, yet she only wore her glasses at times. There was no complaint of headaches or signs of nervous disease, unless excessive biting of the finger nails might be so regarded. She dressed neatly and was rather an attractive girl as we saw her. She had been suffering from enuresis for a year or more previously, but earlier in life there had been no traces of this disorder. In none of the hospital reports do we note any physical findings of significance except the above.

In discussing the mentality of Verna I need not burden the reader with an account of the great irregularities which she displayed on tests, or her variabilities in conduct and general mental reactions. She had attained the seventh grade and her record was fair for scholarship and deportment in school. As a result of her mental tests, we concluded that she could not be fairly called feeble-minded, even though she failed on a few tests which normal children should be able to do. She could do long division correctly and write a fair hand. She had worked for two or three months in a department store, and there had been raised in position and salary.

We studied her after she had been already observed three times in a certain good hospital for the insane, with the result that they considered her "somewhat defective, but not insane", and after the opinion had been given by a well-known superintendent of an institution for the feeble-minded that she was not a fit subject for his place. We were unable to conclude that she was anything but slightly aberrational, showing many inhibitions which caused her to do poorly at times. This immediate diagnosis from general observation and from tests later appeared to be of less consequence than what was found by mental analysis.

About her developmental conditions we learned from a moderately intelligent father and mother — a couple that were willing to coöperate in every way, but who could not go beyond their own intelligence in treatment of the girl. We heard of absolutely nothing abnormal about her early development.

Verna was a happy, healthy child and was formerly very fond of school. She never had any serious illnesses. Certainly before she was ten years old the mother noticed that at times Verna was a very "cranky" child, but her first real outbreaks occurred when she was twelve; her enuresis also began then. On several occasions she had some sort of shivering spells in the daytime, with enuresis. These were the only attacks that were ever noted. Inquiry concerning family antecedents brought out only negative facts; nothing in heredity seemed to bear upon Verna's case.

No little trouble was experienced in getting at the original causes in this case. A good deal of resistance, which itself was easily enough perceived, had to be broken down. Our very first clue to the fact that there was any conflict in the background was Verna's repeated expression to us of secret hatred for a certain girl cousin, who was two or three years older. This was the one from whom Verna had stolen a watch not long since. "I didn't think her worth while to have a watch." Later Verna told us that for years thoughts of her cousin had been continually recurring to her, by night and by day. The gist of the results of our long efforts with Verna may be given as follows:

This cousin — who was regarded as a thoroughly nice girl by the family — had initiated Verna, when she was six and one-half years old, into her first sex experience. For a time they practiced mutual masturbation. Verna grew curious about sex affairs in general, and upon questioning her mother was invariably put off with the statement that she would know about those things when she grew older. After some years, when the two girls had been long separated,

Verna was much distressed by recurring thoughts about her cousin. It seemed to her as if she wanted the cousin near her, and yet she hated her. The first person whom Verna ever knew to take things that did not belong to her was this cousin. They were downtown in department stores a couple of times, and the cousin took some trinkets and urged Verna to do likewise.

When we tried to work back from the clue given us by Verna's expression of complete hatred for this cousin, we were met by the statement that Verna had something she would like to tell us. It took her long to make up her mind to do so, but when she did, the above story came out with great detail and also an account of her own solitary masturbation. The girl, then, had a mental life that her intimates had not even dreamed of; she was continually repressing a lot of knowledge with a lot of sex feeling, but sometimes gave way in the form of bad sex habits, and, especially, to the violent behavior at home. She informed us, too, that these "attacks" that her parents had described to us were the outcome of intense sex feeling coming on during the daytime; the shivering and the enuresis were all part of it. Very intense was Verna's feeling of hatred towards the cousin. "I think she was trying to ruin me. . . . Hate her? I could kill her. I feel inside me as if all the trouble that comes to me leads to her. She was trying to put me in a wrong way. If she does feel that way is no reason why she should go and tell me about it. She said she wasn't going to hurt me, she was just going to have some fun. She said, 'Come on, let's have some fun.' She never said anything about boys. Sometimes I wish I could die. . . . Sometimes I feel as if I should like to have her near me. Sometimes I think she is near me all the time. . . . Something in myself tells me it's bad."

It is to be noted that all of the above came out after Verna had made a great point of her own innocence to several of the people who had tried to help her previously, and also to us at first. This same trait was noted later at the institution for delinquents, where she was sent. One teacher writes that she believes her a constant masturbator, but the girl has a great deal of pride and is most anxious to hide from others that she has such desires.

This case was found most troublesome to handle; there was no one competent to do so in her own family. The mother was already a very sickly and broken-down woman, largely through worry about Verna; she died not long afterwards. Our exploration of this case was not followed by any highly individualized treatment, such as the case demanded. A further diagnosis of "not insane" was made by other observers, and the girl was sent, as a routine measure, to a school for delinquents. There she was regarded by some as quite dull mentally and a great falsifier, while others found her truthful and a faithful worker; a diversity of opinion was forthcoming, as always. However, her conduct improved, and a good prognosis was given. No stealing was indulged in there. After about eighteen months in the institution Verna returned home, and again there was much friction. A little tendency towards dishonesty was observed, but nothing very serious.

In the last two years Verna has sometimes been at home taking care of the younger children, and sometimes has been working in other households. The reports about her in other places are almost uniformly good. She is particularly industrious and fond of working hard at simple types of work. Whenever at home, she has been extremely abusive to the other children and very difficult to get along with. There seems to be little doubt that at times she indulges in her old bad habits, and the girl has never had, at least in her own home, the type of companionship which would lead her to recover herself. There have been no signs of deterioration or further development of a psychosis; indeed, on the whole, there has been considerable improvement, even though the case has never been treated as we had wished.

CHAPTER XIV

CONFLICTS RESULTING IN STEALING

COMING now to the different types of delinquency which may be, respectively, the definite expressions of reactions to elements in mental complexes, examples of stealing are first offered. (Many other cases of this common offense will be found in this volume.) It is most significant for the principles of mental analysis that in many of these cases a specific form of offense affords outlet for the conflict. Of course there may be other delinquencies, but these are generally subsidiary to the one significant type of misconduct. As noted in the chapter on Applications, working back from the special offense to its specific causation is what opens the door to understanding of the part that the mental mechanisms of conflict play in the given case and in misconduct in general.

Case 30. This case shows much stealing by a young boy upon a basis of mental conflict, the account of which was very directly and well expressed.

An agitated father and mother came to tell us about their only child, Manny J., a boy of ten, who had been recently found by the police after having been away from home several days. This boy had begun stealing about a year previously and soon afterwards had run away from home for the first time; this last delinquency he had since committed, after stealing, on numerous occasions.

The parents were foreigners who had been in this country since their boy was three years old. They had been industrious and fairly prosperous and maintained a good home. (We heard from outsiders that the family conditions were unusually good.) The developmental history of the child was entirely normal except for scarlet fever and an ear infection at six years, with a mastoid operation following it. Heredity was said to be negative, and one had little doubt that the sensible parents reported the truth. They had learned to speak very little English, but had placed their boy in a public school from whence came thoroughly good accounts of his deportment and scholarship. The sole trouble was the above mentioned delinquencies.

Manny had stolen considerable sums of money, both from his father's store and from other people. The parents had tried everything, whipping the boy and not whipping him, and the lad would talk most maturely to them about his bad conduct. There were certain peculiarities in his stealing; for instance, the father had repeatedly thought that he would train the boy by leaving money on the counter. When this was done, no money would disappear, but at about the same time money might be taken by him out of the father's pockets or from the clothes of other people. This last time he had broken into his father's strong box and taken one hundred and twenty dollars in cash and some checks; the latter he returned by mail after he had run away from home. When he was discovered by the police, he had bought himself new clothes. He had never stayed away from home longer than a few days, in the meantime sleeping about anywhere that he could. The parents were greatly distressed and found themselves in a quandary, because all their efforts to correct the boy had been unavailing. They maintained that he was a very bright, normal, and affectionate boy, and good in every other particular.

At the very first interview we found that this little boy had a great deal on his mind. He freely acknowledged his delinquencies, stating that when away from home he slept "by kids, in their basement." During the course of his conversation he said, "Sometimes I don't know what I am doing, I get so bothered." We successfully attempted to establish friendly relations with the boy, and these were maintained at this and at all succeeding interviews. "I think about what they say, and then I get all bothered." The boy at this stared off into the distance, and tears came into his eyes. He seemed remarkably puzzled about the whole affair. "I learned to steal from boys. They learned little kids how to smoke. I learned from them, but I don't smoke much now. The worst is the bad things they say. I try to forget, but I can't; it comes up in my mind and I think about it. They talk bad about girls, but I never saw them if they did it. I hear them, and then I get it in my head, and I can't leave go of it. I think and think, and then I forget what I want to do."

It would take many pages to recount even a small part of what this boy told us about his life. We found him a very bright boy, who could do very well on mental tests — a nervous, tense little fellow, who wanted to go home and try all over again to do better. We found there was too much drinking of tea and coffee on his part, but outside of that there were no bad personal habits; his smoking was a very slight affair.

In boyish fashion, he always wanted to deal with more recent matters, not to thoughtfully consider beginnings, but in the course of a few days the beginnings were elicited, and we found we could largely corroborate his story through the parents. The very first money he had taken was forty cents he was intrusted with to deliver to another person. A certain boy was with him who was a lad of poor reputation, according to the parents, but Manny could not remember the exact details of that particular day. Before that he had in his head the idea of stealing, because he had learned about it when they lived at another place. The first person he ever saw stealing was a boy from whom he heard a certain word. He did not ask the lad what the word meant, but he began saying it himself secretly.

Over and over again, Manny insisted with us that these were the things that made him steal, namely, bad words and ideas about girls. Some of the boys who stole little things told him bad things about girls. "I heard what they said, and then I would want to do that myself. I try to forget, and then I can't forget." There were also some attempts by the other boys to tamper with the person of this lad, but evidently nothing much was done to him.

When Manny was asked point-blank to explain his own stealing, for example, in this last instance, his answer was very direct. "That boy got to telling me all sorts of stuff about girls again and robbings, and that got me sore because of the kids telling me, and I went and took the keys and got into that place where my father had the money." Most vehemently he told us, "I get sore lots of times, because that bothers me, about what the boys tell me about the girls. I took the money. I don't know for what I done that myself. I knew where it was, but I don't know why I wanted to take it." After taking this money and leaving home, he apparently spent much upon these boys as well as upon himself. It was true, evidently, that they had told him to steal; they knew that he had taken things before, but he threw little blame on them for this, only for telling him bad sex affairs and getting him so stirred up in his mind about it. One boy had shown him some bad pictures, but it was not that so much as the words they had said which renewed in his mind what he had heard long before from this boy who was the first one whom he had ever known to steal.

We felt much interest in noting this boy's attitude toward himself. He sat with a perplexed look upon his face as he tried to think out his own career, and he seemed to be genuinely interested in his own mental processes as he made them plain to himself and to us. In a typical boyish way he would say certain things, and then later, "Oh, no, I remember", or, "But now I think of that." He frequently told us that he was "worried" and "bothered", using phraseology unusual for a small boy. He expressed himself at times as if he were subject to some sort of attacks of ideas coming into his head, just as an older person might tell about a mental obsession. He was at all times perfectly confident that if these other thoughts would drop away from him, he would certainly cease stealing. Over and over he stated that this was what led him to his delinquencies.

After learning from his father about the peculiar feature of Manny's stealing from pockets, we asked the boy to think back to any early experiences with that form of stealing — he first having told us that no boys that he now associated with stole in that way. It seems that just about the time that he was first hearing about sex affairs — this could be closely placed because of his residence on a certain street at that time — he saw a boy, a member of their group, sneak up to a pile of workmen's clothes and take some coats back into an alley, where he went through the pockets. This he now remembered vividly, although he apparently had never consciously connected the affair with his present troubles, or with his impulse which made him apparently go out of his way to steal in more difficult fashion when he might have taken things nearer at hand.

Of course, it was perfectly clear that nothing could be done for this boy unless his obsessions were corrected. We found that his good father had never known a thing of his inner turmoil nor uttered a word to him on the subject of sex affairs. We at once took up the whole matter with his parents, who, although they said they were at their wits' end in the matter, were willing to make a new start.

(Six months later we heard that a marvelous change had followed our analysis of this case. The previously complaining parents reported to us with many expressions of delight that their boy, Manny, was a changed character. There has been no recurrence of his delinquencies.)

Case 31. The following is an instance of excessive stealing carried on by a young boy over a period of about two years, without the slightest understanding of the essential features of the case being gained either by the parents, teachers, or others who tried to cope with the situation.   Mental analysis quickly revealed the factors in the background.

When he was only eight years and two months of age, Barty M. was brought to us with a long record of thieving.   His father, a fairly intelligent working-man, stated that what he had to pay back for this boy's stealing had been a distinct hardship to the family.   Barty had been thieving for two years, and his behavior in this respect was getting worse of late. Letters from two different schools were sent to us; the boy had been rejected from both.   One principal stated that Barty "seems to have a mania for stealing"; he had twice taken money from his teacher's purse, and warning and scolding had failed to deter him from prowling about when the school was not in session. The report from the other principal read, "The boy seems to be really a kleptomaniac and should be put in an institution where he should have special over-sight."   Articles were said to be missed whenever he was about.   He took keys for which he had no use and hid them.   One teacher stated that he would steal anything he could get his hands on, and that after scolding and punishment on one day, he would be found rummaging in some room on the next day. Many times he had stolen from home.   On one occa-sion he had taken his father's gold watch and sold it for a nickel.   His father said that when the boy went into stores, he seemed to make a definite endeavor not to leave until he had succeeded in stealing some-thing.   From one shop he had taken a violin.   His father insists that he steals things whether they have any value for him or not. His first reported stealing was of pennies from news stands with a boy of his acquaintance.

We found a well-cared-for little boy, with good features, bright eyes, and shapely head. His tonsils had been removed previously. The only abnormality found was a typical habit-spasm of the muscles about the eyes.

The boy was in the second grade and did well on tests up to his grade and age; he was evidently rather a bright type, with a good fund of information. Our findings agreed with the teacher's statement.

Careful inquiry into the heredity brought forth nothing of interest bearing on the problem. The boy's development had been normal in every way. The parents chided themselves for their lack of foresight in leaving the little lad with relatives for two or three months a couple of years previously while they were away from the city. It was clear to them that he had started in delinquency then, but how to check him now was beyond them. They had tried admonitions and all ordinary punishments without avail. The only point of weakness was the fact that the mother, part of the time, was away from home earning money. Barty was the oldest of several children, and the father was keenly anxious that some arrangement should be made so that he would not contaminate the others.

This was another case where we found almost no trouble in getting at the essential facts inside of a few hours. Barty gave us a very remarkable account of mental conflicts, one of the most straightforward that we have ever heard. When approached from the standpoint of beginnings, the inside history of the trouble was rapidly brought to light. There was another boy whom he began to tell us about, a boy he did not see any more because the father would not allow the families to associate. This lad had shown him the trick of stealing from news stands, but more than that, he had taught Barty a lot of bad words. It was only words; he had been shown no bad pictures.

When Barty was asked if anything nowadays bothered him or made him nervous, he made it very plain to us that certain words worried him by coming up in his mind. There were certain words which he sometimes involuntarily started to say, and then, when he found that he didn't consciously want to utter them he usually forced them back. He was not even willing to speak one of these in our office, but finally spelled one, showing the strange reaction that we have known other children to exhibit in a similar situation. Further in the interview the question of what made him steal was taken up. Barty answered us that it was the bad words, and that he spells out these words, or starts to say them, or they come up in his mind, and that is what happens always before he steals. He had never spoken at all of this matter to his parents. No one else had ever talked to him about sex subjects except a little girl, a sister of this other boy; she had drawn some peculiar pictures, the import of which he did not understand, but she indicated to him that they represented such things. The boy himself introduced the subject of his dreams about stealing, but they were incoherently related in childish fashion. Barty insisted that no one had taught him any bad sex habits, and he seemed not to know definitely about these, only in a vague sort of way through the words which he had been taught; indeed, he insisted, and it really appeared, that he did not know the exact meaning of the words themselves.

An attempt to analyze the background of some particular stealing event brought out the fact that before he had looted his teacher's pocketbook, the other day, he had been thinking of the old affairs with the other boy and of the bad words and of the stealing from news stands. When he took the watch from his father, he had also been previously thinking about the other fellow. The father had to sleep during the daytime because he worked at night, and it was supposed to be the boy's duty to be quiet and attend to the house when he was not at school. (Because his mother was so much away from home Barty had been given many hours when his mind was unoccupied and unarmed against the ideas and imageries connected with his earlier unfortunate experiences.) Again and again he reaffirmed that his mind was assailed by thoughts which he endeavored to repress, that it was the thoughts about what this boy had told him, thoughts which he had never mentioned to any one else, that made him steal.

On talking over the matter with the father, who showed rather meager comprehension of the whole situation, it was clear to us that the case would have to be worked out away from home. We advised that the social worker who brought in the case should find another home temporarily for the boy. Perhaps relatives might be found who would take him, and, particularly, we insisted that some one whom he saw often must directly face out with this little lad the real nature of his troubles, as he himself wished to have them faced.

During further trial at home for several months

by the wish of his parents, Barty still engaged in stealing. We felt that nothing really constructive was
being done in the case, and indeed, upon seeing the
boy again, we found that he was still being troubled
occasionally by his old thoughts. He repeatedly
ran away from home during this interval, but evidently did try at times to do better. His naïve statement was, "I try to think about good things now and
to get rid of those bad words. I try, but I can't
always. There is just six words now that I am trying
to get rid of. That one that used to bother me most
I don't think much about any more."

We felt that it was distinctly a bad circumstance
that he had been occasionally seeing the other boy
again. The parents were now ready to take our
advice, and the boy was placed in another home, where
for over a year he has been an entirely different boy;
there have been no complaints whatever of his stealing. He has been with a woman who understands
something of these cases and who has endeavored to
make him confide his difficulties to her.

Case 32. Thoroughly representative and marvel-
ously illuminating is the following career of pathological stealing, or "kleptomania", which we have watched
for years. The misdoer, a young woman of high intelligence, had discernment enough to seek advice herself about her own long-continued aberrations of conduct. Through several favoring circumstances we
were enabled to obtain not only the outlines, but also
many interesting details of this person's conduct and
of her mental life which pertained to her delinquencies.
It is a matter of no small interest that this young
woman was never in the hands of the police.

Mildred E., when we were first asked to study her
case, was attending a noted eastern seminary in her
home city. By a distant relative we were given a
first statement of numerous peculations which had
extended over months, but which did not presume
to include all of her offenses. Mildred had no immediate family, and the widowed and childless aunt, with
whom she had lived for many years, knew very little
about her intimate life. The girl was now eighteen
and had been away intermittently at boarding schools
before matriculating at this seminary. Between times
in the last two years, and even during her attendance
at school, she had readily earned money for herself.
Mildred was looking forward to some, as yet undecided,
kind of professional work; she had always given high
promise of good intellectual attainment. She was
also very well and strong, and for all of these reasons
the aunt had felt that the girl was very little of a problem. Her tendencies to mischief and self-assertion
were no more than many an adolescent girl shows,
and appeared to represent only "healthy outbreaks."

A statement of Mildred's discernible qualities is
easy to give. She appeared to be a very well-developed
and strong young woman; examination showed no
sensory or other defect of importance. She looked
somewhat flabby, and her slightly slouchy attitude
and rather pasty color suggested insufficient exercise.
To this neglect Mildred confessed, and also to a certain amount of constitutional physical indolence, in
spite of the possession of much latent strength which
could be displayed at pleasure.

Mildred's intellectual development was best measured by her scholarship records. We had the opportunity of seeing her school marks for years back and

of judging her ability in other ways. She demonstrated the possession of well-rounded capabilities; she was equally good in mathematics and history and best of all in language. Perhaps Mildred's mental powers may be most significantly summarized by citing a statement of the principal of the seminary, herself a woman of large experience: "Mildred has the best mind in a thousand — comparing her with young women of high school grade." Mildred's further development since we have known her has justified these earlier conclusions. When at times she has not done well with her studies, it has been from downright neglect of them, mostly accounted for by inner mental stress.

We ascertained nothing of great import for us concerning Mildred's developmental history on the physical side, and she showed no signs of having grown in any but the most normal way. She only suffered from very slight attacks of the diseases of childhood. As the result of a fall, she is said to have been threatened with some spinal trouble at two or three years, and wore for a time a special sort of support. Menstruation came rather late, at fifteen years; there have been no abnormalities of this function.

The facts of heredity have no particular significance for us, except in one point, namely, concerning the tendencies of Mildred's father. He was a journalist of ability who showed hypersexual tendencies, and on account of this and some alleged dishonesty, the mother left him. She was a frail woman who soon afterwards died, leaving Mildred at eight years of age, without income, to be brought up by the aunt. Not long after that the father himself was accidentally killed.

A thorough-going account of Mildred's life, even as we have it, would equal a small book in size, with very few uninteresting pages. I shall attempt here merely sufficient statement of the issues of her career, so that the reader may appreciate the extent to which her conduct was motivated by mental conflict. Besides this, I hope to make specific and clear the fact of the conflict itself. For entire confidence in the reality of many of the statements, we are indebted to Mildred's notebooks and diaries, which have been kept since preadolescence including the several years before she knew that her case was ever going to be the subject of professional study. We have known other adolescent delinquents to keep a diary; and even the idea of a cryptogram, such as the one Mildred invented and extensively used, we have heard of in other instances. It is Mildred's superior powers of expression and self-analysis and reasoning which make her own study of her case so extremely valuable for professional people. She is gifted with great powers of objective and subjective "awareness." The mental mechanisms at work in her conflict and the ensuing conduct are entirely typical.

The misdoing that Mildred indulged in should, perhaps, at once be particularized. When we saw her first she had for years been accustomed to steal in the most extensive fashion. Earlier, apparently, her petty thieving had gone on more or less steadily, but of late there had been much fighting against her impulses in this direction, with the result that only from time to time were there definite outbreaks — orgies of stealing would be engaged in.

When Mildren came to us, one of the earliest comments that she made was that she did not think she was exactly a "kleptomaniac." She volunteered this information because she had been thinking and even reading about the subject. She combated the idea of such a classification of herself, and said that she did not believe she took things for which she had no use. However, even a superficial analysis of the facts showed us clearly that this was a weak defense on her part, for she quickly revealed her impulse towards stealing itself and not towards taking objects for their value. In fact, we later studied the remarkable accounts which Mildred kept of her peculations at different times — kept for the purpose of ultimately paying back what she had stolen — and these showed clearly the absurd uselessness to her of many of the articles stolen. This point will later come out more distinctly. It would be difficult to enumerate the thefts which this clever girl had committed, but no doubt the number would range well up in the hundreds.

Another type of misconduct had just been displayed by Mildred at the time we first saw her. She had on several occasions slipped out of her room at night and stayed until daybreak, remaining out under the most incongruous circumstances, sleeping in some one's back yard on an old carpet, or on some back porch. By carefully planned falsehoods, she had been able thus to sleep out for a week in the spring, while her aunt thought that she was at the seminary, and the authorities there supposed she was at home with her aunt.

Falsifying was never a prominent delinquency with Mildred. In general, she was an unusually frank girl with the few who she felt understood her. To her aunt, no doubt, she occasionally told a few lies, "fibs", as she called them. In all of our long acquaintance we have only known her to deceive us, and then slightly, in regard to one or two events; in the main everything has turned out to be as she asserted. During the ensuing years, with the increase of temptations, Mildred has succumbed to sex delinquencies; the phases of this part of her career make the fact of her conflict even more certain.

Mildred graduated early from the grammar grades and began at twelve or thirteen to be an omnivorous and rapid reader. It was no credit to those who were directing her that she was allowed to lose at least a couple of years educationally through change of plans and irregular attendance at her boarding school. To be sure, the necessity for economy influenced her aunt, but the girl was developing, undirected, an un-usual amount of mental life, composed of ill-assorted facts, vivid imaginative processes, and much adolescent introspective reasoning. She first began to earn money when she was about sixteen by working for a few days at a time in shops, and in a department store during one entire vacation.

This account of Mildred's case may now leave her general mental development and proceed to her im-pulses, their origins and outcome in misconduct. The reader will best get some idea of the vividness of Mildred's original case-history from her own words to us and from some quotations from her diary; these are interspersed with our connecting remarks, which are introduced to save scores of pages of quotation which otherwise would be necessary.

Concerning Mildred's stealing we heard the follow-ing: "I have worked at F.'s for the last four weeks, since vacation started, but before that I had not taken anything since December. Then there was a big row

at school, and I was connected with it, but other things
were really the trouble with me. I didn't take anything else until three weeks ago. After once I begin,
I cannot seem to stop. I did stop for five months,
but that seems to be my limit. . . . Sometimes
when I do wrong I feel as if I cannot stand it. It
worries me because I do such foolhardy things. Sometimes I get scared when I get home, scared that I have
done these things for which I might get caught. But
when I am taking things, I just say to myself, 'Well,
I'm not going to get scared just because there are half
a dozen clerks around the counter.' When I get home
it is different; then I am scared. Sometimes I think
I *have* to do these things and get terribly reckless;
it seems then to make life interesting."

"Just what did I take last time? Well, there was
a lot of things. I took a copy of Wells' Algebra at T.'s
on Washington Street; I don't know why, I guess
I just wanted to take it. Then I took a twelve-cent
ring, but put it back; I could have bought it if I had
wanted it. Then I went to F.'s and took a book —
I forget the name of it — then I walked around the
block with it and put it back. I went over to M.'s
and had in mind to take a novel. I had no particular
one in mind, but wanted one of the very latest ones.
I rode up in the elevator, but thought better of it
and came down again. Over at T.'s I inquired how
much the algebra was; I told the clerk I didn't have
the money, and he turned away and I took the book.
I did these things at the noon hour. Then I went
back to work and felt so nervous that I asked the
superintendent if I could come home because I felt
so badly, and he said yes. I have been staying for
a few weeks with my friends, the Smiths, who knew

that I stole last winter at the school, and they are
trying to help me to do better. I have promised to
tell them whenever I take things. Of course, I was
ashamed to go back to the Smiths. Of course, I need
not have told them, but I was ashamed not to tell
them, so I slept out in a back yard after I had pretended over the telephone that I was going home for
the night. The next day Mrs. Smith came down to
the shop, and I went home with her, but I kept right
on stealing things for a time then. I took silk stockings and pearl beads and some booklets and silver
buckles and a lot of other things in the next few days.
I just picked them up and walked out with them;
there was no trouble in doing that. Mrs. Smith asked
me last Saturday if I had been doing well, and I had
to tell her that I had not. I felt so cut up that I
could barely stay there, finally I skipped out late at
night and slept in an old place where I had slept before,
in a back yard on the porch; if it was raining, I would
sleep on the porch. This time I didn't have any
money and didn't have a mouthful of food for break-
fast or lunch. The Smiths called me up, but I just
wouldn't go there that day. I told them I would
go back to my aunt's. They didn't know her very
well, because I had gone to them by myself. I have
always been very well. . . . Look at me now; I
haven't slept in a bed for six days, and that goes to
show I am a pretty strong girl."

"I wonder why it is so different with me on different
days. Sometimes it is not hard at all for me to stop
from stealing. Other days it is. Last year it was
just stealing and stealing, from school and home and
friends. Then I went from June until November.
I am afraid I used to get up schemes. In school I

was always thinking up ideas and then wondering
whether I would be found out or not. Of course,
it took my mind off my work. I got to spending
money freely at one time, and it just seemed as if I
had to. To keep this up I used to take change from
my aunt, and at school I used to take out of girls'
pocketbooks, or even pennies in the dressing room.
It was during the winter there came up one of those
scenes I hate; oh, how I hate them, but they said
they'd give me another chance. The principal says
she does not want to stand in the way of my finishing
my education, but why did I do it; that's just what
I don't know. Why it should be me that should do
these things when other girls don't, is more than I can
tell."

Of course, on numerous occasions Mildred has been
questioned by us about her earliest beginning of stealing; no one else could tell us about that. "Do you
know, I believe that I began from untruthfulness and
worked into little dishonesty. That's as it seems to
me, now that you asked me to think about it. I
would do something I was told not to do in little ways,
perhaps take a little more cream than I was allowed
to take, or maybe two apples instead of one. I am
sure that I went from untruthfulness to stealing. . . .
I have been trying to think why there is fascination
in it for me, and it seems to me I have been led on
from one thing to another; it went from a cookie to
a nickel, from a nickel to a dime. I got much from
my aunt through deception, and I took from many
other people in lots of ways — my aunt had boarders
at one time. One man kept nickels in a drawer for
the telephone. . . . One time it seems as if the
candy habit had much to do with it. It seemed as

if I just must have candy, and if I didn't have money to buy it, I used to take candy from the store; that was a school store, and once I took a book there and sold it to a girl for a dollar and a quarter to get money, which I'd spend in the same store. It seemed wrong to me to be so intemperate about that candy, to have such strong desire for it. One winter I pretended my cough was worse so that I could get money from my aunt for candy. I used to eat so much sometimes that I didn't want my meals. I used to do peculiar things in that way. When I was working, I once went two days without eating at all; I just had water. I well remember the first time I took any big chances on stealing; I was staying with a girl overnight. I got up very early one morning and slipped down to the parlor and took some money that was there. I always thought a good deal of those people, and I don't think they ever accused me, but, after all, I was the only one in the house besides their own family. That was big chances. I mailed that money back to them not long ago without any name. I made a good deal by deceiving as well as by stealing, and I have been terribly untruthful in that way, but I have always tried to have a grain of sense about it, and I have been discreet; I have never told glaring false-hoods. . . . It was always a fascination for me to feel that I could get what I wanted when I wanted it, though later I had the feeling that I ought to pay for it and sometimes did so. . . . But they knew I stole in school. I was getting into a good deal of trouble through disobedience, and I got scolded and pretty nearly suspended, both at boarding school and the seminary."

Mildred was never sanctimonious with us; her

contriteness was shown a hundred times more by what she had written in her diary than by what she said. On several occasions, after a period of excessive stealing, she recorded what she had taken. Her notes of one of the more recent orgies, extending over a few days, stated that she had stolen money from three different people and taken nine separate articles or parcels from shops. The girl made little to us of her attempts to repay what she had taken, but we heard from the Smiths, who made a more detailed investigation of her recent stealing than we ever cared to, that she worked very hard and saved very carefully for long periods to remit, anonymously, conscience money in repayment of what she had taken.

We were, naturally, very keenly interested in the fact that Mildred had been willing on quite a few occasions to do such a strange thing as to slip into some one's back yard late at night and sleep there. We recognized the recklessness and adventuresomeness of the girl, at least as showing strongly at times, but that hardly would explain, it seemed to us, this behavior. Mildred attempted to make light of it, first saying how she liked the open sky, and then, that it was all the same to her because she was accustomed to a sleeping porch at her aunt's. It gradually came out that on all but one of these night escapades she had slept in the same place, and finally we learned that she knew the people who lived in the cottage. It was the home of a former teacher, a middle-aged man and his family. Inquiry into what prompted her in this direction revealed that at one time, a couple of years previously, a tremendous platonic friendship for this man had existed in Mildred's mind, all unknown to him.

"There has always been somebody in my life that
could have controlled me, somebody to whom I would
not tell an untruth. That has been my code of honor.
The summer before last was very hard. It was because I could not see any more some one who was
very dear to me. I don't know whether you would
call it love, or what you would call it; this was a man
that I admired and thought a great deal of in every
way. He seemed to inspire my life. He was a teacher.
He never said anything to me at all, but if you won't
laugh, I'll tell you that for six or eight months there
was not an hour in the day that I did not think of him.
I don't know whether you call love a sweet pain or not,
but that is what it seemed to be. . . . I have always been lonely and gone much by myself. I never
had many friends. I never talked with girls about
boys, but I did think much about them. Ever since
I was eight or ten years old there have always been
some boys in the schoolroom that I have thought a
good deal of. I was always shy and ashamed of it
and maybe did not speak to them at all. I was never
forward like other girls. There would be some one
in every class when I went to public school, but it
would change. I never knew any of them that were
very bad, or who stole. . . . Well, the way I feel
about young people is that I guess a good many of
them are pretty gay. I know that nine girls out of
ten are looser than I would like them to be, and that
is why I never made friends with many of them, even
in the grammar school. There are not many of them
so strait-laced and pure and innocent as I have been.
It has always seemed to me, without the shadow of a
doubt, that I was better than nine out of ten girls.
They will go out once in a while and do things I

would not do, come in early in the morning from dances."

Mildred, in the early days we knew her, made much of the gloominess of life, as it appeared to her at times. She had considered this point and called our attention to the fact that she had checked up in her diary these days of depression and found out that they did not correspond to her menstrual periods. (We were also convinced from our own study of her diaries, which she taught us to interpret, that her stealing escapades were not regularly near the time of menstruation.) "I have times of being very gloomy and depressed, and they come on me when I think of lots of different things. For a long time I have carried around corrosive sublimate with me. I heard about that being a poison, and I had a package with me. I always said to myself if the worst comes to the worst and they catch me, I'll fix it all before I get to the police station." (It was a rather amusing episode that the hem of the long coat into which she had this poison sewed became torn, and the poison escaped, unknown to her, and caused a dermatitis medicamentosa over her ankles.) That Mildred at other times carried poisons we happened to know, for once, after a period of backsliding, she handed over to us a bottle of laudanum. At that time she also gave up a small revolver. It is highly significant that as time has gone on, Mildred's periods of depression have become less heavy and frequent, corresponding to her relief from mental conflict and the breaking up of her habit of stealing.

The high ambitions which Mildred has frequently expressed to us, and which are found stated so ardently in her diaries, have been held with constancy — even

have been reasserted after the young woman had sunk
to great depths. Nowhere are her resolves better
stated than in an idyll written soon after daybreak
one spring morning in a park overlooking the sea,
whence she had repaired after sleeping out all night
on the old carpet on the back-yard porch. We may
excerpt the following :

"Sunday morning. The beauty and peace and
quiet of this spot here in the park fills my heart with
joy and takes from me all worries and cares and anguish.
I feel as the birds and the flowers. God will provide
for me as for them. I will enjoy the moment. 'Use
well the moment. What the hour brings for thy use
is in thy power.' . . . I think I enjoy this sense of
being entirely my own master, of having the day to
do as I please in and go where I want. . . . I have
longed to do this before and yet never dared to when
at home. Now I seem to dare to do anything and
everything. I won't go back anywhere until I feel
surer than I do now that it will never be repeated.
The more I do it the greater the fascination becomes,
and yet it means my ruin if I don't win. As J. said,
it means the 'pen' and a ruined life unless I learn entire
self-control in all things as well as stealing, for it would
be the same thing with smoking, drinking, or opiates
as it has been with candy and everything else. But
I can't go into hysterics and tragedies on this glorious,
beautiful morning in this lovely spot with the bright
sunshine and clear sky and beautiful shades of green.
I want to love life, enjoy the true and beautiful, and
gain strength for this last final effort. The scene
makes me forget circumstances, consequences, and
makes me at rest. 'Whatever line you follow, remember you have the strength for noble endeavor

and grand result, and use it.' 'Resolve to be thyself and know that he who finds himself loses his misery.'"

Various short bits of poetry and record of numerous resolutions attest throughout her diaries Mildred's real desires and her introspective realization of her own moods and tendencies. Sometimes done carelessly, her writing in other places shows considerable literary ability. Two more quotations will show something of her complex nature. On one New Year's eve she summarizes the past year as:

"A year to regret and weep over, but not worth it; a year of wasted opportunities and weakness, and yet all to be forgotten except for the lessons it may have taught me for all time. Let it go, and thank God for the new one — may it be better, truer, and nobler, may I learn from what this year has brought me, the value of self-control, of a good, noble, true and unselfish life; of work, economy, time, energy, and of the good, the true, the beautiful."

On a certain birthday Mildred writes a summary of her own character: "A dreamer and an idealist, romantic and quick-tempered, warm-hearted; life governed entirely by good or bad impulsive moments, lazy and extravagant, yet a good worker when aroused. . . . Capable of great things if only there was some impulse to bring out the best and hold to it. . . . Desperately lonely. . . . Only attracted by a good grown-up man, who has a good influence and a great one on my life. . . . Governed by habits and appetite, continually at war with self, and striving to be better and understand self, a weak, morally useless girl, . . . a strange, self-centered child-woman, for whose condition there is much excuse, who alone knows of her own struggles of the soul and sufferings."

Mildred remembers her own feelings of childhood quite clearly. She tells us that she has always been irritable at home, or at least ever since she was ten or twelve. Her aunt scolded her, and "There was no use in treating me that way all the time, even if I did do things. She used to say I was just like my father. After I started taking things I used to say to myself about her, 'If you talk that way when you know half of what I have done, how would you talk if you knew all?'" Her aunt, in her stern way, was, however, always good to Mildred, as the girl acknowledged; she loved her and wanted her to get an education. After a certain scene at home, Mildred says that she walked up and down the streets, sobbing; not that her aunt was perhaps so much to blame, but Mildred herself felt so irritated at the scolding.

It was when Mildred was asked to analyze the causes of her own irritability at that time when she was so young that she, with the frankness she has always displayed with us, told us of her sex life. It seems that before she was twelve, quite involuntarily, she had a great awakening of sex feeling and developed many auto-erotic phenomena. These experiences were a daily affair with her, and she learned by herself, so she stated, some means of gratification. (More than likely Mildred's story about this is the truth, because her diary gives many indications of the self-centerment and loneliness which would naturally be developed under these circumstances.) She told no one about it, but after a time, through self-realization and some little reading of books, she came to the conclusion that her habits were wrong. She began to put up a fight against her feelings in this direction, and a desperate fight it soon proved to be. There were many indications of her battles, both in her diaries and in what she told us.

It seems that Mildred was only about ten when, from hearing about him, she suspected what kind of man her father was — that he had been very free with women — and when her aunt spoke of her resemblance to him, there may have been more than a little suggestion conveyed to her by the statement. Her aunt had talked nicely to her about sex matters when she was thirteen or fourteen, but already the girl had picked up, in the usual ways, more than her aunt in the least suspected. Mildred made much to us of her excess of sex longing which had already developed at twelve years of age, beginning as merely a physical affair and even before she knew at all what sex functions were. She is positive that the idea never came from others and that she has always wanted to be a good girl. "I have always thought of affairs with boys being so much worse than any stealing I did, but lately I have gotten to think that perhaps a girl who would do one thing would do the other."

Mildred has never been able to trace for us the earliest association of her sex feeling with her impulse to steal. We could never ascertain that the two were related by any definite early experiences. She gave the details of how she first obtained sex gratification by herself, but there were no experiences concerning stealing at this time which impressed themselves in any way on her memory. In a general way, however, it was just about this period when she began taking things; of that she has always seemed sure since we first asked her for her best recollections on the point. It was after she herself evolved the idea that these sex practices were exhausting and generally bad for her, and she consequently stopped them, that her inner life began more intensely; then she commenced her diaries. She manifested platonic friendships and regarded herself as a person who was striving against part of her own nature. Now she began to have definite times of giving way to the stealing impulse, which for two years already had manifested itself, but not in periods.

Mildred looked upon her overweening desire for candy as a temptation, too, that should be striven against, and one that was correlated with her tendency to steal. When about sixteen, Mildred commenced the clandestine smoking of cigarettes; when she was in a troubled, restless mood, they quieted her nerves, she said. She never developed enough of a smoking habit so that any fight against this was necessary; she considered herself justified in occasionally using tobacco, since it helped her through periods of disquietude.

In reviewing the violent attacks of impulse to steal shown during the last couple of years, Mildred realizes now, although she never formulated it before, that these were related to her sex impulse; she remembers that she was fighting off the one when she was giving way to the other. The stealing is an expression of her reckless desire at times for adventure; she craves to do something active and extraordinary, just as she did the nights when she slept out, or when she entered the Smiths' house like a burglar, up the fire escape, after remaining away till midnight.

Considering the whole structure of Mildred's mental conflict, I may enumerate the following constituent parts which enter, one after another, into it, or which appeared as expressions of it: (a) She early learned that her father was sexually immoral. (*b*) She was scoldingly likened to him — a suggestion of heredity that long continued to appear ominous to her. (*c*) Mildred found out, before she was in her teens, that her aunt, in whom she used to confide, was not always a teller of the truth; this caused Mildred to repress much and developed in her a hidden critical attitude towards her relative. (*d*) The child herself then developed a habit of secrecy and untruthfulness, just during the time when she was having auto-erotic experiences. (*e*) At about fifteen years developed the struggle against the sex feelings which had been going on for two or three years. (*f*) This led to the establishment of a particularly vivid inner mental life, including one-sided platonic friendships, great dwelling on ideals as a defense against backsliding, etc. (*g*) At this period a previously existing tendency to slight deceits grew into larger misrepresentations, the intemperate use of candy, and stealing in petty ways. The latter, before long, developed into expert thieving from shops as the expression of an irresistible desire for excitement when fighting off sex feelings. (*h*) Also, Mildred's urgent impulses led her now to be a reckless mischief-maker at school. Later, in the same moods, she indulged in especially foolhardy actions, such as sleeping out at night, walking the streets for long in the rain, leaving and entering her room at night by way of the fire escape, stealing in a spirit of bravado just to prove to herself that she could take things from under the eyes of clerks in stores.

The exact age at which Mildred began stealing was not nearly so easy to determine as it is in many other cases of mental conflict where there has been an original definite event welding a link of association between the idea of stealing and some other emotional experience. We have indicated that in Mildred's case stealing appears to have been preceded by less serious types of misconduct and was gradually developed as a vicarious phenomenon. She was probably between fifteen and sixteen before she really did more than keep pennies and nickels out of her aunt's change in order to buy candy. She evidently experienced at that age her first satisfaction in stealing for its own sake by taking notebooks, paper, and pencils, while she was temporarily working in a store.

Mildred stated very definitely on several occasions that her serious stealing was always the reaction to an inner feeling: "I just wanted to make things more exciting. For some weeks before this last time I had been feeling the same old thing, wondering if I could steal in the same old way, and how it would feel. It was just like playing with fire to see if it was hot." We noted that from time to time she expressed herself — quite unconsciously, since she made no direct reference to any relationship between the two temptations — in the same way about her sex impulses. All these points bear upon Mildred's *abreaction* to her mental conflict. Later observation and interpretation of her conduct greatly aids our understanding of the genesis of her tendencies.

When we first saw Mildred she was already in a period of moral transition, having given up her imaginary platonic friendships and having begun to doubt whether she was so much better, after all, than other girls who were not so innocent as she claimed to be. Mildred had been evidently helped to this last viewpoint by the suggestion of a teacher who had said that "a girl who would steal would do the other thing."

She had also already surprised herself, she who had declared herself recently in her diary as caring for the attentions of no young man, by allowing a young fellow at first acquaintance to caress her. From dwelling on this first real experience with the opposite sex quickly grew intense physical feelings. As a result of these she felt that she might "just as well run away at once and go to the devil"; she could not help herself, she would eventually end by being bad. It seemed like a touch-and-go performance with her, she said; in a minute she might be right down in the depths. She endeavored now to get strength from religion, but really perceived, so she stated, that what she needed was the company of a man.

Mildred's later history includes severe moral lapses that have no excuse for being given here in detail, but the main facts are full of significance for us. As we have seen her at intervals during several years, Mildred has been frank, as ever, with us, and has always showed much intelligent apperception of her own nature and possibilities. Never did she give up her desire for a good education, although its furtherance was much interrupted by her backslidings. She intermittently went on with her schooling until she was adequately fitted for the calling which she had chosen.

For some months after we first knew her, strife against both sex temptations and stealing was bitter. Only once, however, so far as we have ascertained, was there ever any more thieving indulged in. This was during the period when she was first going over her case with us. For her behavior in sex affairs we cannot say as much, but to whatever lengths she went, each time she recovered herself with only a temporary submerging of her ideals. After a time she was established in marital relations and became much

274   MENTAL CONFLICTS

was established in marital relations and became much happier. Now she is an absolutely different person in appearance and bearing, who looks back upon earlier days in the spirit of her recent utterance to us, "It is very curious what some people go through before they settle down."

Concerning the issuance of her conflict: during its exploration with us she faced the facts in straightforward fashion, and the result has been complete cessaation for years past of all impulse towards stealing.

CHAPTER XV

CONFLICTS RESULTING IN RUNNING AWAY

RUNNING away from home as a type of delinquency sometimes originating from mental conflict has special interest for us because of the suffering which frequently accrues to the delinquent during his wanderings. The strength that an urge evolved within may show towards anti-social behavior is nowhere better demonstrated than by these foreseeable unpleasurable results, sometimes oft repeated. From our many cases where this comes out clearly I have selected for citation here three examples, one of which is an instance of intermittent *vagrancy*. (Further illustrations of this topic are Cases 6, 10, 14, 17, and 21.) Some of these exhibit behavior reactions which in present-day terminology might be designated as *nomadism.*[1]

Case 33. We have known this boy, who began giving an immense amount of trouble at a very early age, during a period of seven years. Not until after several years did we feel persuaded that we really knew the main cause of his delinquent tendencies. It was easy enough in this instance to blame other factors, because with superficial knowledge of his background in heredity and environment these appeared distinctly.

---

[1] The term *Wanderlust* is too loosely used to be of value in our discussion.

Deeper consideration and more thorough knowledge,
however, revealed mental conflict as the main cause.

Emil V., born in Vienna, was brought to this country
when he was six years of age.   On the eighth day here,
in this strange city of Chicago, Emil ran away for the
first time.   Up to the present, it would be difficult to
enumerate how many times Emil has taken to flight.
We do not pretend to have a complete story of his
escapades.   At nine years he had already been to the
truant's detention school for two periods.   Between
the July when we first saw him and the previous April,
when he had last been released from this school, he
had run away from home fifteen times by actual count.
On one occasion he had remained away for a week,
sleeping principally in parks.   His stepfather lost two
positions on account of looking for him.   Once Emil
got away by jumping down eight feet out of a window
at home.   Before leaving on several occasions he had
taken a little money from home; he had stolen his
baby brother's bank.   Emil was known as a great
liar.   It became plain to us, however, that his false-
hoods were merely attempts to evade punishment for
his delinquencies.   We ourselves visited his home at
this time and found a neat little mother who gave us an
intelligent history of the case, a clean home, and a stepfather who had a more reasonable attitude toward the
boy than the mother herself.

Following our first study, Emil was placed in a
country home where he enjoyed himself, and from which
he did not run away.   Unfortunately, although the
people had become attached to him, they had to break
up their housekeeping arrangements and Emil was sent
home.

When he came back to town, Emil began running away again, sleeping in sheds, sometimes getting as far as the suburbs, occasionally stealing money for expenses. He attempted to board a train for the country town where he had been happy. He was then tried in a home for children in a suburb. From there he did not run away, but his parents being unable or unwilling to pay anything at all for him, he was taken home again.

Ten months later his mother appeared, again distracted. There had been one trouble after another with Emil. He had run away many times; he had taken small sums. His mother had found, through advertising, a place in the country for him, which proved a failure, although while there four months the boy had not run away. However, he had done many sneaking things, even at this place, and had tried to get hold of small sums on every possible occasion. There had been much complaint of him. The woman out there said he was the greatest criminal for his age she had ever heard of, and she was really much afraid of him. He had been taken away from her place at her request. Then he reappeared one terrifically stormy night at her home, thoroughly drenched and worn out, having walked all the way out and suffered much in consequence. The fact of his having shown so much desperate will power seems to have frightened her more than anything else. Once more he was taken home, but we heard ourselves that at a still later date he had been hanging about this country town again, perhaps seeking a chance of getting another home in which to remain. The boy at this period was still only ten years old, and it is to be noted that his own home was not then a particularly bad sort of place; indeed, the boy said himself that it was "all right."

Then Emil was sent to an industrial school for boys. He remained there sixteen months and had a good record. He was considered an exceedingly sweet and polite boy. He seemed happy and never ran away, although he had constant opportunity to do so. Then he was returned home and after a short time began his flights again. After a few weeks of this, he was again returned to the industrial school and remained there a year, and again had a good record. He came home now, being almost fourteen years of age, and, finding his people in a state of poverty, he did well in helping take care of the two younger children and worked at odd jobs until he was old enough to get his working certificate at fourteen. He then proved himself efficient as a messenger boy for over three months, being discharged because of some boyish altercation. He immediately, and without any other reason, took flight again, being picked up by the police as a vagrant while wandering through a town some twenty miles distant. On returning home, he worked again until there arose some trouble with his mother, who by this time has grown peculiarly irritable. He took his week's wages and stayed in cheap lodging houses for a few days until it was all spent, and then hung about a police station waiting to be taken in as a runaway boy.

Our study of Emil at this time seems to bring out clearly some points which had been *sub judice* previously. In explanation of his most peculiar delinquencies, which involved considerable suffering on his part, we had at first considered the possibility of hereditary traits breaking out in him. (We heard early that the father was a bad character.) Certainly something was vigorously at work within him making for a delinquent career. Then we considered the home situation itself, although on the surface it seemed fair enough. There was early complaint on the part of Emil about his home treatment; we ourselves never felt satisfied that there was sympathetic appreciation of his needs. We considered home conditions certainly a factor in the case, perhaps more of a factor later than earlier. In our first summary of the causative factors we dictated that "although we have not succeeded in getting much that bears on the question, still it may possibly be that the boy continually has rankling in his own breast the problem of his parentage." The step-father himself suggested this, without any recognition of its deep significance.

Physically we found Emil at first to be in poor general conditions. He was anemic; at nine years of age he weighed only fifty-three pounds; his poorly developed chest showed remains of a rachitic rosary; his teeth were in very poor condition; he was then a biter of his finger nails, as he has remained since. He showed no sensory defect, and his reflexes and other nerve findings have been normal, with the exception of over-action of the facial muscles when he was younger. Examined at fifteen years of age we found he weighed only one hundred pounds, although he showed many points of gain through the healthy life which he has led in the country for many months.

Since the time seven years ago, when it was suggested to us by his people that this boy was not normal, we have had the opportunity of testing his mentality many times. We found him always eager and interested in doing the tasks we set before him. On account of his truancy he was somewhat backward in school work, but on a wide range of tests calculated to evaluate his mental abilities, he did so well that we were persuaded that the only diagnosis could be that he had fair mental powers. This diagnosis has been corroborated by the observations and testings of a number of people. The boy now grades perhaps somewhat below his years and has not profited by all of his opportunities in school. He writes a rather childish hand and misspells many words; he finds it difficult to concentrate when given more arduous tasks, but his perceptions and apperceptions and memory processes are sufficiently good, and in nothing does he show evidences of mental aberration. He is still a childish boy; he is lacking on the side of mental interests, which, however, may never have been presented to him in a stimulating way.

The developmental history of Emil is comparatively uneventful. The mother was under a certain amount of stress during the pregnancy on account of being unmarried, but the situation seems not to have been taken very hard. The boy suffered almost no illnesses during his early childhood, although we find evidences now of poor nutritional conditions. He was brought up away from the mother during all of his early years. The things which we found wrong with him might have been due to early malnutrition, poor hygiene, and to his over-use of coffee, but as I stated above, his physical conditions have steadily tended to become better.

Heredity is another matter. The boy's father is said to have been a bad sort of a man, alcoholic, a spendthrift, and a fighter, who came from a fairly good family. Emil's mother states that she refused to marry him after her condition became known. Conception took place at a forest party, when both were probably more or less under the influence of alcohol. On the mother's side also there are some unfortunate traits. Her mother was a deserter of her large family and a quarrelsome woman, who remarried a couple of times and became somewhat notorious in her later years on account of her marriage to a criminal. The step-siblings of Emil are quite normal children.

Any good account of Emil's home life must include the story of his mother's peculiarities. Until he was six years of age the boy was brought up by estimable people to whom his mother paid part of her earnings. He loved them, and they loved him, and there was absolutely no trouble on account of bad behavior. He saw his mother at such rare intervals that he can only nowadays remember that he saw her a couple of times in the old country. Suddenly, when he was six years of age, she appeared on the scene and at once brought him with her to America. He had lived a pleasant life in Vienna, with a chance to play in pretty, open places. In Chicago he was set down in a crowded and poor part of town, and through his mother living with the grandmother, who had been here for years, quarreling began. In a few weeks the mother married a very decent young fellow who had known her in Vienna.

Always since then there has been more or less trouble at home on account of the comparatively poor earning capacity of the husband and the bad temper of his wife. At times she has been pleasant, but she has attempted to manage her household with a shrewish tongue and the laying on of hands; all this she has distributed fairly between her husband, her children by him, and her first son. Emil cares much more for his stepfather than he does for his own mother, on account of her quarrelsomeness.

Far more significant than anything else is the history of Emil's mental experiences. Although always a remarkably pleasant and polite boy — "a child of sunshine" as he was called by an enthusiastic woman in the country, we got little from him about his inner life during the first year or two we knew him. Perhaps the fault was ours, inasmuch as we were not then so alive to the existence of mental conflicts. Later we have extended our knowledge of him through his confidences and through the many reports we have received of him from his family and others. The stepfather always thought Emil peculiar from the moment after his own marriage when he told the boy to call him "father." Emil quickly looked him in the face, burst out laughing, and turned away.

Recounting his own worries of that period it is revealed in Emil's more recent interviews with us that his relationships to others were a great puzzle to him from the time when his mother brought him away. He has always insisted that he loved the T.'s, with whom he lived in Vienna. He called them mother and father. They were kind to him. "They cried when I left. I didn't want to come. Things seemed strange to me. I didn't know my mother. In those days the only thing I wondered about was about my father. I've asked her sometimes since then about him. She never told me what my father's name was; she said it was none of my business. I always worried about my father. I don't know anything about him. I don't worry now any more. My stepfather said he would tell me all about my life when I grew bigger. . . . I used to think a good deal about it. I always used to wish I knew. I wondered if my mother was my real mother."

It is now nine years since Emil was brought to Chicago, but his mind still reverts to Vienna: "When I was there I played out in the open. I always liked it out of doors. I always wanted to get out more when I first came here. I wouldn't mind if I was back there now. I like it out in the country. I'd like now to drive and run around. Out in the country you're out in the fields all the time, not in the house. It was closed in when I first came."

One of the first statements this boy ever made to us was concerned with his desire to be out in the open. His early running away began in the summer time, when he first slept in some sheds; later, when his people moved nearer a park, he used to sleep out of doors a great deal. He said he liked the air in the park, liked to get up at five o'clock in the morning. He used to subsist on the few pennies which he had sometimes taken before he went, or on what he could beg from bakeshops or picnickers. In those days he asked to go on a farm because then he could be in the "open country." Although he described his excursions to us then he always stated that he didn't know why he ran away.

The upshot of this whole case, as it has become clear through our more recent studies of it, is that this boy had a most terrific mental conflict in his earlier years, the elements of which he was forced to repress through the unreasonableness of his mother. His emotions centered about the puzzle of his parentage. Just the association of running away with the repressed elements does not stand out clearly, but we may be allowed to surmise that possibly the flight of his mother with him from the old country may have brought the idea to his mind. Certainly, some suggestion there must have been to have started his flights on the eighth day after he arrived in a strange city.

Emil's phrasing of his own troubles at home have, until recently, been vague, and he was inclined to exaggerate his mother's behavior. We have intimated above that the boy early lied to us, translating her scoldings and occasional slaps into actual beatings. When cornered, however, he always would say that he was only punished when he was bad. About his own inner mental states, he told us a couple of years ago, once when he had been picked up as a runaway: "I didn't feel as if things were right at home." At our first interviews he used to say that he liked his mother and stepfather, and that he didn't know why he would not stay at home. As he looks back nowadays on those earlier years, he tells us plainly that he then was always worried about his parentage.

Any one might naturally ask why this boy still occasionally runs away for other reasons than mental conflict about his father. On the last two occasions he has taken flight after either leaving or losing the position which he held, and once after spending his wages. In explanation, we may remember that home conditions, with regard to quarreling, are no better, and that the boy has a good deal of dissatisfaction on account of this and because of the idea which he still holds, that life in Vienna would be much pleasanter, and that he would like to have all the facts of his parentage cleared up. But I am inclined to believe that here, as in many other cases, a habit of delinquency has been formed. He early developed the conception of flight as a way out of unpleasantness and difficulty. It relieved the immediate situation in some way, even though it led to considerable suffering on his part.

The idea of running away still recurs to him when he is
in trouble, and he has twice in the last year given way
to the impulse.   We have often found evidences that
a type of conduct was persisted in even after the original
cause was removed, largely as the result of the formation of an habitual reaction.

(To bring this history up to date, we may state that
Emil was once more placed in a good farm home where
he was very happy and from which he did not run away
for several months.   Then his parents separated, his
mother finally following his stepfather, who had taken
the other children to a new residence, a thousand miles
west.   Emil heard of this after a time, and again suddenly took flight.   He has not been heard of since.)

Case 34.   A strong impulse to vagrancy on the basis
of mental conflict is illustrated here.   The origin of the
conflict is clearly shown.

The mother of Chester N., an intelligent woman,
stated to us that Chester got along very well in every
way till he was fourteen years old.   During the two
years since there had been an immense amount of
trouble with him.   It began with truancy and staying
away from home all night.   He withdrew from school
at fourteen, but has held no job for long.   If he works
for a week he goes off with his pay.   He stays away a
week or more at a time, sleeping under sidewalks or
in parks.   The police have taken him up for vagrancy.
He has frequently helped himself to small amounts
of money at home, but he can hardly be said to have
shown much tendency to stealing.   Altogether he has
run away many times.

In disposition Chester seems rather sullen at home;
he likes to be by himself or to play with small children.

He always talks sensibly; he finished the seventh grade and plays the piano well. He is fond of moving picture shows. So far as the family knows, Chester always goes alone, both to the picture shows and when he wanders away. The mother knows nothing of his associating with bad boys, now or formerly.

The family history seems quite negative in respect to this boy's tendencies. He comes from strong, healthy stock, where neither mental ailments nor nomadism figures. Chester passed through a rather sickly infancy, but no nervous troubles developed at any time. He walked and talked as early as the other four children, all of whom are normal. He finished seven grades in six years, having begun school rather late.

We found a well-developed boy on the physical side, without sensory defect. Mental tests showed him to be quite bright, without peculiarity in any direction. We particularly noticed that tests for mental control were done fairly well. But Chester evidently regards himself as somewhat of a weakling; he seems to lack self-assertiveness, although he is not without confidence in his mental powers. Beyond this we found him a talkative lad, anxious, upon sympathetic inquiry, to go into all the details of what led to his tendencies.

The essence of the analysis of Chester's troubles can be told largely in his own words: "I have temptations, temptations to steal and temptations about those bad habits. *I don't give way to them*, but those things are in my mind. How can you help it; it's all you hear about down our way; every word they say is a dirty one. It used to put me all upset. *I never can get over Dickson*. It's like a picture of him comes in my mind.

. . . Dickson used to be away from home about four days a week. His mother didn't care if he went off; she went off herself."

The story of Chester's environment and companionship included much that is important for understanding his case. When they lived on another street, about four years earlier, he was first taught to steal by Dickson. He remembers a half dollar that they took from a grocery store; Chester paid that back. Then there was another extremely bad boy there whom he came to know. (It curiously happens that we ourselves were acquainted with both these other boys as delinquents.) The stealing would not have been so bad if these boys had not told him other things. They used dirty words. "I'd come up there, and they'd talk about girls; that's one thing I didn't like to hear. I never said a bad word to my mother or father in my life. They'd talk about it all the time till it got on my nerves. I got to wondering if it was true. I didn't believe it, but they'd talk about it till I'd get all excited."

This other boy, Dickson, was the first one who told him "about girls." Yes, and he was the first who told him about stealing, too. "I was ten or eleven then. They'd go out to meet the girls, but I wouldn't go along." To our inquiry if he had seen pictures that bothered him, he replied that he had. "One kid down that way has a book, and there ain't a good thing in it. . . . I keep thinking how can that be true, the things that the picture shows."

The former acquaintance, Dickson, he has not seen for a long while, but he thinks of him and of his talk about girls. Particularly when he gets his pay, it comes up in his mind about "Dickson with the money, running away." Chester considers that stealing is not right, and, as a matter of fact, he has sometimes later paid back to his mother money which he has stolen from her when he was going away. He has not stolen from others, except that this last time he took four or five dollars from a woman next door to use as a start to make his own way in the world. He did not much mind taking it from her, because she has a grudge against him and frequently has said to his mother, "Why don't you put that kid away? He's crazy."

The neighbors think he is queer, he says, because he plays with the little children. The reason for this is that all of the boys over eight or ten years old around there are bad; they do daylight robberies; some of them have been arrested and sent away. Chester does not want to do these things; he wants to stay good and keep away from the bad boys.

With the exception of this last adventure, Chester has not run away for a long time with money other than his own. He takes his pay and stays away from home.

He makes much to us of the sex affairs that the boys showed him and of how he was affected thereby. "They have bad habits . . . I would never do that. I don't get in any bad habits that will spoil my health. I've seen good Irish kids in our neighborhood that were good when they came get into that. They ain't good no more." At another time he told us of his curiosity. "Once, when I said I didn't believe it, they said, ' We'll show you if it's true,' and I wanted to know and went with them. The sight of it sickened me."

There is no doubt of Chester's good behavior ordinarily at home; when his mother was in the hospital, he even did the washing. He never talked to his father about his troubles; he was afraid to do so. Earlier he thought his father would get after Dickson, and Dickson in turn would get after Chester. Then he put off telling about the affair.

(The several months that have elapsed without further complaint of Chester's behavior are not enough to warrant us in declaring Chester cured of running away as yet.)

Case 35. In this instance the genesis of the impulse to run away was unmistakably traced.

Philip R., just ten years of age, has been running away from home for two years. This, with the truancy which it entailed, was his sole delinquency. He has gone away many times, usually staying about a couple of days and nights, sleeping in hallways, parks, or peddlers' wagons. Philip always goes alone. He has been taken by the police at least six times, always somewhere in the city.

In other ways Philip enjoys an enviable reputation. He is said by both his parents to be unusually kind and helpful at home, willing to scrub, wash the dishes, or to take care of the younger children. He is also very generous; given a nickel, he takes only a penny for himself, giving the rest to the others. In school he has, naturally, not advanced rapidly, but is in the fourth grade.

Developmental history brings out nothing of importance, except that he has been free from severe illnesses and walked, talked, etc., at the normal age. Inquiry into the family history elicited no abnormality on either side.

Our examination showed a normally developed little lad with no sensory defect or physical trouble of any sort. Tonsils and adenoids had been removed at seven years. On mental tests he graded above age by Binet; on other types of tests he did exceedingly well for his years.

A summary of what we discovered by analysis is as follows: Philip began his running away as the direct result of an experience which his parents knew nothing about. A group of much older boys ran away to another city, while there being arrested for robbery. As Philip blurted out to us in the midst of conversation about another point, "The first time I ran away; that's how I started it. They told me about their running away and how fine it all was, and I got it in my mind. . . . They started me when I was eight years old running away. . . . They talk about girls; they say lots of dirty things; they don't say anything nice. . . . I dream about what they do to other kids. . . . It is these boys who ran away. . . . It is these things I think about. . . . They don't live there any more, but I think about it and what they did to Frank; he lives next door. . . . They begged me to go robbing, but I never did."

Discussion of the facts with the mother and in more detail with Philip showed the probable truth of what he said. Two older boys were notorious in the neighborhood for stealing, and they did engage in the escapade which the boy described. The mother, however, knew nothing of their introducing her little lad to sex affairs in such flagrant fashion. It was soon after they came back that he started running away alone. He has never to her knowledge stolen or been in bad habits or used bad language of any kind. Her statement on these points was all the more interesting because it was she who made the complaints.

A fact of no small interest in this case is that our first study of Philip, undertaken in somewhat routine fashion, merely asking for causes and trying to get the boy to talk out his troubles, was a failure. He was a pathetic figure under detention then, crying much and lying much in self-defense. He wanted to go home, he said, and do better, but we obtained no good understanding of his case. His parents made extra efforts after this time to make home attractive, but after a few weeks, Philip relapsed and ran away again on two occasions. The last time he was again taken by the police, and now more prolonged efforts on our part were rewarded by getting at the fact and essentials of his mental conflict as given above. His parents again were willing to do all that they could, and it remains to be seen how well, with their limited resources, they can succeed. Our own advice was for them to go carefully into all details of his connection with this group of boys and also for them to move to an entirely different neighborhood, where suggestions of the old kind would not be so likely to arise.

CHAPTER XVI

CONFLICTS RESULTING IN OTHER DELIN-QUENCIES

FROM among the other kinds of misconduct we have observed following upon mental conflicts, the following cases offer a fair variety. They illustrate homicidal attempt, extreme bad temper and violence, extreme willfulness, destructiveness and disobedience, malicious cruelty and sadism. The favorable outcome in some of these cases deserves earnest consideration.

Case 36. The interest in this case centers on the fact that a desperately criminal attempt at taking life developed directly upon a basis of mental conflict. The inmost depths of the mental trouble were never known and the needs of the delinquent were never met under home conditions.

Octave M., a well-mannered and rather good looking quadroon girl of about fifteen, was held for attempting to poison her family. She had mixed Paris green with some apple sauce which was ready for the table. Fortunately, her mother had detected the unnatural color in time to prevent disaster.

The intelligent and affectionate mother was concerned not only about this particularly vicious offense, but also about the welfare of the younger children.

She felt that Octave was having a bad influence at home. The girl had been going about for several months with an older girl of poor reputation, and to this the mother attributed much of the trouble. The matter of her conduct in general needed thorough looking into, the mother told us.

We found Octave in good general physical condition and well developed. With the exception of slight signs of anemia and some complaint of headaches, we found nothing whatever wrong. She had menstruated early, at twelve years. There had been a former diagnosis of recurrent appendicitis, but no symptoms had been complained of for some time.

Mentally the girl proved herself to be of quite normal ability. She had attained the sixth grade in spite of being away from school a great deal, taking care of the children on the days when her mother went out to work. There had been no complaints of any kind from school. Octave did fairly good work on a wide range of tests given to her at two periods, a year apart, and she serves, incidentally, as an illustration of the fallacy of mental testing when the subject is under emotional stress. She failed badly on one occasion and then, when inquiry later was made about this, she said, "There is something resting on my mind." A day or two afterwards, when she was feeling better, she did very well on the same tests. She passed through all the Binet series up through twelve years and made good records on the more difficult tests. We saw no reason at any time to consider her either defective or aberrational, although this had been suggested.

The developmental history given by the mother proved negative. Pregnancy and birth were normal. During childhood Octave had several infectious dis-

eases, but all were light attacks.   The most serious illness she ever had was a rather severe attack of bronchitis.

The family background was not so favorable.   The
father had been at times a heavy drinker and did not
support his family.   The mother had to work, but
within the last year or two the father had been doing
much better in every way.   As is frequent with colored
families, we got no satisfactory account of heredity,
but such facts as were known were evidently negative.

Octave proved very willing to do what her mother
asked, namely, to go thoroughly into the matter of her
bad conduct.   She appeared shamefaced, but talked
quite frankly.   During the course of our study we
ascertained the following vital points:

The girl whom the mother had told us about, Octave
readily acknowledged to be bad.   "She did a lot of
bad things and taught me to do them.   She says bad
words.   They are so bad I can't tell them to you.
She does things with boys, too.   Her mother works
out, and she waits on the street corner for the boys
and takes them home with her. . . .   I just can't keep
my mind on my work any more.   When the teacher
here tells me something, I forget what she has told me
to do."

For a long time Octave contented herself by continually reaffirming that she could not remember what
it was that came into her head, but something does
come which makes her forget things and worries her
greatly.   On reviewing home conditions in detail,
Octave stated that her father was always unkind to
her; that he scolded her without cause, and that she
really does not care for him.   Then more came out
about her companion.   This older girl told Octave of

the money she made through immoral practices, both
at home and in hotels, and urged Octave to do likewise. The other girl's mother, too, was probably immoral. Although Octave had similar opportunities
for indulging, she evidently resisted all the temptations,
but insisted that she was much disturbed mentally
by the knowledge conveyed to her, as well as by the
imagery which this called up in her mind. Doctor
Bronner's opinion, dictated at the time, was that this
seemed to be an innately clean-minded girl who apparently wanted to remain good, but who was much
afraid of her thoughts.

Concerning Octave's major delinquency, we obtained some interesting information by putting together
what we learned from the girl and her mother. The
objective facts were that on that day there had been
some quarreling and some abuse of the girl by her
father. The mother noted that Octave seemed particularly provoked, but Octave's own account of the
affair included no statement of this abuse by the father,
which was usual. She dwelt entirely upon what was
going on in her own head all that afternoon. "I had
been thinking about those bad words for the last
month. That afternoon I was standing on the porch
nearly all the time, and I couldn't get those words
out of my mind. I put that stuff in the apple sauce
about five o'clock in the afternoon." Some details
were gone into with the mother and the girl together.
It appeared that the father was the one in the family
particularly fond of apple sauce and would be the only
one likely to eat much of it then. Octave stated that
she only intended to injure him because he was "no
good and was mean to the family." However, she
had given us no hint of self-justification previously.

Her own explanation had all to do with the subjective content of her own mind during that day, — things that she had never mentioned to anybody which were continually worrying her. The mother insisted on the great penitence of the girl directly after the poison was found and she was accused. There was no attempt at self-denial. It seemed almost as if Octave then awoke from some dreamlike state and only at this time first realized what she had done.

The outcome of this case with Octave living at home, as could have been foreseen, has been most unsatisfactory. The family moved, and it is probable that she saw no more of her evil companion, but the father got to drinking again, and Octave alleged, one year later, that he had sexually assaulted her and repeatedly made attempts. The man was tried for this offense. But Octave finally denied before the jury all that she had alleged previously and accused another man. All felt there was considerable probability in the truth of what she had first stated, but many things had come up to make her retract, and the mother herself changed her earlier stories of her husband's misdoings. In such cases there is frequently an economic factor which has to be accounted for — if the husband is taken away, who will support the children? He was doing this properly just now. Octave at this later time made much of the stress that she had been under through not wishing to tell her mother and yet ward off her father. We found that she had become very untruthful; her word was not to be relied upon in many respects. All this was a change from her previous character. She had gone to a hospital and alleged that she was pregnant, at the same time complaining of her old appendicitis pains. Later examination showed that she was not pregnant. It was clear that she had grown entirely beyond parental control; that she had been given almost nothing of what she needed in the way of better mental life following our original exploration of her troubles. She had to be sent to an institution for delinquent girls.

It is of no small interest in this case to note that although conditions for all of the six children had been the same in the family life, there had been absolutely no trouble with any of the others, one of whom was older. Another main point is that there had been absolutely no delinquency on the part of Octave until three months prior to the attempted poisoning. At this time the family had moved into a new neighborhood and it was then that Octave met this older girl and herself became perverse.

Case 37. How extreme irritability and display of violence may be the result of mental conflict is shown in the following short narration:

An unusually intelligent relative brought to us from afar the problem of Ella T., eighteen years old. For several years Ella had been extremely quarrelsome at home; even the neighbors complained of the disturbances she created. Her mother had been kicked and pounded by her frequently. An older sister on several occasions she had actually beaten. Once Ella pulled to pieces a scarf belonging to her sister, and on another occasion seized music that a visitor was playing at the piano and tore it into bits. More than once she had thrown a drinking glass at a brother to whom she was formerly devoted, and repeatedly she had tossed such objects as scissors and lighted matches at her relatives. Some days she was said to appear thoroughly quiet

and well behaved, but she was always beyond the control of her mother, and between the two there had
never been full confidence.

We found a well-cared-for young woman who had
been recently thoroughly investigated from a medical
standpoint, with negative findings. Physically she
was attractive and well developed.

On the mental side she showed herself intelligent
and capable. She had done well in school whenever
she had pleased to exert herself. Her conversation
was coherent and to the point. She showed some
resentment and resistance at first, when essential
points of her experience were approached, but only
in a very natural way. We found every reason to
believe that, as her relatives stated, she was truthful
by nature.

Brought to the point of considering herself a delinquent, Ella expressed herself as desirous of doing differently and willing to go into causes. At an early
interview we learned of certain experiences that were
corroborated for us by the family. It seems that five
or six years previously this young woman at an Eastern
girls' school of high standing had become deeply
attached to another girl. This had developed into
homosexual relations which were continued for long.
There had been a quiet scandal, and without any complete exploration of the affair and without any real
understanding on the part of the mother, Ella had
been sent home. After this she experienced a great
deal of sex temptation which she kept absolutely to
herself; her attraction now, however, was to thoughts
of the opposite sex. There was a frequent turmoil of
inner feeling, ideation, and imagery, which she endeavored to suppress, consciously quite acceding to

the social point of view, namely, that giving way to sex desires was wrong. She evidently completely downed voluntary thoughts of her original experience and those earlier habits. Any external show of feelings which assailed her was always rapidly and successfully repressed. Even her relatives said that she was an entirely modest girl, thoroughly quiet in her attitude towards men.

With the exception that the father had been at times unfortunately addicted to alcohol, the family history showed no neurotic tendencies or mental abnormality on either side. The mother was a woman of fine temperament. Ella herself had never had a physical ailment of importance.

Putting it all together, it seemed sure that, in the main, here was a girl of thoroughly good antecedents. She had a splendid physical background; she had ceased, after her first experiences, the bad sex habits; she had not developed any psychoneurosis. The intense mental conflict and repression had found vent in her vicious display of violence.

After discovery of the essential facts, the relation of cause to effect was realized by all, and a new régime, beginning with confidence between mother and daughter, was instituted. The outlook seemed good because of the intelligence and common sense of the parties concerned.

Case 38. The following instance of general bad behavior arising very largely upon the basis of mental conflict, can be given in a few words. It illustrates the type of child who is frequently misunderstood, the child who is adjudged simply or willfully or "naturally" bad.

Andrew M., a boy of twelve years, was brought to us by his vigorous parents. He was reported by them and by the school people as being utterly disobedient, destructive, and possessed of a peculiarly mean temper. The teachers simply would not have him in school on account of his bad behavior; they stated that he was bright when he wanted to study, but most of the time engaged in malicious mischief. He had repeatedly torn up his school books. Recently he had written a letter to his mother stating that he would run away from home, and he had already been truant. In spite of much warning he had persisted in going with bad companions; his parents believed that he was an accomplice in their stealing, but that he never undertook anything of the sort by himself. His misconduct had been kept up for two or three years, and his people were thoroughly out of patience with him. His father had whipped him a great deal in the past, but finding it futile, had entirely stopped these tactics.

Physical examination showed a boy decidedly poorly developed for his age, for he weighed only sixty-seven pounds. Tonsils and adenoids had been removed a couple of years previously. No sensory defect. Bit nails excessively and had been doing so for long. Complained of occasional headaches. Sometimes badly constipated. Very good features. Eyes bright. Expression intelligent.

The mental findings indicated that the boy was unquestionably bright and intelligent; could do good school work. He passed well on many kinds of tests; by the Binet scale he graded slightly above his age.

Nothing in heredity or developmental history was found to have any significance for us. Concerning environmental influences, his parents knew that when he was about eight years of age he saw a girl in a barn "doing bad things with a boy." He came and told them then; they had thought nothing more about this until we questioned them.

In studying Andrew, we found at once that we had to deal with a very frank and nice boy, who plunged at once into his own story as follows: He volunteered that he has been disobedient and bad in school, but does not know why. His parents are very good to him. He has been going with bad fellows who steal and give him some of the proceeds. His recreations are going to nickel shows and playing with these boys. His father frequently is away from home on business. He really wants to live at home; he was fooling when he wrote that letter. He says he is nervous and irritable, and knows he has a bad temper; for instance, when he tries to tie his necktie and it does not go well, he just has to say a lot of bad words.

Very interestingly Andrew tells us at some length how he fights against certain thoughts. He finally narrates in detail just what these are; they are what the boys told him long ago, or at least what he heard them say, about bad sex affairs. They did not directly tell him, but he has wondered a good deal about it, and the ideas flash up in his mind. He denies that they had ever led him into bad sex affairs of any kind. "I try not to think about it when it comes up in my mind, I think about going out to play or something like that. I don't care for it."

Andrew tells us he has taken to smoking. He insists that he doesn't care for girls, nor would he engage in any of the sex things of which he has heard, but he cannot help thinking about them. He proposes that he be sent away for a time to some school and then perhaps he could control himself better.

To us Andrew showed evidences of possessing a decidedly strong character. He has a good chin and a rather stubborn look on his serious face. We should also characterize him as being a quick, careless, rather nervous type. It is here impossible to do justice to the ingenuous account which we received, after becoming friendly with this boy, about his own inner mental life and the things he fought against in it.

On our advice, this boy was placed in a private school. We knew that he would be subjected to the usual routine, but we could see nothing better for him, since his father's business did not permit his being a companion to the boy, and since neither of the parents, although intelligent, seemed to have any capacity for understanding the real causation. The father blamed the boy's physical conditions, his constipation, the school teachers, or anything else, except the real underlying cause which we discovered and which the boy acknowledged. The father never exerted himself to obtain the full confidences of his son.

Taken away from his old associations, the boy has done right well, except for occasional outbreaks of his former misbehavior. We felt that very likely he would gradually get hold of himself, even though we saw clearly that the most direct method of re-education to greater stability would never be utilized. From the school the report comes that this boy is not considered abnormal in his conduct, although somewhat erratic in deportment. His class work is consistently fair. (The latest report, a year and a half after his entrance in the school, is that he is still doing well.)

Case 39. In one case of a little boy who showed
extreme tendencies towards cruelty and other malicious
misbehavior, complete evidence of repressions was
obtained, although the boy's own reaction to inquiry
was always that of obdurate resistance. An uncommon feature in this case was that with the original
overt expression of sex tendencies there was no other
form of delinquency; coincident with repression, violent forms of misconduct appeared.

Lawrence L., seven years of age, was adopted by a
highly intelligent family. Their methods of upbringing were model, but in this instance the result was a
complete failure. They had had the boy for about a
year, and there had been on his part one offense after
another, until even their unusual patience was exhausted.

Lawrence as seen by us was in splendid physical condition. In general developmental characteristics all
points were normal, and he had been cared for admirably. Mentally we classified him as being unusually
bright, in fact, somewhat precocious. The boy used
good language and talked well, but one soon found
on approaching any question of his delinquencies that
one had to deal with easily discerned self-contradictions,
and a mass of material that was part truth and part
lies, all mixed together under the impulse of a defense
reaction.

The family history of this child was atrociously bad,
including criminality on the part of both his father
and mother, and more than this, his early environment
had been equally poor. For scientific interpretation
of heredity the details of the peculiarities of the widely
scattered families are imperfect; our knowledge is

simply that several members of the families were addicted to alcohol and had been guilty of crimes.

The delinquencies of Lawrence were very remarkable.   Soon after he came to live with his foster parents he was caught showing his sex feelings towards a little cousin of the family, who lived next door; he had undressed her.   At this time he was tremendously demonstrative in his affections towards the women in the family.   He was very fond of getting up close to them and kissing them, for instance, all up and down their arms.   Later he was caught in masturbation on several occasions and was circumcised.   Following this operation, there had been no further overt display of sex tendencies.

Soon after this change, however, Lawrence began showing inclinations towards cruelty; with older boys he seemed normal, but with little children he was always inclined to be mean and brutal.   He exhibited these tendencies in the most deliberate way.   Once his foster mother had warned the children about the danger of stepping on broken glass which she had observed near the house.   Later it was found that on four occasions Lawrence had deliberately distributed broken glass where the children might possibly step on it.   He later stated that he did this so that they would get cut.   He also threw down needles for the same purpose.   A succession of accidents to the little cousin had been reported, and after the family became suspicious, it proved that Lawrence several times had hit her thumb with a hammer.   He once put some glass down her neck and once cut her with glass.   He had also beaten her.   In their childish pleasures it was always noted that he showed extreme selfishness and jealousy of her.

(To the student of these problems it will be interesting to note that this little girl seemed to stand these attentions with remarkable equanimity. In spite of his behavior towards her, she always took his part and, whenever he was jealous, divided with him what she had received. She did not make any complaint of his hurting her until the elders of the family had suspected the cause of her bruises. In this, of course, she showed masochistic tendencies.)

Lawrence was deliberately cruel to animals; he picked insects to pieces, in spite of having been taught that this was very wrong. Other children reported that he was very abusive to an unusually gentle dog who was their playmate. In the most malicious way he had lately stolen highly valuable articles from his foster mother, the stealing of which benefited him not at all and gave her a great deal of trouble. He secreted these articles so well that they were never found, and told lie after lie about what he had done with them.

When he first came to these people, he was recognized as being quite untruthful, but his stealing, as well as his bad temper and maliciousness and cruelty, was not displayed until after his show of bad sex tendencies had ceased. We obtained this point very clearly from his guardians, although they had never thought about the significance of these facts. They had kept close account of his development for its human interest and as a measure of what might be accomplished with a child apparently physically and mentally normal who came from bad surroundings and bad stock.

Latterly Lawrence had been doing better in his studies; at first it had seemed as if he were not able to concentrate well. He was regarded as a merry-hearted boy; he often played nicely with other children.

Our own study of Lawrence brought out very little that is not already mentioned above. He was willing to tell us that he had known of sex affairs long before he had come to this new home, but we gained no clue whatever to the exact mechanisms of his inner satisfactions resulting from his acts of cruelty. The student of mental analysis can readily understand, however, the nature of the mental life that was going on below the surface.

The subsequent history of this case is of the greatest interest. The foster parents found a new home for the boy, where there were no small children. I felt that taking him away from the little girl who had been the object of his sex feelings and whom he later had treated so cruelly was absolutely essential. The result under changed conditions has been most gratifying. The behavior of Lawrence has been entirely free from his old misconduct for considerably more than a year, and no further sadistic tendencies have been reported. It is very evident that the latter had received considerable impulse from continued suggestion in the associations of his previous home; the people themselves, the mother and the little girl, had been the objects upon which he had centered his ardent feelings. To remain with them could mean nothing but continuous demand for repression. Living in another home proved to be the best safeguard against renewal of original causes.

Case 40. We have here an instance of the development of tendencies to cruelty (sadism) correlated with premature arousal of sex impulses leading to mental conflict.

Abel S. was brought in from a school for half-orphans for us to study. He was then ten years of age and had been at the school for three years. He was recognized as a bright enough boy, but he had become exceedingly troublesome within the last six months or so. The main complaint was that he frequently showed a violent temper, even to the point of attacking the other children with any object he could lay his hands on; once he had threatened another child with a knife. Besides this, however, Abel had repeatedly pinched smaller children and had been observed sticking them and scratching them with pins. There was some complaint of bad sex habits on the boy's part, but this, apparently, meant that the matron had seen him occasionally touching himself in a suspicious way. No account of real masturbation was forthcoming.

The father came in to give us a history of the case. His wife had committed suicide four years previously. After he had married her, he had discovered that she was epileptic. There was nothing further especially interesting in the family history. Abel was the third child. Developmental history was quite negative; indeed, the boy had all along been considered as unusually healthy and bright. Before he had been sent to the school, and after his mother had died, the father knew that some boys had taught him bad sex habits, but the older brother had told him to stop these, and it was presumed that he had done so. The father knew of no way in which to account for Abel's present type of behavior. From both father and child we carefully inquired for attacks of any kind which could be interpreted as evidence of the inheritance of an epileptic taint. We found nothing whatever to indicate this.

Working with Abel we soon found him to be a boy

of quick and sharp mental reactions, not suggestible even to the ordinary degree for his age. The boy showed unusual powers of introspection. He answered our questions and outlined the history of his mental life in a very thoughtful manner, using exceptionally good language for his years and in spite of the fact that a foreign language was largely spoken at home and in the school to which he had been sent. Abel showed a normal childish lack of memory, particularly in regard to time, but his veracious tendencies were shown in the fact that he did not attempt to fill in these lacks or to romance in any way. With us he seemed willingly truthful all through, with the exception of his first reaction to our inquiry concerning the causes for his cruelty to children. This was the only delinquency that he denied, and even this he later freely acknowledged.

On mental tests, in spite of some difficulty with language, he graded as being rather precocious. On Binet tests he scaled a little more than a year above his age. There was no doubt about his being a boy of good mental parts.

Physically Abel presented a normal picture in every way. He appeared strong, upright, alert, with good features and firm expression. We were particularly interested to note that he seemed the reverse of a child who could be indulging in sex habits.

From Abel we got a story that was vital to understanding the situation. He assured us that he did not like it in the school, he got in trouble altogether too easily there; the boys were continually getting him angry, they would punch him and then he would be so "mad" that he tried to hit them with anything that he could reach. Then there were boys who started something going in his head. "Sometimes the boys in our school say the bad word. Sometimes when they say it, my head would be going round, like this."

Bringing up the question why any word should affect him peculiarly, we led back to his earlier life, before he went to the school. It appears that the boys on the street where they then lived were not good. He could not remember their names at all, but he remembers well what they told him. He saw them go with a girl into a big box and also into a shed, and sometimes the boys went in by themselves; they locked themselves in, and he did not see what went on, but they told him about it. He was then too little to understand what they meant and what the word signified. Then, some of the same crowd started him on masturbation. During these years at the school he has given way to this but very little. He has never seen any others do anything of the kind, nor has anybody ever done anything bad to him, but when certain words are uttered, a great deal of this comes back to him, and he tries desperately not to think of it. "I tried not to. I always tried not to think. I tried not to keep it in my mind. I'd play marbles, and then some boy maybe would swear, and it would get in my mind." As evidence of just what did bother him, Abel cited to us a most curious anagram, the like of which we had never heard before and would not have understood except that he showed us that the first letters spelled a bad word.

About his actual temptations Abel gave us a strikingly good account. He maintained that he often felt like doing what he learned about earlier, but he would not do it. He showed how he placed his hands under

his arms so that they should be away from other parts
of his body. "I'd put my hands like that, and I
should think about happy things and not about them
things. I don't let my hands feel like that no more.
I read 'Good Health', and I don't do it no more.
The boys say it, and write it, those bad words, but I
never said it to no one."

About his continual fighting and bad temper, Abel
tells us that it is all on account of the other boys.
"They made me so mad, I said I would kill any one
of them." A threat that he made to set the place on
fire, was "just for fun", because he was "mad."
"The boys get me mad, and I have my teeth together,
like this, I get so mad." Abel tells us that he sometimes gets all "shaky" inside. He thinks this is
mostly when he is angry. He does not sleep well at
night, dreams mostly about ghosts and devils and
stories which the boys make up about such things. In
his sleep he starts fighting and wakes up. Sometimes
he dreams about girls and particularly of seeing boys
and girls kissing.

Inquiry about specific events when he has hurt
other children brought out that another boy was badly
cut by him on the head and rendered unconscious,
but that was done distinctly in anger because the boys
were pushing him on the slide. When it came to the
matter of his use of pins on the little children, we found,
for the first time, considerable resistance. After some
hesitation, then, and at later interviews, Abel acknowledged that he did pinch these children or stick pins
into them. He did it at times when he was excited.
He had told us about local sex irritation previously,
and we were interested to ask if this occurred at the
times of hurting other children. Abel felt sure that

he did have some feelings of this sort, but they were not at all definite in his mind.

There seemed little doubt about this fact, because on all negative points Abel was thoroughly accustomed to reply in the negative, firmly and sharply. Vague though his explanation and memory of his feelings seemed to be, yet it was clear that some sort of sex stimulation occurred at these times.

Abel was strongly of the opinion that he ought not to remain in the school or to live anywhere with other boys. He wanted to go to a farm, he thought, where he would be away from other children. Asked what prevents him from being good, he said, "It's what is bad that comes up in my head." This "bad" seems to be entirely based on what he heard when he was only six years old, and this was what he had fought against. The seriousness of his attitude towards his own problem was one of the most remarkable points brought out by our study.

Through our advice, Abel was placed in a country home under the care of a woman who has special ability for handling boys who are problems. During the ten months he has been under her care, he has given no trouble in school nor in her household where he is in daily association with other children. It is interesting to note the report that he is considered "a kind boy, good to others."

CHAPTER XVII

CONCLUSIONS

What remains to be said in this chapter on Conclusions is in summary of the findings, not only in the cases given above, but from our entire experience with misconduct developed from mental conflicts. Much in the way of generalization has been given in the opening chapters which needs no repetition here.

An important query, often made, concerning mental conflicts and their consequences, is whether or not mental conflict represents a reaction that implies a *peculiar constitution* of the person so reacting. Are there traits and characteristics which render some individuals susceptible to this type of mental mechanisms, whereas others escape? Freud and his followers have already suggested that this may be true, that an inherited or a congenital predisposition is needed, if not for the genesis of a mental conflict, at least for it to produce the nervous and mental symptoms which these medicopsychologists have so carefully studied. We have taken this topic under consideration, with the following results:

In the first place it will be wise, since conflicts have been so generally observed in relation to the psychoneuroses, to inquire to what extent misdoers through mental conflict are neurotics. We can determine this in a general way on the basis of sufficient cases to make the verdict thoroughly reliable. While, of course, we have studied numerous cases of conflict and misconduct accompanying psychoneuroses, we have, nevertheless, found conflicts existing in dozens of instances where the misdoer was in first-rate physical condition, and where neither the physical examination nor the history gave any evidences of nervous disorder. On the other hand, if we compare this group of misdoers with others whose delinquencies are not the result of conflicts, we find no marked difference between the average nervous make-up. In many neurotic offenders there is no trace or hint of mental conflict as a cause for misdoing. The main point is thus clear, namely, that mental conflict commonly produces misbehavior in individuals who prove themselves by examination and history to have apparently normally stable nervous systems.

Concerning the problem of *heredity* in its relation to our topic, I may say, in short, that there is no good evidence that our instances of conflict have arisen upon any specific hereditary basis. If any predisposition is inherited, it is not, in general, such as may be identified and traced in any ordinary family history. We have seen enough parents and obtained enough outlines of family traits to show us that if foundations for the mental conflicts we have studied do exist in characteristics of the family stock, that recognition of these characteristics is quite beyond present powers of discernment. None of the ordinary, categorized abnormalities of mind and disposition are to be found among these families with any great degree of frequency. Our histories given in the preceding chapters show over and over again normal ancestry, as far as we have been able to find out by first-hand observation and information. In regard to the instances where heredity is defective, I may again suggest comparison with other groups of misdoers, — it being well known that offenders in general come from stock that averages poorer than that of non-offenders.

The *age of onset* of conflicts has always been a matter of exceeding interest to students of mental analysis. The analytic method of investigating human motives and reactions has proved nothing better than that at hitherto unsuspected early ages there are in the mental life forces at work, transmuting elements derived from experiences into reaction tendencies, — tendencies which may not be recognized at the time. The reader of the previous chapters will be struck by our practical findings in confirmation of this point. It seems doubtful whether complexes of much significance for students of misconduct ever arise beyond the early days of adolescence. It remains for observers of older offenders to show us how long conflicts as moving forces in misconduct may persist.

The *length of time a conflict may lie dormant* before producing reactions in misbehavior seems to vary according to the nature of the individual, the strength of repressions, and outward opportunities or incentives for misconduct. In our experience we have been more impressed, of course, by those cases where the unfortunate conduct has broken out after long periods of repression, during which no one has known of the prior disturbing experiences, than by what seems the more natural order of events, namely, reaction within a comparatively short time. That children can keep affairs, important to themselves, hidden in mental life for long months and years is a fact of great human significance.

Passing on to consider *special mental traits* as possibly characterizing those who are susceptible to mental conflicts which produce misbehavior, we can offer at least the following conclusions: Any preconceived idea that these victims of conflicts must be individuals inordinately given to moody introspection falls to the ground, in light of the facts. Our experience is that many of these misdoers are finely frank and open and not given to depression. Anything approaching the "shut-in" type is very rarely seen. Even when imagery and impelling ideas amount almost to obsessions, healthy-mindedness in other directions is often clearly apparent. We can find, then, no evidence of conflicts especially afflicting individuals of a general subjective temperament.

On the other hand, there can be not the slightest doubt that those who suffer from conflicts are so tuned that they respond to certain experiences in a way that some others would not. It must be that those who are affected are decidedly sensitive beings, but whether or not beyond the average of normal people it would be hard to say, particularly since we have no norms with which to compare them. (Certainly it is extremely rare that we find any case of conflict among offenders of the "rough" type, such as comprise a considerable percentage of delinquents in general.) We recognize that in some instances we have had to do with hypersensitive individuals, but even that does not imply hypersensitiveness in other directions. Indeed, the reader of case-histories can but wonder at the coupling of great sensitiveness on one point with obvious callousness in other ways;

the delinquencies which are entered into bring out this latter fact.

Reviewing other qualities of character, temperament, and disposition, it can fairly be stated that no special type predominates among our cases. Individuals exhibiting many varieties of traits are affected by mental conflicts which react in misbehavior. The fact that neurologists who use mental analysis in the treatment of the neuroses continually emphasize the limited or retarded emotional (affective) development of their patients has made us consider this point in particular. While we, too, have observed immature emotionality in hysterical and neurasthenic misconduct cases, I can with surety state that in many others we find no traces of anything but generally normal emotional reactions. Neither do we find very frequent evidences of over-assertiveness and egocentrism.

The question of whether different *races and nationalities* possibly present specific characteristics that have bearing upon the development of conflicts and reactions thereto may be answered in a word. Our cases are drawn from many different nationalities which seem, respectively, to give no intimation of special susceptibilities to conflicts being correlated with national characteristics. Of course, it is obvious that peoples who conceal little and immediately display their emotions are less likely to suffer from repressed elements in the mental life.

In *general abilities* we find our conflict cases ranging far above the average of our entire group of delinquents. Comparing one hundred and thirty cases of mental conflict with a thousand repeated offenders carefully classified on the basis of mental ability, the percentage of those above the class designated poor in ability is twice as great in the mental conflict group. Of the latter, seven per cent. grade as supernormal, and at least eighty per cent. of the remainder are fair or average in ability, although eight per cent. of these have had distinctly poor educational advantages. (Of the one hundred and thirty cases only four and a half per cent. were classified as abnormal, that is, either feeble-minded or psychoses.)

In order to ascertain whether any *special mental characteristics*, as judged by reactions to mental tests, are common to this group of conflict cases, we have tabulated the results in a number of the tests which were most frequently used; not all tests being given in every case. (Of course, on the Binet scale, the normal cases graded practically to age or above. This was taken into account in their general classification.)

There is little use discussing certain of the performance tests given, such as construction tests, because there is no reason to suppose that this conflict group would not show the usual variability. Indeed, this is what we find. In tests where one might with some show of reason suspect results to be significant, we discover the following:

General mental control as evidenced by such tests as controlled associations, our code test, the continuous subtraction test, and general observation on other performances, shows no defect or peculiarity belonging to this group. Indeed, the tests are done well on the average, as compared with the larger group of other mentally normal delinquents.

Psychomotor control: Leaving out the cases with definite nervous diseases and the very young who are not expected to make an average record on our tapping test or any other test which involves good motor control, we find quite the usual and average reactions. Individuals of ordinary ability over twelve years of age may be expected in our motor coördination test to tap at least sixty squares in thirty seconds with not more than three or four errors. Our present conflict group reaches this standard, the median score being seventy, with .5 as the median error, this being calculated on the basis of the average of two trials.

Control of association processes has been directly tested by the opposites test. The results are well up to the usual scores, both for time and accuracy. Considering language and educational differences the range of response from one to four and a half seconds is very moderate. The median time record, one and four-fifths seconds, is decidedly good. The median error, being only one, shows even better.

Powers of *mental representation* as estimated by the well-known cross-line tests stand out more strongly, perhaps, than any other discovered mental abilities. These tests happen to have been given in a large majority of the cases. The first cross-line test was given in eighty-one cases, none of which failed. Of these, seventy-five per cent. did it correctly on the first trial. We were surprised to find that the scores on the second cross-line test, usually supposed to be a fit test particularly for those twelve years old or above, in spite of numbers of cases being under twelve years of age, was done almost equally well. In the ninety-four normal cases in which it was given, there were but two failures. Almost eighty-five per cent. of these successes were on the first or second trials. This is a record that compares very favorably with the results on a selected private-school group as tested by Doctor Clara Schmitt, formerly of our institute. Inasmuch as powers of mental representation are by some suggested as being the foundations of foresight, and the use of normal foresight might be expected to keep these misdoers from repetition of their offenses, the above findings are of great interest.

Apperceptions as evaluated by the pictorial completion test may be considered. Previously we have stated that this is a test which should be performed by individuals of ordinarily good intelligence above ten years of age in at least five minutes, with not more than one illogical and two total errors. It has been given in sixty-seven cases in this group. The median number of illogical errors is zero, range of such errors is zero to three. The latter record was made in only one instance. The median number of total errors is one, range of total errors is zero to four. The last occurs only in two cases, both young children.

Memory powers, as estimated in general by results on Binet and other tests, are certainly at least up to the normal. The good records on many tests which involve memory are proof of this.

If the reader raises a question concerning the functioning of *will*, on account of these individuals being so patently the victims of impulses, we may state that as far as tests which require attention and some continuity of effort are concerned, there is no indication of deficiency in will, nor do the histories often show such weakness. These cases are not at all like our instances of defect in self-control. However, will from the psychological standpoint is hardly a unitary function. Individuals may show all sorts of strong powers of attention and sustained effort in one field or in one sphere of interest and apparently be woefully lacking in ability to carry out activities in another direction.

Summary of the tests, then, shows our cases to possess good mental abilities, but we find no one test or a group of tests of diagnostic worth either for discovering the general fact of conflict [1] or indicating the type of personality that is particularly prone to conflicts.

We have been asked whether our findings tend to prove the existence of exceptional *sex consciousness* on the part of children who develop complexes and conflicts upon the basis of the experiences we have described. In reply, the suggestion is offered that these results (to wit, the conflicts) should be compared with what takes place in other children who have had somewhat similar experiences, and particularly with the behavior of close companions, perhaps the very ones from whom our conflict victims gained their unfortunate knowledge. Over and over again we have learned of companions who have shown no hesitation in overtly expressing what they knew or felt concerning sex matters, giving no evidence of conflicts or vicarious delinquencies. Is there greater proof of sex consciousness, I would ask, in the fact of repression of sex knowledge and experience, or in the fact of unrestrained expression of such knowledge and experience through the medium of language or of physical practices? Turning impulse inward undoubtedly tends to prolong the consciousness of its activity and to magnify it in mental life, but that this implies a special innate tendency to over-consciousness in sex matters, I fail to see.

---

[1] Concerning the use of the association-reaction method for determination of the specific nature of a conflict, *vide* p. 62.

We confess to being unable to satisfy even our own inquiry about the complete *normality or abnormality in reaction type* of those who develop mental conflicts. It boots little to say that this or that individual or kind of individual would not have reacted thus, because it would be very rare to find identical circumstances obtaining. I must bring to the front once more, however, the fact that the experiences which start the complexes under consideration have had peculiar settings, with ominous secrecy and the like, and have come from socially abnormal sources. Besides this, they often have certainly arisen at moments and ages of special psychological import and, as I have frequently emphasized, always when there has been no normal opportunity for confiding the experiences to sympathetic elders.

The possibility of the existence of general predisposing causes of conflicts many readers will feel has not been exhausted by the above statement. With regard to correlation of conflicts with *physiological malfunctioning*, it may be said that, while perhaps outbursts of reactive tendencies may in some occur more readily in periods of special stress, such as menstruation (*vide* p. 265), on the whole there is no sign of there being any such relationship.

Environmental circumstances in our cases are most diverse. The histories show misdoers coming from all classes and conditions of society. There is one common feature, however, that belongs to what may be termed the psychical environment. These misdoers with mental conflicts never have had any one near to them, particularly in family life, who supplied opportunities for sympathetic confidences. Repression has gone on very largely as the result of this need.

Concerning *origins of tendencies* to misconduct and particularly to specific forms of misconduct which are displayed in our cases, to be specially thought of is the genesis of relations between repressed elements of the complex and suggestion of misconduct which later is engaged in. The accounts of our cases often set forth very plainly the immediate juxtaposition of these as matters of experience. Whether it is necessary for the two to be in close bonds of association at the first development of the complex, often long before any reaction to conflict is exhibited, we are not sure. It is quite conceivable that at a time after the original complex was established there might have been a renewal of the emotional state, and then first occurred association of it with the suggestion of a form of delinquency which would be in some measure compatible with the individual's ideas of action possible for him. We have perceived some hint of this being a fact in several of our cases, but it must be confessed that a definite statement of beginnings when all the elements were from the very first in close association is so frequent that the burden of proof must rest upon any one to show the facts to be otherwise.

In the search for characteristics of our conflict cases, we have seen reason, and undoubtedly the reader of our histories has also, to wonder whether they have made normal attempts at *escaping detection*. Again, we should warn against the interpretation of any facts except in the light of comparison with another group of offenders; in this matter with those of the same age. When this is done, we should have to conclude that, after all, there is very little difference. Those of wide experience with adolescent offenders know very well how impulses are given way to without consideration of results or the attempt to avoid consequences, both evidences of a lack of the sense of precaution which usually develops first at a later age.

Even though it savors of reiteration, I would emphasize here that our histories frequently show the building up of *criminalistic mental and social habits*, and that these form one of the greatest evils attendant upon the development of misconduct as reaction to mental conflicts. There can be no doubt that the neural pathways worn by habit, as well as the various outer associations formed, lead to unfortunately easy repetition of the same behavior. For the reformation of a case we must, from the findings, infer that habit as well as original sources of impulse may have to be combated.

We find that conflict cases brought to us have been viewed ordinarily with all sorts of *misconceptions* concerning the nature and cause of the trouble. This stands out on many preceding pages in this book. Considering that extensive careers of delinquency may be founded on mental conflicts, and taking into account the fact that many of the misdeeds seem to be undertaken with slight cause and apparent lack of normal social consciousness, I may be justified in suggesting the likelihood that even some cases of so-called moral imbecility and constitutional immorality are really instances of misconduct reactions to mental conflicts.

Our findings, naturally, are of worth in formulating some of the data of *prognosis*. The reader will have learned already that in some instances there have been immensely favorable outcomes. In the chapter on Applications I have dealt with facts which partially cover the topic of prognosis, as far as it can at present be safely set forth.

The limits of age at which cures may possibly be accomplished are not yet determined. It should go without saying that we find individuals in the plastic ages, when habits are less strongly formed, most susceptible to improvement, for this is merely in line with what every student of genetic psychology would expect. I have commented already on the fact that exploration is greatly aided, as a rule, by being carried out during the age of naïve communications. Here, as always, there is some variation according to the individual temperament, but the general rule is well established.

Among the main elements to be considered for prognosis, it comes out repeatedly in our histories that environment plays a great part, and particularly mental environment. The possibilities of establishing new interests, new confidences, new ways of looking at life, have all to be taken into account.

The effect of institutional life on the type of cases we have been considering is shown in some of the instances cited in the foregoing chapters. Some of them have been made much worse by institutional experiences; others have not suffered particularly, but have met their own problems later and have reformed; still others have been distinctly benefited by the breaking up of the delinquent habit through forced removal from opportunity. I fear we know of no case of conflicts which in an institution has had its individual problem met in the straightforward and economical way that scientific acquaintance with the fact of mental conflict should demand.

Most of the good results observed have followed individual treatment of the definite problems which have been formulated through diagnostic studies.

Parents or other older persons have been intelligent enough to meet the actual and specific needs of the situation.

Certain types of individuals, particularly the mentally abnormal and those with peculiar temperament, and cases of conflict following upon certain types of experiences, for instance, homosexual or incestuous experiences, offer especially difficult problems. I should advise that these cases be treated by the most thorough social and professional methods.

In all the above I would not have the reader lose sight of the fact that sometimes the individual himself may, as it were, institute his own treatment, as when religion or any other commanding activity is taken up. Sublimation of the conflict may then take place without full exploration and diagnosis. Recently a young man whom we knew as a victim of conflicts years before, but with whom we could never accomplish a thorough exploration, reported to us. After wandering in many lands and after many attempts at controlling himself, his conflict seems to have been resolved. He states the fact and shows by his normal conduct that he has lived down the conflict. No doubt many others by themselves have found after a time some method of sublimating earlier misconduct impulses.

No one of our findings is so important as the general discovery that *the study of mental conflicts is a scientific method of approaching certain problems of misconduct*, and that in this method lies the possibility of rendering great human service.

INDEX